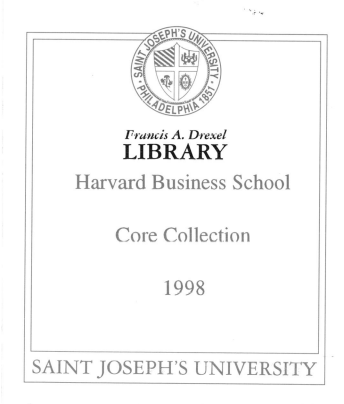

THE U.S. BUSINESS CORPORATION

THE U.S. BUSINESS CORPORATION
An Institution in Transition

Edited by
John R. Meyer and
James M. Gustafson

Published for the
American Academy of Arts and Sciences

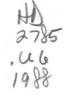

Ballinger Publishing Company
A Subsidiary of Harper & Row, Publishers, Inc.

International Standard Book Number: 0-88730-354-4

Library of Congress Catalog Card Number: 88-22062

Printed in the United States of America

Library of Congress Cataloging-in-Publication Data

The U.S. business corporation : an institution in transition / edited
   by John R. Meyer and James M. Gustafson.
        p.   cm.
     "Published for the American Academy of Arts and Sciences."
     Includes index.
     ISBN 0-88730-354-4
     1. Coporations—United States.   2. Industry—Social aspects—United
States.   I. Meyer, John Robert.   II. Gustafson, James M.
HD2785.U6   1988
338.7′4′0973—dc19   88-22062
89 90 91 92 HC 5 4 3 2   CIP

CONTENTS

LIST OF FIGURES

LIST OF TABLES

ACKNOWLEDGMENTS

This book came about as a response to a suggestion several years ago by Elmer Johnson, then of General Motors Corporation, to James Gustafson, who was chairman of the Midwest Center of the American Academy of Arts and Sciences, that the Academy undertake a study of corporate social responsibility and governance, in light of recent economic and social developments in the United States. Johnson cited as a model an earlier Academy study, *Public-Private Partnership: New Opportunities for Meeting Social Needs* (Ballinger 1984).

With the advice of Elmer Johnson and Ira Millstein, the Academy convened several exploratory meetings of scholars from various disciplines and practitioners from the corporate world. The participants in these early meetings represented a broad spectrum of professional activities in both academic and business worlds. A steering group was formed, which included Johnson, Millstein, Winthrop Knowlton, and the editors. The group quickly agreed that recent developments in corporate social responsibility and governance could best be examined against a broad background of the evolutionary and environmental changes that are modifying the role of the U.S. business corporation. Rather than creating yet another contribution to the growing number of specialized legal or economic analyses of corporate activities (of which there are several splendid examples already available), the objective became a broader overview, to bring together insights on the corporation from a wide range of perspectives and expertise. This approach seemed especially appropriate for the American Academy—an association reflecting not only virtually all groves of academe but the world of affairs and administration as well.

To finance the study, a group of law firms engaged in corporate work was approached. Ultimately seventeen firms contributed, including: Bodman, Longley & Dahling, Detroit; Carpenter, Bennett & Morrissey, Newark; Fulbright & Jaworski, Houston; Gray, Plant, Mooty, Mooty & Bennett, Minneapolis; Honigman, Miller, Schwartz and Cohn, Detroit; Irell & Manella, Los Angeles; Jones, Day, Reavis & Pogue, Cleveland; King & Spalding, Atlanta; Kirkland & Ellis, Chicago; Latham & Watkins, Los Angeles; O'Melveny & Myers, Los Angeles; Pepper, Hamilton & Scheetz, Philadelphia; Rumberger, Kirk, Caldwell, Cabaniss & Burke, Orlando; Sutherland, Asbill & Brennan, Washington, D.C.; Thelen, Marrin, Johnson & Bridges, San Francisco; and Weil, Gotshal & Manges,

New York. For this support, the Academy is most grateful. The remainder of the funding came from the Academy's Research and Planning Committee.

In addition, the editors wish to acknowledge the intellectual contributions of those people who attended the exploratory, planning, or review meetings, or with whom we discussed these issues, as we and our colleagues on the steering group developed the organizational concepts and outline of this book. One person, Corinne Schelling, coordinated and participated in all these activities. As Associate Executive Officer of the American Academy, she was the key individual who gave the project continuity, focus, and eventually closure; her contributions were literally indispensable. The developmental editor, Sarah St. Onge, not only improved every chapter but earned the respect and thanks of all authors while doing so.

Finally, several other people gave generously of their time to the project. Prominent among them were John S. Strong and Leslie Meyer-Dean, who read, critiqued, and otherwise helped with the editing and organization of this volume and of the preceding conferences. Eleanor Lintner, Jane Wilson, and Patience Terry checked references and oversaw the production of several revisions of the prospectus, introduction, epilogue, and other materials. Without their help, and that of countless others not mentioned, this endeavor would not have been possible. The only "contributions" that remain those alone of the editors are any errors or oversights.

John R. Meyer
James M. Gustafson

INTRODUCTION

A major U.S. institution, the business corporation, has been subjected to substantial stress and change in recent years. Demands, particularly on the large corporation, now go far beyond the traditional economic goal of efficiency to include complicated and controversial social and political functions, as reflected, for example, in expectations concerning such diverse activities as job creation in the inner city and operations in South Africa. Major changes have also occurred in the ownership of U.S. corporations and in the political and financial environments in which they operate. The emergence of global markets has raised serious doubts about the long-term competitiveness of many large U.S. industrial corporations and stirred countless debates over the appropriate nature of business-government and management-union relations. Current management structures and practices, too, are receiving serious scrutiny.

These developments suggest that a comprehensive review should be made of the American business corporation as an institution. This volume attempts such a review, focusing mainly on the new problems of governance and social responsibility that have come into prominence in recent years. The approach is explicitly multidisciplinary, with contributions by historians, ethicists, sociologists, and political scientists, as well as by economists, lawyers, and corporate executives.

Special attention is given to the difficulties of defining corporate legitimacy and of distinguishing clearly between public purpose and private gain. A comparison is made of selected features of corporations in several foreign countries (particularly Japan) in order to highlight differences in characteristics of ownership and management and of financial and legal conditions that may be especially relevant to understanding the changing nature and function of U.S. corporations. In particular, many questions are raised by the phenomena of takeovers, mergers, and buyouts that came to the fore in the early 1980s. Do these represent attempts to bring the corporation back to a narrower, purely economic focus, which may eventually conflict with the growing social/political demands made on this institution? What are the implications for corporate financing? For example, it has been argued that buyouts and takeovers may benefit stockholders disproportionately at the expense of creditors: Will this make debt less available or only available on more rigid terms? And what is the effect of these restructurings on the incentives of managers and executives and on their performance and competitive strategies? Will these changes also evoke important changes in the legal environment? Will defenses against certain takeover practices become so common that they are incorporated routinely into corporate charters, perhaps to the point of making the removal of incompetent management inordinately difficult?

Many of these questions suggest that the applicability of the traditional corporate form may no longer be as universal as it once was. Business entities in the United States now include several public-private hybrids, such as government-sponsored "for-profit" corporations (e.g., Comsat, Amtrak, Conrail). Partnerships, trusts, joint ventures, and cooperative arrangements with other companies and labor unions are also used increasingly. Among other consequences, decisionmaking authority and responsibility are shared in ways so new, complex, and little understood that it has sometimes become difficult to define the boundaries of a particular corporation's operations and responsibilities. The corporation as an authority system, a system of action, and a social system— within the corporate organization and in relation to the family and the community—may thus have assumed a new character. These changes, if they endure, will inevitably affect relations among the corporation's many constituencies, including stockholders, employees, management, and the community. Specifically, if public and political demands for corporate responsibility are increasing, *to whom and for what are corporations responsible?*

In keeping with this emerging diversity, the chapters of this book are informed by very different "visions" or models of society. The most radical difference involves inclinations toward more individualistic or contractual models or toward more interactional communitarian models.[1] Indeed, one approach to analyzing the chapters of this book is to see how the explicit or implied social visions underlying them affect analyses of corporate activities.[2]

Different visions are, of course, often correlated with different general moral viewpoints of what constitutes the well-being of corporations and the societies in which they function. Such moral, or normative, visions may affect not merely the general ends of corporate activity but also the values that inform policy choices. The more contractual vision tends to favor maximizing the range of liberty, to extend the scope of individual choice, and to place great weight on the responsibilities of individuals as rational agents to determine what is in their best interests. The more communitarian vision tends to express a preference for cooperation, for compromise among individual and group interests and values for the sake of some larger public interest or the common good. An extension of this vision might involve promoting the common good through social mechanisms to coordinate the activities of various participants in society. By contrast, a more conflictual vision would stress the inequities in the distribution of economic and social power. It would be highly suspicious of the benevolent intentions of persons with great power and acutely sensitive to issues of distributive injustice.

It is hoped that the different visions and preferences represented in this volume will stimulate a broad audience to ponder these complex and controversial issues. The first chapter, by McCraw, provides an historical overview documenting important changes that have occurred since the inception of the U.S. corporate form over one hundred years ago. This is followed by Peck's chapter contrasting U.S. corporate experience and practices with those abroad, specifically in Japan. Scherer's statistical survey then analyzes the changes in corporate ownership and their effect on corporate performance. In the fourth chapter, Badaracco explores organizational alternatives to the simple unitary corporate form, including joint ventures, cooperatives, and other associations. In Chapter 5, Coleman takes a more introspective look at the corporate institution, assessing it as a social organization. Brooks and Maccoby in Chapter 6 also look inward, evaluating how work relationships have evolved in response to changes in technologies and society. In Chapters 7 and 8, Weaver and Bower develop sharply different positions on what they consider to be the overall responsibilities, political as well as economic, of the modern U.S. corporation, while, in Chapter 9, Knowlton and Millstein suggest changes in corporate governance that they feel would make the typical large corporation better able to cope with modern circumstances. In Chapter 10, Gustafson and Johnson outline what they see as the social responsibilities of the corporation. In the final chapter, the editors (Meyer and Gustafson) return to synthesize and summarize these various contributions and to relate them to other contemporaneous and earlier writings on the role of the U.S. corporation.

John R. Meyer
James M. Gustafson

NOTES

1. One significant social vision, however, is not represented in this book—a Marxist one. A chapter from that perspective would undoubtedly feature a conflictual interpretation of corporate activities and their social settings.

2. The various models could be assessed for their relative adequacy, or comprehensiveness. Do they prematurely foreclose or unrealistically expand the information used to understand the issues and to provide some manageable response? Is the descriptive and analytical account adequate to the circumstances under study? Is a model so inclusive that the complexity of variables renders it difficult to determine their relative importance? Is it so restrictive that important features of corporate activity are neglected?

1 THE EVOLUTION OF THE CORPORATION IN THE UNITED STATES

Thomas K. McCraw

Across a broad spectrum of industries, American companies now face intense and unrelenting competition from foreign producers. Never before has there been anything like the trade and fiscal deficits of the 1980s, and, until recently, the locus of foreign challenge has been the older industrial powers of Europe, not the formidable new competitors of East Asia.

Even so, in the broad historical sense, American corporations have always confronted serious challenges. Usually, they have handled their problems by changing their behavior or transforming their structures or both. The corporate form has not remained static over long periods but instead has exhibited a striking and perhaps intrinsic flexibility. Compared with other important institutions—governments, military services, churches, and business proprietorships and partnerships—the corporation as a dominant form of economic organization is not only young, it is still evolving. When we speak of it, therefore, we are discussing a moving target, and we should be wary of pronouncing timeless truths.

The modern corporation emerged in the last half of the nineteenth century. At that time, the economy of the United States was still organized around small farms, business proprietorships, and partnerships. There were a few corporations, but, except for railroad companies (which had become important in the 1840s), they were not very large. Outside the railroad industry, modern business management was completely unknown.

In the years since 1850, a span about equal to two human lifetimes, all of this has changed. In the United States today, some three million corporations are doing business. There are also about ten million sole proprietorships and one-and-a-half million partnerships, but corporations account for about 90 percent of all business receipts. Of the three million American corporations, a significant number are solo operations, and most of the others are very small companies. Only a few hundred thousand firms take in more than $1 million per year, yet these account for more than 92 percent of all corporate receipts. By the mid-1980s some 287 firms had assets of more than $1 billion each, and these few hundred accounted for about two-thirds of all corporate assets in the United States.[1]

In the past, such statistics were often cited as alarming proof that American industry was becoming too concentrated and that "corporate power" was threatening democratic values. More recently, two circumstances have muted this criticism. First, industry concentration ratios have stabilized over the last few decades, even though diversified businesses and conglomerates continue to grow in size. Second, and more important, the American pattern of corporate growth has been replicated in many other countries, suggesting that concentration has more to do with the inherent structures of different industries than with the legal system or culture of a particular country. Some types of business, such as automobiles, steel, and oil, are oligopolistic wherever they occur, while others, such as furniture, printing, apparel, and shoe manufacturing, remain atomized in the pattern envisioned by Adam Smith. The statistics, therefore, may be taken less as evidence of some ominous trend within the American economy than as symptoms of the natural evolution of different types of industries within market economies everywhere.

This chapter examines separately four chronological periods: first, preindustrial times to about 1765, the year James Watt achieved his breakthrough with the steam engine and thereby made possible the modern factory system; next, the era of the first industrial revolution (roughly 1765 to 1850); then, that of the second industrial revolution (about 1850 to 1950); and, finally, what I believe to be a third industrial revolution, which began in about 1950 and continues to the present.[2] Together, these four sections are designed to suggest the malleable nature of the corporation and its intimate connection with the overall economic setting of each period.

BEFORE 1765: THE LEGAL AND INSTITUTIONAL FRAMEWORK IN ENGLAND AND CONTINENTAL EUROPE

The legal history of corporations can be traced at least as far back as the time of the Romans. Corporate bodies within the Roman Empire were set up to formalize the management of towns, villages, guilds, and, after Rome's conversion to Christianity, monasteries and abbeys as well.[3] During the late Middle Ages in England, the Crown conferred charters on universities and numerous trades as a means of identifying legitimate practitioners and regulating the quality and price of products. Weavers received from Henry II the first corporate charter of a guild, followed by goldsmiths in 1327, mercers in 1373, haberdashers in 1407, fish mongers in 1433, and so on. The principal idea behind the charters was formal participation in a group with some legitimate common interest, and this remains the primary link between these early bodies and the modern business corporation.[4]

An additional link appeared during the years of exploration, as the English Crown awarded corporate charters to "foreign adventurers" such as the Russia Company and the Turkey Company. The East India Company, chartered in 1600, was the first joint-stock enterprise of any importance. Its members subscribed stock for each separate ocean voyage, pooling their resources for the large initial investment and agreeing to divide the expected profits according to their percentages of participation. Later, share participation became longer term.[5]

By the end of the seventeenth century, much of Britain's colonization in the New World had been carried out by chartered joint-stock companies: the Massachusetts Bay Company, the London Virginia Company, the Hudson's Bay Company, and the Royal African Company. As businesses, the last two were far the most important. Like the East India Company, they were not only profit-making organizations, but de facto instruments of the Crown as well. Each was endowed officially with monopoly status in its business, along with quasi-governmental power to pursue its assigned mission—an odious one in the case of the Royal African Company.

Similar privileges within the domestic sphere of England were granted to a number of incorporated guilds. By the early eighteenth century, the principle of private corporate activity undertaken for a public purpose and possessed of monopoly rights was lodged firmly within the body of the English legal system. In many charters of the period, including that creating the Bank of England in 1694, the text included references to the public interest and the great expense these undertakings represented as justifications of the monopoly power bestowed.

Movement toward general incorporation had been retarded by some notorious abuses. By the early eighteenth century, the establishment of corporations and the trading of their shares had become conspicuously loose. As of the year 1720 about 200 companies had been formed for all sorts of purposes. The most dubious of these was a scheme for exploring the South Seas, and a frenzy in the buying and selling of shares in the South Sea Company ended in the bursting of that famous "bubble" and the passage by Parliament of the Bubble Act in 1719. This legislation put a damper on the spread of the corporate form, and, for the rest of the eighteenth century, it remained the province of Parliament or the Crown (or both) to grant a corporate charter. Both proved to be selective in exercising this power, and the practice of giving charters reverted to the earlier pattern of public-purpose corporations. The Bubble Act remained in force until 1825; in fact, not until 1844 was it possible for any group in England to incorporate without a special grant, and not until 1855 were such corporations given the right of limited liability.[6]

Meanwhile, similar developments were taking place on the Continent. In 1807 the Napoleonic *Code de commerce* set forth regulations for all kinds of businesses, including the share corporation—the *société anonyme*, as it was and still is called in France. From the beginning in a *société anonyme*, no member's name could appear as part of the company's title, shareholders enjoyed limited liability, and— unlike later American practice but typical of European law down to the present— stock securities were issued to "bearer" and their purchase and sale were not very closely regulated. Until 1867 in France, the privilege of organizing a *société anonyme* could be received only by specific government authorization. Similarly, in Germany, the use of the corporate device was closely held as a special grant from the authorities until 1870, when a law was enacted to permit freedom of corporate organization.

THE FIRST INDUSTRIAL REVOLUTION (1765 TO 1850): THE EMERGENCE OF THE CORPORATION IN AMERICA

Meanwhile, the setting across the Atlantic was proving to be even more hospitable. "In America," Adolf Berle and Gardiner Means wrote in 1931, "the corporation has developed along distinctive lines and to a more advanced stage than elsewhere." They noted that the American Revolution left the English common law in force, "thus perpetuating the principle that a corporation is a franchise but granted by the sovereignty of the state [and not the federal government] instead of by the crown."[7] Federal power to grant corporate charters was omitted from the Constitution deliberately—it was neither given nor withheld—and, afterward, federal charters were seldom issued, except to banks.

In the early years of the industrial revolution in America, numerous corporations were chartered but not solely for industrial purposes. Between 1783 and 1801 nearly 350 enterprises were incorporated, mostly in New England. This was a remarkable total by European standards, especially since the United States was still a sparsely populated, agricultural country. As previously in England, the reason so many appeared seems to have been the desire of the political state to use the corporate device for a public purpose. As Oscar and Mary Handlin put it in an important article on early Massachusetts, "turnpikes, not trade, banks, not land speculation, were [the corporation's] province because the community, not the enterprising capitalists, marked out its sphere of activity." Indeed, in the American setting, the corporation turned out to serve a doubly democratic function. First, by privatizing public activities, it helped keep down the overall size of the government. Second, as the Handlins noted, "Creation of many corporations spread the benefits of this aspect of government among many citizens, instead of confining them to a favored few as in Europe, and thus transformed the old institution."[8]

This is not to say that the corporation immediately lost its historic association with monopoly power in the minds of many Americans. That process took several decades to accomplish, and the major milestones were the laws of general incorporation—broad measures permitting groups to incorporate without a special act of the legislature. In 1799 Massachusetts passed such a general incorporation statute but restricted it to aqueduct companies. More important was the New York law of 1811, which allowed freer incorporation of manufacturing enterprises. By 1850 this practice had spread to many other states, and by the 1870s it had become the usual way for a group to incorporate. In the closing decades of the nineteenth century, several states—most notably, New Jersey and Delaware—actually vied with each other in the realm of "charter mongering."[9]

Although charter mongering was hardly undertaken in the interest of disciplining corporate behavior, the movement from special charters to general laws of incorporation was regarded consistently as a reform. Especially during the first half of the nineteenth century, special charters had been a prominent issue in American politics. In the prolonged "war" between the Jacksonians and the Second Bank of the United States, it became almost impossible to disentangle anticharter sentiments from antimonopoly and even anticorporate feeling. Consider, for example, this passage from William Gouge's widely read tract of 1833, *A Short History of Paper Money and Banking in the United States*:

> Against corporations of every kind, the objection may be brought that whatever power is given to them is so much taken from either the government or the people. As the object of charters is to give to members of companies powers which they would not possess in their individual capacity, the very existence of monied corporations is incompatible with equality of rights.

Gouge went on to say that monopoly power and "control of the market" inhered in almost every aspect of corporate life.[10]

The movement away from special charters and toward free incorporation represented a reform that gained momentum throughout the nineteenth century. Ironically, this movement produced a situation in which American corporations enjoyed much greater autonomy and general freedom from public control than did their European counterparts.

THE RAILROAD ERA AND THE SECOND INDUSTRIAL REVOLUTION (1850 TO 1950): ADAPTATION OF THE CORPORATE FORM INTO AUTONOMOUS ENTITIES FOR THE EFFICIENT MANAGEMENT OF LARGE UNDERTAKINGS

The corporation proved to be far more important in the second industrial revolution than it had been in the first. While the first industrial revolution produced a number of incorporated factories, canals, turnpikes, and banks, many of these enterprises could have been, and often were, conducted successfully as partnerships or proprietorships. By contrast, during the second industrial revolution, the corporate form proved to be absolutely essential. It was a very useful way to aggregate the unprecedented amounts of money required to construct large-scale railroads, factories, mills, refineries, and pipelines and was also an extremely effective device for administering the affairs of these enterprises. From a primarily *legal* construct, with quasi-public functions, the corporation now evolved into an inward-looking, private, and very complex organizational hierarchy—a *managerial* revolution within the private sector.

The second industrial revolution can only be understood within the context of the burgeoning railway industry. The first railroads were constructed in the 1830s, and by the 1850s a few had grown to substantial size, connecting cities and towns several hundred miles apart. During that development, severe management difficulties began to appear, and, it was often impossible to pinpoint responsibility for particular problems. The operation of a railroad required the most up-to-date techniques of civil engineering, finance, accounting, and management. Some precedents existed for the engineering and accounting functions, but there was practically no experience (with the exception of military operations) in financing and managing large, far-flung enterprises. The railroad business required an endless variety of decisions, ranging from the immediate (when to take a locomotive in for repair) to the very long term (whether to build a track into the interior of the country). In addition, entirely new issues arose: the marketing of securities in America and, because of the amounts of money required, in Europe as well; the handling of cash by large numbers of employees; and, most prominent of all in the new railroad era, the issue of safety. This industry introduced unheard-of possibilities for accidental death and destruction to a society accustomed to the speed of the horse and the mass of the wagonload.

One of the earliest railroad managers to try systematically to solve some of these problems was Daniel McCallum, the general superintendent of the Erie Railroad. McCallum's line went from New York City to Lake Erie and eventually stretched to Chicago and beyond. With the New York Central, the Pennsylvania, and the Baltimore and Ohio, it was one of the vital "trunk lines" that opened up the American West. When the Erie first began to grow, McCallum tried to figure out how to meet the new challenge of management. In 1856 he proposed a new system of organization for the railroad in a report to the company's president. This document, a milestone in the history of corporate management, vividly expresses why a new form was essential:

> The magnitude of the business of this road, its numerous and important connections, and the large number of employees engaged in operating it, have led many, whose opinions are entitled to respect, to the conclusions, that a proper regard to details, which enter so largely into elements of success in the management of all railroads, *cannot possibly be attained by any plan that contemplates its organization as a whole.*

Some way, McCallum went on to say, had to be found to divide responsibilities:

> In the government of a road 500 miles in length . . . any system which might be applicable to the business and extent of a short road, would be found entirely inadequate to the wants of a long one: and I am fully convinced, that in the want of a system perfect in its details, properly adapted and vigilantly enforced, lies the secret of their failure. . . .

By "failure," McCallum meant an unacceptable number of accidents, a confusion of responsibilities, and the inability of a long railroad to charge less per ton-mile than a short one, which was feasible in theory, given the enormous scale economies inherent in the railroad business. He persuaded the owners of the Erie to reorganize the company into six "divisions." While McCallum remained "general superintendent," each of the new units was put under a "division superintendent" who had full authority over his section of the railroad, usually about a hundred miles of track.[11]

The division superintendents were analogous to line officers within the military—those who actually led troops and did the fighting. They were, in effect, managers of people. Of course, the railroad needed managers of things as well, and, in the same 1856 report, McCallum identified a separate group of railroad officers: "general ticket agent, general freight agent, general wood agent, [and executives in charge of] telegraph management, and engine and car repairs."[12] These managers corresponded to military staff officers (medical, supply, engineering). This line-and-staff pattern based on military organization eventually became the precedent for most large corporations of any type.

The only other realistic way to manage railroads—tried in Europe with some success—was through direct government ownership and operation, again derived from military practices. In anti-statist America, however, public operation of any large industrial enterprise was never in the cards; the corporate form evolved under private initiative and ownership.[13] Corporations gradually drifted away from their historic public-purpose status and became separated from government. The focus of managers shifted from the relationship of corporations to government to internal operations. Each company began to conceive of itself as a freestanding entity, just as individual Americans characteristically insisted on independent citizenship for themselves. Corporate managers saw their organizations as autonomous bodies beyond the interference of government or any other powerful institutional force. The corporate form was hardening into a mold that was so efficient for the conduct of business that it would prove almost impossible for public authority to crack. By the time serious regulation and antitrust prosecution materialized, the mold had set like reinforced concrete, and the modern corporation constituted the very foundation of the American economy.[14]

This evolution of the corporate economy occurred with extraordinary speed. There were only 23 miles of railroad track in America in 1830; by 1890 there were

208,152—the result of the largest and most sustained construction program in human history up to that time. Once the national railroad system was built, the manufacturing sector took off as well. The total capital invested in American manufacturing stood at only $2.7 billion in 1879; it grew to $8.2 billion in 1899 and $20.8 billion in 1914.[15]

Meanwhile, the multidivisional structure pioneered by Daniel McCallum on the Erie Railroad transformed the corporation. This structure is best illustrated by an organization chart, such as the one reproduced in Figure 1–1.

The invention of the multidivisional structure was revolutionary, quite as important as the scientific breakthroughs characteristic of the same period of American history. "M-form," as it came to be called by economists, represents the key innovation in the entire history of corporate organization in America and the world. First proposed in 1856, it spread gradually during the first half of the twentieth century. In the years after World War II, the M-form became a virtual craze, spreading to hundreds of large corporations in both the United States and other market economies.[16]

For companies such as Du Pont and General Motors in the 1920s and the numerous diversified corporations of the post-World War II period, the preferred organizational form was a multidivisional structure with product (line) divisions on the one hand and the advisory (staff) divisions on the other. Figure 1–2 shows a generic organization, in this case, a chemical company. Note the formal separation of hierarchies within the organization: top management, represented by the board, president, and executive committee; middle management, comprising the general (staff) offices and the product (line) division offices; and lower management, the functional offices within the divisions. Such hierarchies appeared to be essential to the smooth working of corporations, as a way to exploit scale economies and facilitate the flow of materials in production and marketing, as a means of transferring resources among divisions when a firm operated as an internal capital market, and as a device to formalize the separation of ownership and control.

This last characteristic, so memorably articulated by Berle and Means in their book of 1932, *The Modern Corporation and Private Property*, was actually noted long before that, at the beginning of the second industrial revolution. The observation became commonplace during the 1890s, often appearing as a complaint about the loss of accountability among the new breed of managers. Yet this loss seemed to be more than offset by corresponding gains. In 1914 Walter Lippmann sketched a compelling outline of the importance of the change: "The real news about business is that it is being administered by men who are not profiteers. The managers are on salary, divorced from ownership and from bargaining." Standing outside the model of Adam Smith, they seemed immune to petty haggling and other ancient commercial practices. "The motive of profit is not their personal motive. That is an astounding change."[17] Although

Figure 1–1.   Simplified Organization Chart of a Large Railroad in the 1870s.

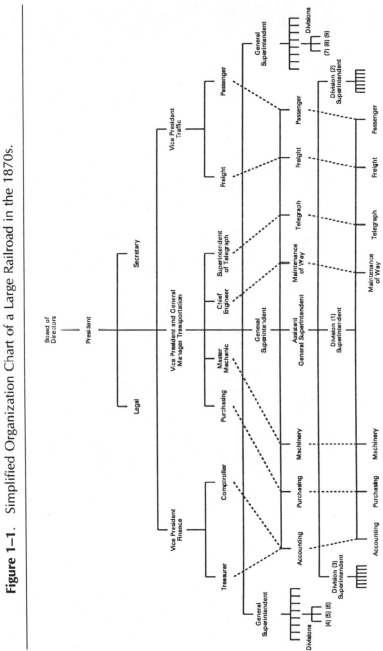

Figure 1–2. Multidivisional Structure in an Industrial Company.

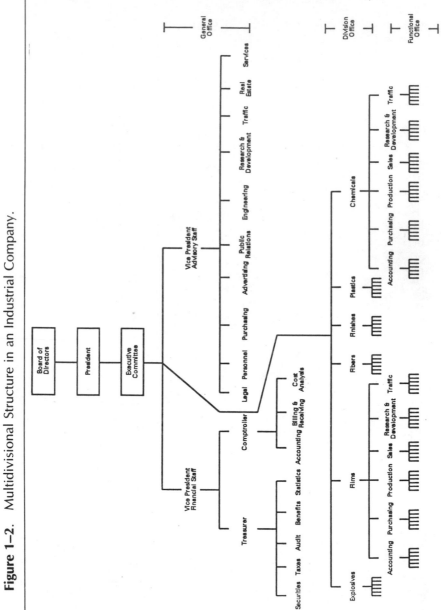

Lippmann overstated his case here, he did draw an accurate dividing line between the old style of owner management and the new corporate hierarchies.

THE THIRD INDUSTRIAL REVOLUTION (1950 TO THE PRESENT): THE CHANGING GLOBAL ECONOMY AND ITS IMPLICATIONS

In the first industrial revolution, the distinctive technological innovations were Watt's steam engine, followed seven decades later by the railroad and the telegraph. In the second industrial revolution, the key developments were electricity, new chemical and metallurgical processes, and the internal combustion engine. Within corporations, the second industrial revolution produced the unification of mass production and mass marketing and the rise of the multidivisional structure, with its complex managerial hierarchies.

In the third industrial revolution, the appropriate *organizational* symbol is the diversified multinational corporation, with its matrix governing structure: a multidivisionalization based on a mixture of product, functional, and geographical units. The *technological* hallmark of the new era is electronics, particularly the transistor and the computer. The technology of electronics, in addition to making possible entirely new products and services, has ushered in profound changes in the ways nearly all other important industries do business. Financial markets have become truly international, the focus of instantaneous transactions at orders of magnitude that dwarf anything that went before. Most important of all, manufacturing becomes global, with the result that American producers find themselves not only operating factories abroad, but facing unprecedented competitive pressures in their home markets.

This new era cannot properly be understood as a "postindustrial" society. While it does emphasize knowledge-based undertakings and service industries far more than did either the first or second industrial revolutions, in most respects, it represents a logical continuation of those earlier movements. Just as the first and second industrial revolutions were not exactly "postagricultural," but instead made agriculture more efficient, so the third industrial revolution has helped to induce productivity gains in the industries typical of the first and second.[18]

It is impossible to predict where the third industrial revolution might eventually take us. What is clear is how very far we have come already, in the brief space of a single generation. In addition to its many cultural impacts, such as an almost unbelievable amount of television watching, the third industrial revolution is having numerous subtler effects. It seems, for example, to have broken down some of the characteristically sharp divisions between large and small corporations. As recently as the early 1980s, American Telephone and Telegraph was by far the world's largest private company, with total employment of about one million persons. But in 1984 AT&T "unbundled" itself, subdividing into numerous local, regional, and national firms. The background of the AT&T divestiture had many political and legal aspects, but, in the most basic sense, it was the direct result of a technological breakthrough—cheap microwave tele-communications, which led to competition in long-distance calls.[19] In the 1960s, U.S. Steel, once the very symbol of American industrial might, was almost swept away by wave after wave of competition, not only from foreign manufacturers but also from American steel companies operating minimills. Like some bewildered dinosaur, it now lurches about in a desperate effort to survive.

These two examples suggest how conventional big businesses might shrink in the third industrial revolution. Yet the same kinds of technological innovations have had the opposite effect on some small firms. In the old order, the prototypical small businesses were restaurants, hotels, auto repair shops, and laundries. Now, however, McDonald's hamburger stands, Holiday Inns, Midas Muffler shops, and Martinizing Cleaners have sprung up everywhere. Tokyo has a Disneyland, as well as numerous 7-Eleven, McDonald's, Wendy's, and Kentucky Fried Chicken outlets. Nor is franchising limited to inexpensive items or services. The upscale Meridien hotel chain, owned by Air France, operates establishments in North American cities. Airlines of many countries fly global routes with airplanes leased from banks or other companies.

Are these franchised operations and new kinds of relationships best understood as big business, or small? Are they manifestations of local entrepreneurship, since most are locally owned and managed, or of creeping giantism, since the prerogatives of local management are sharply limited? Should we regard them as blessings or curses? Will there be a McDonald's on the Champs-Elysées? Is there one already? Will popular culture everywhere be standardized?

Global Competition

Perhaps the most distinctive characteristic of the third industrial revolution is the rise of global enterprise and international competition. The evolution of this situation was quite complex, and it should be understood against several different backgrounds. The first important condition was the end of the Great Depression and World War II and the onset of Keynesian demand management in many industrial countries (though not all: Germany and Japan remained notable exceptions, generally following supply-side strategies). Then, too, between 1946 and 1971 the world economy experienced unprecedented growth—an economic miracle that multiplied real per-capita incomes by factors of two, three, or even five or six in some countries, all within the narrow span of one generation. Third, this era of miracle growth came to an end during the 1970s. Stagflation and the two oil crises struck powerful blows against most national economies, slicing growth rates approximately in half, back to the rates typical of the second industrial revolution. Fourth, this halving of growth rates, together with escalating military expenditures and the installation of thoroughgoing welfare states, brought heavy fiscal deficits in nearly every country.[20]

For the United States, the salient problem now became competitiveness with foreign producers. The closest proxy for a nation's competitiveness is its balance on international trade and its balance on current account (an indicator that adds short-term capital movements to trade). In both areas, American performance became steadily worse during the 1980s, to the point of potential disaster. If the American economy as a whole were to be evaluated in the way a corporation is studied by securities analysts, its two most striking characteristics as of the late 1980s would be rapidly declining market shares for its products as reflected in the trade deficits and a quickly deteriorating balance sheet as reflected in the fiscal deficits and the onset of heavy foreign borrowing.

This situation is too recent for any mature historical understanding of its causes and consequences. Nor is present economic theory developed sufficiently to explain the relationship between a nation's macroeconomic performance and the microeconomic circumstances prevailing in its most important industries. When the appropriate theoretical and empirical studies are done, the best are likely to be cross-national, comparing the United States with Japan, Germany, and other high-performing industrial countries. They are also likely to emphasize organizational capabilities at the level of the firm and to develop some way to relate the skills of corporate managers to national economic performance. Such studies will almost surely review themes prominent in the business literature of the last decade: the short-term horizons of American managers and the limited attention span of workers; the low national savings rate and the emphasis on consumer values; the breakdown of the American educational system; the decay of craftsmanship; the atrophy of institutional commitment.

In historical terms, the most remarkable aspect of the decline in national competitiveness has been its speed. As late as 1960, well into the third industrial revolution, American companies were producing nearly half of all motor vehicles manufactured in the world. In that year, Japanese firms turned out about 2 percent of the total, or one twenty-fifth of the volume of American companies. By the late 1970s, however, Japan, with only half the population of the United States, drew even with the Americans in motor vehicle production and emerged as the world champion in product quality for a given price. Similar statistics showing the relative decline of American manufacturing could be adduced for steel, heavy machinery, electronics, and other industries.[21]

During the third industrial revolution, no single country dominated in the way England did during the first industrial revolution and the United States during the second. To the extent that any national economy emerged as a leader in the third industrial revolution, that economy was the American until about 1970, then the Japanese. Not only did Japan's manufacturers displace American competitors in many product markets, but in 1986 Japan's GNP per capita actually overtook that of the United States—an event that would have been impossible to imagine even a few years earlier.

The internationalization of industrial competition consists of two specific business operations. One is "direct foreign investment"—wholesaling and retailing products through foreign outlets, putting together "knock-down kits" manufactured in the home country, and even manufacturing those products from scratch in the host country. Such direct foreign investment has grown very rapidly in recent years, after a sluggish historical beginning. True, even in the middle nineteenth century, such companies as Singer Sewing Machine and the McCormick reaper company erected factories in a few European countries. General Electric, Standard Oil, General Motors, Ford, and many others sent their managers abroad to manufacture and sell their products. British firms such as Courtaulds and Cadbury's, German companies such as Siemens, Bayer, and Hoechst, and many Japanese trading companies established important foreign direct investments in many countries, as did numerous banking houses: Citibank from the United States, Barclay's from Britain, and so on. So international business was already well established by World War II.

After the war, however, as the third industrial revolution began, international investment shot forward with unprecedented speed. From $11.8 billion in 1950, direct investments abroad by American companies leapt to $232.7 billion in 1985, with much of that growth occurring since 1970.[22] At the same time, investment by foreign corporations in the United States grew rapidly. Long considered a safe haven, the American market became even more attractive when protectionist sentiment began to rise in the United States. Just as U.S. companies had constructed factories in European Common Market countries during the 1960s to get behind the EEC external tariff wall, so in the 1980s non-U.S. companies began to move more heavily into the American market. Japanese corporations, for example, which as late as 1974 had only about $300 million invested in all their American operations, in the single year of 1986 poured $27 billion in investments into the United States.[23]

An equally striking manifestation of the internationalization of business was the immense growth of imports and exports throughout the world. During the first twenty years of the third industrial revolution, world trade increased at a rate two or three times that of general economic growth—itself in a "miracle" phase. The fundamental cause of this spurt in world trade was the reduction of tariffs and other forms of protectionism, a movement led by the United States and followed by most countries in the industrialized world. From the late 1940s to the early 1970s, the General Agreement on Tariffs and Trade, the Kennedy Round and Tokyo Round of tariff cuts, the end of intercountry barriers within the European Economic Community, and other actions all represented effective attempts to create a free-trade environment unlike anything in economic history. The result was a mushroom growth of international commerce, which in turn created a new level of global competition and a profound economic interdependence.

To put this into perspective, consider Table 1–1, which lists the top ten companies exporting manufactured goods in Japan and the United States as of the middle 1980s. For the Japanese companies, the average of exports as a percentage of total sales is a whopping 48 percent, whereas, for the American companies, it is only 15 percent. But, in both cases, the dollar amounts are immense, reflecting the important role of exports in these companies' strategic planning.

Reliance on exports, however, could set a trap for corporate management. Suppose, for example, that the dollar/yen exchange rate suddenly changes—as it did beginning in late 1985, when the yen began an appreciation against the dollar that eventually reached more than 40 percent. At that time, Japanese companies' reliance on exports represented a tremendous problem, as their exports automatically became much more expensive, regardless of their production cost. This issue, with which Japanese executives are now struggling, was endemic to American corporate management throughout the first two decades of the third industrial revolution (1950 to 1970), when the dollar was systematically overvalued. American authorities had pursued this policy in order to create a climate conducive to the growth of Japanese and European exports to the American market. The larger goal was geopolitical: to strengthen those economies as bulwarks against Soviet and Chinese expansion.

The third industrial revolution, then, created unprecedented economic growth plus unprecedented levels of trade and economic interdependence. In many product markets, this meant increased competition. In the early 1950s only a small fraction of American manufacturing was subject to serious competition from

Table 1–1. The Top Ten U.S. and Japanese Companies Exporting Manufactured Goods in the Mid-1980s.

	Japan			U.S.A.	
Company	Exports (in billions of dollars)	Exports as a Percentage of Total Sales	Company	Exports (in billions of dollars)	Exports as a Percentage of Total Sales
Toyota Motor	10.4	45	General Motors	7.3	9
Nissan	8.9	58	Ford Motor	6.0	12
Honda	5.8	71	GE	3.9	14
Matsushita	5.1	37	Boeing	3.6	35
Hitachi	4.7	37	IBM	3.1	7
Nippon Steel	4.1	34	Chrysler	2.7	14
Mazda	4.0	67	Du Pont	2.7	7
Toshiba	3.1	29	United Technologies	2.4	15
NEC	2.7	34	McDonnell Douglas	2.1	22
Sony	2.6	69	Eastman Kodak	1.9	18

Source: *Japan 1985: An International Comparison* (Tokyo: Keizai Koho Center, 1985), p. 45.

foreign producers; by the middle 1980s the great majority of American manufacturing was vulnerable. On the whole, these new developments represented good news for both consumers and producers: Competition and regional specialization benefited consumers in all countries and forced business managers everywhere to become more sophisticated about economic relationships.

Yet, in some respects, this situation has also increased the possible dissonance between the interests of corporations and those of their home countries. As an example, consider the long-standing controversy in Great Britain about the export of capital to other countries and the investment of British funds abroad—to the great disadvantage, contends the British Left, of employment and industrial revitalization at home. The argument has been going on for about one hundred years now and seems unlikely to be resolved. More recently, in the face of a revalued yen, should Japanese bureaucrats and corporate executives continue their emphasis on home production and exports and attempt to become still more efficient? Or should they build factories in the United States, their major foreign market? So far, they have decided to do both, partly because they are loath to lay off workers in Japan and partly because they know that investment in the United States serves as a hedge against protectionism.

These same pressures are felt by American companies, perhaps even more keenly than by Japanese. Firms such as General Electric routinely calculate whether or not the company's interests are best served by continuing U.S. production of a particular item or by moving such production offshore. In recent years, pressures from foreign manufacturers have compelled GE to relocate some factories to Mexico, Singapore, and other foreign countries. When plants move, so do manufacturing jobs. Although much of the slack has been taken up by the concurrent rise of the service sector, that phenomenon cannot compensate fully: first, pay scales in the service sector are customarily lower than in manufacturing; second, and more important in the long run, high-value-added portions of the service sector, such as banking, accounting, and legal services, are closely tied to important manufacturing industries. Sooner or later, a substantial number of service firms must follow their manufacturing clients abroad.[24] The dynamics of the world economy have led intelligent corporate managers into investment decisions that help ensure the survival of their own companies, but do not necessarily help the American economy as a whole. A new dimension has been added to the old dilemma over the tradeoffs between public and private interests.

CONCLUSION: THE FUTURE FUNCTIONS OF THE AMERICAN CORPORATION

In the seventeenth century, Sir Edward Coke wrote, ''corporations cannot commit treason, nor be outlawed nor excommunicate[d], for they have no souls''; in the

1950s, however, during the flush early years of the third industrial revolution, many observers advanced the reverse proposition. In *Big Business: A New Era*, the formerly militant New Dealer David E. Lilienthal argued that giant corporations represented the vanguard of social responsibility. In an even more widely read book, *American Capitalism: The Concept of Countervailing Power*, John Kenneth Galbraith suggested that the traditional American suspicion of large corporations, especially as expressed in the antitrust laws, had become obsolete because of balancing forces represented by Big Labor, Big Government, and buyer-seller relationships among the giant companies themselves. And in 1957 Carl Kaysen startled an audience at the annual meeting of the American Economic Association by announcing that corporate behavior "[now] can be termed 'responsible': there is no display of greed or graspingness; there is no attempt to push off onto the workers or the community at large part of the social costs of the enterprise. The modern corporation is a soulful corporation."[25]

By the 1980s the corporation had become even more soulful. Sometimes, companies accepted their new responsibilities willingly; more often, they were forced to do so by federal law. During the three decades after Kaysen's declaration, corporations acquired novel duties with respect to the environment, civil and gender rights, occupational health and safety, pension planning under ERISA, product liability, employment at will, and numerous other matters that would have looked very strange indeed to John D. Rockefeller and other titans of the second industrial revolution.

Nor were business corporations the only entities to be charged with these new duties. Institutional employers—universities, schools, military services, government agencies, labor unions, churches, foundations, law firms, and so on—like corporations, have acquired responsibilities that transcend their specific missions. Like corporations, these other agencies offer benefits to their employees: retirement plans, health programs, life insurance, and a welter of other perquisites that workers in all such American organizations have come to take for granted. When we begin to analyze the additional burdens placed on the corporation, we should recognize that these same responsibilities have been thrust upon many other institutions as well.

For each of them, the same question now arises: How many diverse duties can a given organization perform simultaneously and still fulfill its original task? In the case of universities, for example, where should the line be drawn between open admissions on the one hand and academic standards on the other? And where is the proper boundary between the fiduciary responsibility to manage endowments in a way that maximizes income for the chronically strapped universities and the equally clear responsibility to divest the shares of corporations doing business with South Africa and other nations with immoral public policies?

In the case of corporations, the question can be posed more simply. We might stipulate that the law need not retreat from its commitment to equal opportunity, a clean and safe environment, and other issues on which the political voice of the people has spoken. Beyond this, however, given international competition and the poor recent performance of American business, we must question whether the corporation can afford to retain its new-found soul. I use the word "afford" in its literal sense, because if the corporation becomes too soulful, it will have difficulty making a profit. If it cannot make a profit, it will cease to exist. If it ceases to exist, soulfulness is no longer a consideration. Therefore, the national interest requires that corporations have just the right amount of soul. If they try to have too much, they will become generous but short-lived institutions. Foreign competitors will displace American companies, employment will decline, and the national interest will suffer. Yet, if corporations have too little soul, they will alienate their employees and customers, lose their efficiency and their markets, and again, ultimately injure the national interest.

Whether or not the corporation is "the greatest single discovery of modern times" (as Nicholas Murray Butler termed it in 1912), it does represent a golden goose. In that sense, any discussion of the "role of the modern corporation" takes on a slight tinge of luxury. For it could be that the answers we give, however wise, may be in response to the wrong question. In a setting of global competition, the most important question may not be the American business corporation's *role*, but its adaptability and even survival.

NOTES

1. U.S. Bureau of the Census, *Statistical Abstract of the United States* (Washington, D.C.: U.S. Government Printing Office, 1986), pp. 517, 532.
2. Historians and economists by no means agree that there have been three industrial revolutions. I use the terms here to facilitate the identification of four very different historical settings in which corporations have operated.
3. A thorough treatise on this subject is in John P. Davis, *Corporations: A Study of the Origin and Development of Great Business Combinations and of Their Relation to the Authority of the State* (1904; reprint, New York: Capricorn, 1961).
4. Ibid. See also Samuel Williston, "History of the Law of Business Corporations Before 1800," *Harvard Law Review* 2 (October 15, 1888): 105–8.
5. Williston, "History of the Law of Business Corporations," pp. 109–10; A. A. Berle, Jr., and Gardiner C. Means, "Corporation," *Encyclopaedia of the Social Sciences* (New York: Macmillan, 1931), vol. 4, p. 414.
6. This paragraph and the next owe much to Berle and Means, "Corporation," pp. 414–16.
7. Ibid., p. 416. See also Edward S. Mason, "Corporation," *International Encyclopedia of the Social Sciences* (New York: Macmillan, 1968), vol. 3, pp. 398–99.
8. Oscar Handlin and Mary F. Handlin, "Origins of the American Business Corporation," *Journal of Economic History* 5 (May 1945): 22–23. The most thorough treatment of the early history of American corporations is E. Merrick Dodd, *American Business Corporations until 1860* (Cambridge: Harvard University Press, 1954).
9. Berle and Means, "Corporation," p. 417; Mason, "Corporation," p. 399; John W. Cadman, Jr., *The Corporation in New Jersey: Business and Politics, 1791–1875*

(Cambridge: Harvard University Press, 1949). During the decade spanning the turn of the twentieth century, an extensive muckraking literature examined the practice of charter mongering.

10. Quoted in James Willard Hurst, *The Legitimacy of the Business Corporation in the Law of the United States, 1789–1970* (Charlottesville: University Press of Virginia, 1970), p. 30. Hurst comments: "Muddled together here are objections based on (1) egalitarian values, (2) balance-of-power values, and (3) values of functional efficiency. Gouge embodies the heart of the confusion of mid-nineteenth-century debate when he links a particular attack on banks to an indiscriminate attack on the corporate instrument in any use or with any character. It took another generation to disentangle the questions of special-action franchises from those of corporate status proper, which Gouge brought under a single attack" (pp. 30–31).

11. Quoted in Alfred D. Chandler, Jr., and Richard S. Tedlow, *The Coming of Managerial Capitalism* (Chicago: Irwin, 1985), pp. 201–3. Emphasis added.

12. Ibid., p. 203.

13. Why extensive public ownership never took root in the United States represents a complex historical problem. For an introduction, see Thomas K. McCraw, "The Public and Private Spheres in Historical Perspective," in Harvey Brooks, Lance Liebman, and Corinne S. Schelling, eds., *Public-Private Partnership: New Opportunities for Meeting Social Needs* (Cambridge, Mass.: Ballinger, 1984), pp. 31–60.

14. I am speaking here primarily of the self-perception of executives rather than the legal theory of corporations as "personal" entities. The two are related, however, and a useful and controversial technical literature exists on the subject of entities; see, for example, Hurst, *The Legitimacy of the Business Corporation*; and Morton J. Horwitz, "*Santa Clara* Revisited: The Development of Corporate Theory," *West Virginia Law Review* 88 (Winter 1985–86): 173–224.

15. U.S. Bureau of the Census, *Historical Statistics of the United States: Colonial Times to 1970* (Washington, D.C.: U.S. Government Printing Office, 1975), vol. 2, p. 731; Paul Uselding, "Manufacturing," in Glenn Porter, ed., *Encyclopedia of American Economic History* (New York: Scribner's, 1980), pp. 409–11. The money figures cited are in current dollars.

16. Alfred D. Chandler, Jr., *Strategy and Structure: Chapters in the History of the Industrial Enterprise* (Cambridge, Mass.: MIT Press, 1962). Chandler's research into the evolution and spread of the multidivisional structure was applied to other settings in a series of Ph.D. dissertations done at the Harvard Business School in the 1970s: see Derek F. Channon, "The Strategy and Structure of British Enterprise" (1971); Gareth P. Dyas, "The Strategy and Structure of French Industrial Enterprise" (1972); Robert D. J. Pavan, "The Strategy and Structure of Italian Enterprise" (1972); Richard P. Rumelt, "Strategy, Structure, and Economic Performance" (1972); and Hans T. Thanheiser, "Strategy and Structure of German Industrial Enterprise" (1972). The dissertations of Channon, Dyas, Rumelt, and Thanheiser were later published as books.

Among economists, the most influential proponent of the importance of the multidivisional structure has been Oliver E. Williamson. See *Markets and Hierarchies* (New York: The Free Press, 1975), chapter 8; and *The Economic Institutions of Capitalism: Firms, Markets, Relational Contracting* (New York: The Free Press, 1985), chapters 4, 5, and 11.

17. Walter Lippmann, *Drift and Mastery* (1914; reprint Englewood Cliffs: Prentice-Hall, 1961), pp. 42–43.
18. This point is explicated in John Zysman and Stephen Cohen, *Manufacturing Matters* (New York: Basic Books, 1987).
19. See Peter Temin with Louis Galambos, *The Fall of the Bell System*, (New York: Cambridge University Press, 1987).
20. In the early and middle 1980s, the United States government ran deficits of about $200 billion per year (or about $1000 for every man, woman, and child in the country). What had been a total national debt of just under $1 trillion in 1980 grew to $2 trillion in 1986 and threatened to top $3 trillion by 1990. In Japan, a country noted for its thriftiness and fiscal conservatism, the very same economic forces (minus heavy military expenditures) more than quadrupled the national debt as a percentage of GNP in the short space of a decade (from 9.9 percent in 1975 to 41.0 percent in 1984). The Japanese people, however, saved such a high proportion of their incomes (far more than twice the American rate) that the entire Japanese debt could easily have been financed through domestic savings. In the United States, the continuing fiscal deficits necessitated extremely heavy foreign borrowing, to the extent that in mid-1985 the nation became a net international debtor for the first time since 1914. This extraordinary development held enormous, potentially negative consequences for the American economy and for American corporations' ways of doing business. Estimates were that, at the existing rate of foreign borrowing, by 1993 the United States would owe about $1 trillion in foreign obligations (principally U.S. government securities owned abroad)—a sum that dwarfed the $500 billion owed in the middle 1980s by all Latin American governments combined, which caused so many alarms about the international debt crisis.

    For source citations to the above figures, together with a fuller discussion of their implications, see Thomas K. McCraw, ed., *America Versus Japan* (Boston: Harvard Business School Press, 1986), chapters 1, 9, and 11.
21. Ibid., chapters 1, 2, and 3.
22. Mira Wilkins, *The Maturing of Multinational Enterprise: American Business Abroad from 1914 to 1970* (Cambridge: Harvard University Press, 1974), pp. 30, 329; U.S. Chamber of Commerce, *Survey of Current Business* (Washington, D.C.: U.S. Government Printing Office, August 1986), vol. 66, no. 8, p. 40. All figures are expressed in current dollars.
23. McCraw, *America Versus Japan,* chapter 4; *Newsweek,* February 2, 1987, p. 42.
24. A qualification should be noted here. It is not yet clear to what extent the vastly improved world telecommunications network will reduce the need for service firms to follow their clients. Thus far, the internationalization of some service industries has reflected something of a herd instinct, in which firms seem to move abroad irrespective of pure cost-benefit considerations.
25. David E. Lilienthal, *Big Business: A New Era* (New York: Harper & Row, 1953); John Kenneth Galbraith, *American Capitalism: The Concept of Countervailing Power* (Boston: Houghton Mifflin, 1952); Carl Kaysen, "The Social Significance of the Modern Corporation," *American Economic Review* 48 (May 1957): 313–14.

2 THE LARGE JAPANESE CORPORATION

Merton J. Peck

In its broad structure, the Japanese economy is similar to that of the United States. It, too, is a market economy with large corporations and small businesses, unions, stock markets (the Tokyo Stock Exchange is now larger than the New York Stock Exchange in value of the shares traded), and even an FTC (although the F stands for Fair in Japan and for Federal in the United States). Like its U.S. counterpart, the Japanese large corporation is a private enterprise owned by its shareholders, who elect a board of directors, which, in turn, appoints the corporate officers. Yet the Japanese large corporation possesses many unique characteristics, which, to many Americans, seem so instrumental to its notable success that they should play a role in the evolution of the U.S. corporation. Such a view implies that the Japanese corporate organization is superior to that in the United States, a very controversial contention.

In this chapter, we will analyze the validity of this claim through an overview of Japanese corporate structure and practices. Inevitably, we have had to rely on generalizations for simplicity's sake—there are many exceptions to the broad truths discussed here. The Japanese economy is highly decentralized; its large firms are diverse, and themselves in transition. Its special features have depended in part on insulation from the world economy and a high rate of economic growth. Yet the Japanese economy is becoming more internationalized and its annual rate of growth, although still high, is no longer at the double-digit level of the sixties. These changes are forcing large Japanese corporations to modify their distinctive practices; however, they are not likely to lose all the characteristics that distinguish them from the large American firm.

CORPORATE GOVERNANCE, OWNERSHIP, AND CONTROL

The Japanese board of directors is elected at the annual meeting of the stockholders, but, in contrast to the United States, the directors are usually full-time managers who head an operating division or a corporate function. Boards are usually large—for example, Mitsubishi Electric Company, a large Japanese electronics firm, has thirty-seven directors. Boards do tend to include one to three directors who come from banks, insurance companies, or other corporations, but, once they join the board, these individuals usually become full-time company executives. Rodney Clark, in his fascinating book, *The Japanese Company*, reports that:

> Some [such] directors may be possibly slightly more inclined than directors promoted from within the company to give more weight to the shareholder's interests. In normal circumstances, however, the outside directors will share the point of view of their colleagues in the firm's management, partly because their backgrounds will be similar and partly because most of them will be doing full-time jobs in the company since their appointment to the board.[1]

The Japanese commercial code requires voting by stockholders on such major issues as changes in the corporate charter, the sale of significant assets, or mergers and acquisitions, and such decisions must be approved by a two-thirds majority in order to be implemented. Even so, these powers are largely dormant. At the annual meetings, management arrives with sufficient proxies from large stockholders to determine the outcome, and questions from the floor are not encouraged.

Clearly the protection of stockholders' rights, "corporate democracy," evokes little interest in Japanese stock exchanges and the Ministry of Finance (which has powers equivalent to the U.S. Securities and Exchange Commission). Apart from a 1974 change in the Commercial Code that increased the responsibilities of the auditors and a 1978 requirement that the financial reports of majority-owned subsidiaries be consolidated, these bodies have done little to strengthen the position of the stockholder.[2]

The lack of concern over stockholder rights is explained by the fact that the majority of shareholders are financial institutions and business corporations, many of which own stock in each other's companies. Table 2–1 shows that in 1982 financial institutions, business corporations, and government agencies owned 64 percent of the shares of large corporations. Differences in the share of stock held by individual stockholders in the United States and in Japan are particularly striking: F.M. Scherer in this volume reports that individuals held 55 percent of the shares in U.S. corporations in 1979, while in 1982 individuals held only 27 percent of the shares in Japanese corporations.

Predictably, ownership of large blocks of stock by individuals is relatively rare in Japan. Of the 78 largest publicly traded nonfinancial corporations in 1979, only seven counted individuals or families among the ten largest stockholders. Employees, including managers, do hold stock in their companies, yet in only 19 of the 78 companies were employees as a group among the 10 largest stock owners, with the largest ownership share being 15 percent.[3]

Table 2–1. Distribution of Stock Ownership in Japanese Corporations Listed on the First Division of the Tokyo Stock Market, 1955–1982 (percent).[a]

	(1)	(2)	(3)	(4)	(5)	(6)
Year	Banks and Insurance Companies	Nonfinancial Corporations	National and Local Government	Individuals	Investment Trusts and Securities Firms	Foreigners
1955	19.5	13.2	0.4	53.1	12.0	1.8
1965	23.4	18.4	0.2	44.8	11.4	1.8
1975	34.4	26.3	0.2	33.5	3.0	2.6
1982	38.0	25.8	0.2	26.8	2.9	6.3

a. Data are for fiscal years.

Source: Stock Market Distribution Section, Ministry of Finance, Government of Japan, Tokyo, 1984.

The Evolution of the Japanese Group

When the American occupation began in 1945, many large Japanese corporations belonged to one of the four major zaibatsus—Mitsubishi, Yasuda, Sumitomo, and Mitsui—which controlled 32 percent of national corporate investment and 50 percent of the nation's bank deposits in 1941. In addition, there were a number of other smaller zaibatsus. Each prewar zaibatsu consisted of a holding company with large stock ownership in core companies; the holding company, in turn, was controlled by a family trust. The core companies, which had stockholdings in many smaller companies, included large manufacturing enterprises in most of the major industries and a trading company, as well as a bank, a trust company, and an insurance company to provide financing for the zaibatsu companies.

During the occupation, the zaibatsu family trust and holding companies were dissolved by being required to sell their stock in the core companies to the public "to broaden the base of ownership in the modern sector from a handful of business families of giant fortunes to ownership by the many."[4] As a result of these public sales, by 1955 individuals held 53 percent of the stock and investment trusts (similar to U.S. mutual funds) held another 12 percent (see Table 2–1).

The managements of the former core companies considered this diffusion of stock to be a threat to their continued control, especially since a relatively small equity investment could take control of a large company, because Japanese companies are largely financed by renewable short-term bank loans. With the exchange rate of 360 yen to the dollar in the fifties Japanese companies would have been particularly good buys for American investors. The exchange control laws provided immediate protection against such purchases, but only in the short term. Managements wanted their companies' stock to remain in friendly hands. The most friendly hands belonged to other former core companies that had been part of the same zaibatsu. With the ending of the occupation, these former core companies had established presidents' clubs with regular meetings which furthered this thrust toward mutual stock ownership. As Table 2–1 demonstrates, the percentage of stock held by nonfinancial corporations, banks, and insurance companies grew from about 33 percent in 1955 to about 61 percent in 1975, while the percentage held by individuals declined from 53 to 34 percent. Mutual shareholdings of group members were responsible for much of the change, and this pattern of shareholdings achieved its aim. There have been only four attempts at hostile takeovers of large Japanese firms, all by foreign investors. None succeeded.

The Keiretsu

In the seventies, a common view among both American and Japanese economists was that the large Japanese group (keiretsu) was a prewar legacy, which would disappear as the individual companies grew larger and financially more secure.[5]

Table 2–2 shows the present equity ownership of the six major keiretsu. Mutual equity ownership remains high—indeed, there has been little change since 1973, except that each keiretsu has grown larger and includes more companies. Not all firms in a keiretsu are equal, for they are divided between nucleus firms, which are members of the president's club, and non-nucleus firms, who attend only less frequent, larger meetings. The arrangements vary among keiretsu, with the older and larger keiretsu being more exclusive. Thus, the Mitsubishi keiretsu has 28 out of 101 firms in its president's club, Sumitomo 21 out of 87, Mitsui 21 out of 65, and Fuji 29 out of 87. Samwa has two-thirds of its keiretsu members in the club and DKB, in a fit of democracy, includes all of its members.[6]

Nucleus firms are usually older and significantly bigger—the average sales of nucleus firms are 15 times greater than those of non-nucleus firms. Keiretsu financial institutions have much larger equity holdings in nucleus firms than in non-nucleus firms; the one or two outside directors come mainly from these institutions. Equity holdings by nonfinancial keiretsu members are largely by other nucleus firms and are dispersed fairly widely.[7]

In contrast, keiretsu equity in non-nucleus firms is held by a few nucleus industrial companies and the one or two outside directors are drawn from those companies. Non-nucleus firms are generally former subsidiaries of keiretsu members that have progressed to the status of full-fledged members, though not to the status of nucleus firms. The nucleus/non-nucleus distinction replicates the core/non-core distinction of the prewar zaibatsu.

As of 1980, the six major keiretsu accounted for 18 percent of sales, 14 percent of corporate profits, and 6 percent of the employment in Japan.[8] Although this

Table 2–2.   Intercorporate Links of the Six Largest Japanese Groups (1981).

Group	Number of Companies	Average Percentage of Equity Held in Group Companies by Group Banks and Trust and Insurance Companies	Average Percentage of Equity in Group Companies Held by Nonfinancial Group Members	Average Percentage of Group Member Debt Held by Group Financial Companies	Average Number of Directors Coming from Group Members
Mitsubishi	101	9.0	22.9	33.0	1.0
Sumitoma	87	8.6	31.4	34.7	1.0
Mitsui	65	8.4	22.5	27.8	0.5
Fuji	87	10.2	20.3	33.3	1.0
Sanwa	61	6.7	21.5	26.7	0.6
DKB	43	8.2	21.0	21.5	1.2

Source: Lisa Klein, "The Impact of Group Structure on the Strategy of the Japanese Firm" (Yale College senior essay, Yale University, 1987). Reprinted with permission.

is only half of their prewar share and they have grown more slowly than the Japanese economy as a whole—largely because of disproportionate investment in slower growing heavy industries—the keiretsu still constitute a major part of the Japanese economy, particularly of its large corporations.

There are, of course, important large firms outside the six largest keiretsu, such as Hitachi, Matsushito, and Toshiba in electronics, and Toyota, Nissan, and Honda in the automobile industry. Such firms, often termed independent or industrial keiretsu, are composed of one large manufacturing company and several smaller companies that serve as suppliers, distributors, and spin-offs of the large firm. No large Japanese firm stands totally on its own; each has partners, allies, and subordinates. The mutual stockownership of the keiretsu carries over to these industrial or independent keiretsu, with the large firm holding equity in its suppliers and its suppliers holding equity in the main company.

THE LARGE JAPANESE FIRM AND ITS EMPLOYEES

Some economists aver that the distinctive labor practices of the large Japanese corporation are more prevalent in theory than in practice and have counterparts in the United States and Western Europe. This claim is only partly justified—Japanese labor practices are indeed unique and influence greatly the behavior of the large Japanese corporation.

The Practices

With seniority wages, a worker receives a low entry wage, which rises annually for the next two decades even if he continues in the same job. Workers of the same seniority receive the same pay, except for those who become managers or foremen.[9]

A neoclassical economist would expect that even wages set strictly by marginal productivity would rise with age as an employee accumulated experience that made him or her more productive. Comparisons with Britain and Germany, however, show that wages in these two countries peak between thirty-five and forty, while Japanese wages peak just before retirement. The premium for seniority is some 50 percent higher in Japan.[10] Furthermore, it is difficult to reconcile marginal productivity with an explicit commitment to a wage schedule that rises in annual increments throughout most of a worker's tenure.[11]

A seniority wage system, of course, reinforces a lifetime employment system. The worker with seniority has little incentive to leave since the alternative is usually employment in the lower paid small-business sector. With lifetime employment, a worker also knows that he will not be replaced by a younger and lower paid worker. In a 1980 survey, 52 percent of the university graduates and 29 percent of the high school graduates aged 40 to 44 employed in large firms had never changed employers since leaving school.[12]

Semiannual bonuses are paid to all employees—from the janitor to the president—and average about 25 percent of annual compensation. They are largely deferred wage payments and only minimally a form of profit sharing.[13] Yet, as various observers have pointed out, the widespread perception among Japanese workers that bonuses are dependent on corporate profits could be a significant factor in productivity.

Enterprise unionism is almost universal in large Japanese corporations. This form of union organization is strictly by company—there are a Toyota union and a Nissan union, not a United Automobile Workers of Japan. The enterprise union reflects a commitment by the Japanese worker to his firm that offers a corresponding lifetime commitment to him.

Implications for Firm Behavior

The most striking advantage of these practices is intangible—the cooperation and even enthusiasm of the typical Japanese worker. There is no quantitative measure for such an advantage although it is visible in the 1980 national average of paid vacations taken by employees: 8.8 days relative to an entitlement of 14.4 days.[14] Cooperativeness is also demonstrated by the much-discussed Japanese quality circles, periodic group discussion by workers about improving productivity.

Another advantage is the absence of strict job classifications and work rules. The Japanese worker thinks of himself as working for a particular firm rather than at a particular occupation. He is relatively willing to move from one job to another as the needs of the firm dictate. A striking example of such flexibility is the practice of job rotation, in which particular assignments in a production unit are rotated among employees every two months.[15] More senior employees can perform every job in their sections. Maintenance and repair, a separate job category in most Western plants, is performed mainly by machine operators. Such accumulated knowledge facilitates adjustment to varying levels of operations and to technical change.

The Japanese worker's loyalty to the employer and flexibility regarding his assignments are sometimes attributed to a deep sense of group mindedness characteristic of Japanese society. But it is most marked in large rather than small firms and is surely enhanced by the labor practices of the large firm.

The disadvantage of Japanese labor practices is that the large firm is saddled with a work force whose total size is fixed in the shortrun. Flexibility in using labor within the firm is purchased at the cost of little flexibility with regard to layoffs and firings. Japanese firms do employ temporary workers (paid daily wages, in contrast to regular workers paid monthly salaries), who are outside the lifetime employment system. Union contracts, however, typically limit such employees to 5 to 10 percent of the work force.[16] Japanese firms can also place regular workers on leave, but they must pay such workers 50 to 85 percent of their regular salaries. In extreme situations, they can shift workers to other employers, continuing their pay and being paid, in turn, by the firm in which their employees are working. Early retirements, attrition, and the cessation of hiring are the usual ways to reduce the firm's work force. Firing employees is penalized by the high level of severance pay.

For the large Japanese firm, then, labor is largely a fixed cost, as is much of its capital, which comes from bank loans with fixed rates of interest. Given such fixed costs, firms tend to maintain production even during a downturn in demand. To sell their rising inventories, Japanese firms have been aggressive exporters, cutting prices during worldwide recessions. There have also been price wars among large firms in Japanese domestic markets. Short-term recession cartels authorized by the Japanese government are intended to prevent such price wars, which are felt to jeopardize the commitment to fixed wage and interest payments. Semiannual bonuses are necessary to the system, because foregoing or cutting bonuses provides downward wage flexibility when a firm is in serious trouble.

These adjustments are not adequate, however, for what are termed in Japanese policy "the structurally depressed industries," such as shipbuilding, which is experiencing a worldwide slump in demand, and aluminum smeltering, which is internationally uncompetitive because of energy costs. Special legislation provided government aid to allow firms in these industries to meet the substantial costs of severance pay required in their union contracts. Keiretsu ties also helped—about half of the redundant workers in aluminum smelters, for example, were reemployed by other keiretsu members.[17]

Management Workers

Japanese managers like to call themselves "management workers" and so stress their identification with other employees of the firm. And, indeed, in some ways "management" is a less distinctive group in Japan than in the United States or Western Europe.

All regular employees of the large firm—management, white collar, and blue collar—are treated the same formally; all have monthly salaries, semiannual bonuses, lifetime employment, and flexibility in job assignments. Even the chief executive officers of large firms are more like employees than are their U.S. counterparts. Salaries with bonuses are in the $200,000 to $300,000 range, half to a quarter those of comparable U.S. company heads. Stock options are rare; the Japanese chief executive has few chances to build an independent fortune. Yet this egalitarianism is mostly superficial—the Japanese company head ranks high in a hierarchical society.

Managers in Japan are generally recruited from universities and join their companies upon graduation. University training is commonly in engineering, economics, law (an undergraduate degree in Japan), or recently, business administration, although the MBA has little standing. There is intense competition among graduates for positions in large firms, and large firms, in turn, seek out the graduates of the best, most selective universities. The institution attended is more important than academic performance. Some companies use written examinations for preliminary screening, and the final selection is based on interviews to determine the individual's compatibility with the management group and his potential in a variety of assignments.

A university graduate joins a company at the standard entry grade, as an ordinary company member, with a salary only slightly higher than that of an entering high school graduate. In most companies, he spends the first few years at this rank; promotion into a management rank occurs only at age twenty-seven to thirty, followed by successive promotions at three- or four-year intervals. Clark summarizes the promotion policy as follows:

> Passage through the standard ranks of a Japanese company is rather like promotion in a civil service or army in the West. A man will rise through the first few ranks more or less automatically, but as he reaches the top of the company, his prowess will depend very much on what he has achieved and whether he is thought to be a good manager. Automatic promotion ends and competition begins between the ranks of section head and department head.[18]

To be sure, young, exceptionally promising executives are given greater responsibility than their contemporaries. They may complete two years of a U.S.

MBA program at company expense—more to perfect their English than to learn management skills—and may also spend some time on a trade association staff or at a subsidiary.

Japanese managers often are rotated at two-year intervals among a wide variety of functions. The aim is to create managers with a broad knowledge of the company rather than a command of one functional specialty. Managers at all ranks frequently attend company or external short courses, often at a company lodge or resort hotel.

Decisionmaking in Japanese companies is quite different from its U.S. counterpart. Clark summarizes its elements:

> Decisions are taken not by one man with specific authority but collectively, by a group of managers. The most frequently cited example of the actual mechanism by which decisions take place is the circulation of a ringi: A ringi is a proposal that emanates from one manager or one department, and passes first around collateral departments and then to the senior managers of a company, the directors, managing directors, and the president of the company. All those who see the proposal make their comments on the attached form. When it finally reaches the top, the president takes the decision on the basis of what his subordinates have said.[19]

The success of this shared decisionmaking has mystified Western observers: decisionmaking by committee is considered slow, indecisive, and risk averse, yet Japanese corporations are quick, decisive, and bold in competition. Of course, the large U.S. corporation is also characterized by group decisionmaking; the differences may relate more to rhetoric than to reality. Furthermore, group decisionmaking has certain advantages: More information can be brought to bear on a decision; greater participation raises management morale; and the greater knowledge facilitates implementation.

Shared knowledge could encourage risk taking, since no one manager can be assigned the responsibility for a mistake and so damage his career. Yet senior management is accountable; a bad decision is held to be the responsibility of a senior manager or even the president. Clark describes the situation:

> When something goes wrong, the senior man or group of men presiding over the mistake will take "responsibility" to lift the blame from their subordinates. Symbolic responsibility, which for the individual is simply the price of status, has some value for the company community. It encourages conscious mutual dependence of seniors and juniors. Those below know that those above will protect them. Those above must rely on their subordinates not to make mistakes that will lead to responsibility having to be taken. When a mistake is made, the resignation, transfer, or other penance of the leader of the group allows everyone to make a fresh start.[20]

To promote mutual trust and informal information sharing, there is extensive socializing among Japanese managers. Corporate life involves expense account dinners at the upper levels and barhopping at the lower levels. There are frequent weekend outings to the corporate lodges that populate Japanese resorts.

The style of Japanese management provides several advantages. Lockstep promotion in the early years sustains the morale of those who will not reach the senior levels, yet will stay with the company until retirement. The lack of executive mobility means that a company can keep its high-talent juniors without rushing them through the ranks. The emphasis on wide experience within the company and heavy socializing with fellow executives reinforces the notion of lifetime commitment to the company, as does the willingness to invest in management training. Sharing information is more feasible when managers can be expected to remain with the company.

The pattern has many exceptions. There is some manager mobility, though nothing like that in the United States. Corporations have long hired retiring senior government bureaucrats, particularly those from the Ministry of International Trade and Industry (the famous MITI) and from the Ministry of Finance. They bring in scientists and engineers at midcareer from universities and government laboratories. And there has been some hiring, now increasing, of midcareer executives from small firms and even large companies, though mostly within the same keiretsu. Finally, some large companies have a tradition of a strong president, despite a formal adherence to the ringi system. This is particularly true in companies that have grown big only recently, where the founding executives are still active and have substantial stock ownership.

SUBSIDIARIES AND SUBCONTRACTORS

The large Japanese firm is surrounded by affiliates. Some are partly owned subsidiaries, others are subcontractors, that is, suppliers who operate under long-term agreements with the central corporation. Subsidiaries and subcontractors, in turn, have their own subsidiaries and subcontractors, making the total network very large indeed. Central firms are significantly smaller than their U.S. counterparts; for example, in 1981 Toyota produced 3.22 million cars with 53,000 employees, while General Motors produced 4.62 million cars with 758,000 employees.[21] On the other hand, 46 percent of all Japanese manufacturing workers are in establishments of less than 50 employees, as compared to about 20 percent in the United States.[22]

The terms subsidiaries and subcontractors are often used interchangably, yet two distinct types of smaller firms exist within the network of the large Japanese manufacturing firm. The first, subsidiaries, are typically incorporated, medium-sized firms with a substantial minority stock ownership by the parent and the remaining shares held by individuals (often in the locality of the subsidiary), employees, and other members of the keiretsu. Management includes executives retired from the parent and many retired employees of the parent who are on the subsidiary payroll. The parent often founds these firms, providing the initial cadre of executives and start-up financing.

The second type are family-owned firms which have sought out contracts with the large firm to manufacture particular components and parts. They are usually family-managed proprietorships in which the large firm has no ownership interest. Usually small in size, they are often second-tier affiliates, making parts that will be assembled by first-tier subsidiaries before reaching the parent.

Affiliates are treated as part of the large corporation. Both parties regard their relationship as long term; indeed, the arrangement is sometimes termed "quasi-vertical integration." The large firm, however, expects its affiliates to keep their prices down and their quality up, although it generally avoids pressing an affiliate to the point of jeopardizing its financial health. It will commonly shift business from poor to good performers. Occasionally, an affiliate will be cut adrift if its performance is consistently unsatisfactory. In return, the large firm provides its affiliates with technical assistance, financing, and management advice.[23]

The prevalence of small firms in Japan was once attributed to late industrialization, and it was assumed that their numbers would decline with economic growth. Instead, small manufacturing firms have maintained their relative importance, with more becoming affiliates. This is, in part, a response to the labor practices of the large firm, with its lifetime commitment to its workers, which demands strict hiring standards to ensure that recruits are dedicated and highly trainable, and an enterprise union opposed to special arrangements for particular classes of workers. Large firms must aim for as homogeneous a work force as possible. The Japanese labor market, however, has a heterogeneous supply of workers, and small firms provide a way to accommodate this diversity. They can pay lower wages, which allows them to hire less selectively. Some specialize in tapping special segments of the labor force—the paato (housewives seeking part-time work), the retired, and students.[24] These firms also employ retired workers from large firms, who must retire between the ages of fifty-five and sixty.

Risk reduction is a rather common explanation for subcontracting, although a survey revealed that only 8 percent of the responding parent firms cited it as the most important reason, whereas 75 percent named "long-run reliable relations." Even so, affiliates do cushion large firms during demand downturns. Affiliates can absorb some of the labor force adjustments, an easier process for small firms, which do not guarantee lifetime employment. Yet the large firm cannot be too ruthless vis-a-vis its affiliates because it will need them when demand takes an upturn. Diversification can help carry the smaller firm over a slump in the parent's demand for its main product, by providing other sources of sales, which also permit economies of scale to be realized. Still, affiliates remain highly dependent on the parent; in the survey mentioned above, 1,592 subcontractors reported that an average of 82 percent of sales were to the parent, even though they averaged over six customers, and 65 percent wanted to maintain or to increase this ratio of sales, while the large firms wanted more diversification by their affiliates.[25]

A third explanation for affiliates lies in the management structure of the large firm itself. Large Japanese firms tend to be far less diversified than their U.S. counterparts, maintaining a limited number of product lines by spinning off new operations as separate corporations. In 1976, for thirty large firms in six manufacturing industries, the median percentage of sales in unrelated industries was only 15 percent.[26] To be sure, some Japanese firms are diversified: Mitsubishi Heavy Industries makes cars, ships, aircraft, and industrial equipment, and most large Japanese electronics firms cover a range of products from semiconductors through consumer electronics to computers. Still, there is nothing comparable to the United States' ITT, whose activities run from electronics to hotels, car rentals to insurance.

The existence of enterprise unions may account, in part, for this narrow focus. Union demands for annual increases depend in part on the recent prosperity of a firm's major industry. For example, a firm with major activities in both shipbuilding, which has been depressed in recent years, and automobiles, which have been booming, presents a problem for both the union and the firm. If demand for all the firm's workers is based on the automobile industry, labor costs in shipbuilding will be out of line with competitors; if the demand is based on shipbuilding the automobile workers will fare less well than other workers in the same industry. Differential increases are no solution, since they would undermine the unity of the union and the commitment of the firm to wage uniformity.

The narrow focus also suits Japanese management practices. Japanese firms are seldom organized in the American multidivisional form, with profit centers, transfer pricing, and bonuses geared to divisional as opposed to company profits, although there is much discussion of the option in Japanese management literature. Moreover, Japanese practices emphasize detailed knowledge of one industry by managers and tend to reject the pursuit of generalized management skills applicable to a wide range of activities.

Finally, diversification may be discouraged by keiretsu membership. Moving into a new industry might bring one keiretsu member into direct competition with another. Historically, keiretsu have been composed of one large firm in each industry which compete with firms from other keiretsu. There are exceptions—both Mitsubishi Petrochemicals and Mitsubishi Chemicals are substantial producers of low-density polyethylene—but more often the apparent competition is, in fact, the operation of the spin-off process.[27] Thus, the Sumitomo group has four firms producing household electrical appliances, but three are partly owned by the largest of the four, and they all produce different though overlapping product lines. Direct competition among them is more analogous to that existing between different car lines of General Motors than head-to-head competition.[28]

An even more significant constraint may be the difficulty of arranging mergers in Japan. As noted earlier, mergers require approval by a two-thirds majority of the stockholders of both acquired and acquiring companies, and some large stockholders may be banks, customers, or suppliers, concerned about the impact of a merger on their existing business relations. A merger also upsets standing enterprise union arrangements and may require a corresponding union merger. Individual managers and employees generally oppose mergers, which may upset existing labor and promotion practices.

In one respect, the absence of diversification is puzzling, since a diversified firm would find it easier to maintain its commitment to lifetime employment. However, the health of the Japanese economy has meant that these commitments have seldom been tested. The recent appreciation of the yen, which has introduced the prospect of reduced exports, has prompted much more discussion of diversification as a way to stabilize sales and avoid layoffs.

THE OBJECTIVES OF JAPANESE MANAGEMENT

One model of the corporation portrays it as engaged in continuous bargaining among its employees, affiliates, lenders, shareholders, and the government, trying to leave each party sufficiently satisfied that it continues to contribute to the firm. Among the many bargains meeting that condition, some are superior to others, in that they make the firm more efficient. And, of course, if the firm is more efficient, there is more to be distributed to all the claimants.[29] This view contrasts with the more neoclassical view that management is the agent of the stockholders, charged with maximizing the present value of their stock.

There is little question that the Japanese corporation adheres more closely to the bargaining model, largely because the characteristics of stockholding provide Japanese management an unusual degree of freedom from pressures to behave as the stockholders' agent. They can pursue corporate immortality without threat from stockholders.

Furthermore, the large Japanese corporation appears at first instance to be a leading example of the "blurring of the boundaries of the firm" discussed by Badaracco in his chapter on "Changing Forms of the Corporation" in this volume, given its many long-term relationships with its affiliates, its lenders, and its employees, involving unwritten and vague (at least by American standards) mutual obligations and responsibilities.[30]

Yet, a Japanese firm makes a clear distinction between a supplier with whom it has a long-term relationship and one who supplies a particular item on a short-term basis. And the large firm sharply distinguishes between its regular and its temporary employees. Even among insiders, there are sharp gradations. Japanese managers want to see their partly owned affiliates prosper but with nothing like the intensity with which they nurture the financial status of their own firms. Who is in and who is out is well understood, if mysterious to external observers.

Market Share as a Specific Corporate Objective

More insight comes from comparing the stated objectives of Japanese and U.S. managers, as shown in Table 2–3. Japanese managers placed improving products and market share (surely, closely related) at the top; in contrast, U.S. managers gave top billing to return on investment and higher stock prices. The differences are in degree—return on investment ranks third for Japanese management, and market share ranks third for U.S. management. A striking similarity is that, for all the talk of social responsibility in both countries, these objectives come near the bottom.

A long-noted feature of Japanese business is its fascination with market share. Market share is an easily observable index of long-run profit maximization, particularly when today's share influences tomorrow's and the overall market is growing.[31] The ratio of after-tax profits to sales is consistently lower in Japanese firms than in U.S. companies. The disparities are quite large; in 1978, for example, the ratio of after-tax profit to sales was 1.68 percent in Japanese firms, compared to 5.36 percent in the United States.[32] Japanese firms have never surpassed those in the United States in this area. These lower current profits may indicate greater investment in market position and hence be a sign of strength rather than weakness.

Market share also determines relative labor cost within the seniority wage system. A firm's rate of growth determines its proportion of newly hired, lower paid workers and hence its average labor costs. A declining market share means higher labor costs than competitors.

The Japanese concern over market share, however, has still another significance. Since the firms are not highly diversified, it is relatively easy for the press to cull market shares from publicly available data. A rising market share is interpreted as a signal that the company and the managers are doing well; workers and junior managers, in particular, can anticipate a better promotion rate, and affiliates more business than their counterparts in the same industry.

Workers as the Dominant Claimant

Who gets what in the many-sided bargaining characteristic of the Japanese firm? One view holds that the workers have priority over other groups. As T. Nishiyamai puts it:

> [The large Japanese corporation] exists to supply workers with the means of daily living, to satisfy their common interest, and further to provide for their common destiny. The management workers, on the basis of their position and dominant

Table 2–3. Comparisons of Japanese and U.S. Corporate Objectives.

Japan	Score	U.S.	Score
1. Improving products and introducing new products	1.54	1. Return on investment	2.43
2. Market share	1.43	2. Higher stock prices	1.14
3. Return on investment	1.24	3. Market share	0.73
4. Streamlining production and distribution systems	0.71	4. Improving products and introducing new products	0.71
5. Net worth ratio	0.59	5. Streamlining production and distribution systems	0.46
6. Improvement of social image	0.20	6. Net worth ratio	0.38
7. Improvement of working conditions	0.09	7. Improvement of social image	0.05
8. Higher stock prices	0.02	8. Improvement of working conditions	0.04

Source: Tadao Kagawa, Ikujiro Nonaka, Kiyoneri Sakakkibara, and Akihiro Okumura, *Strategy and Organization of Japanese and American Corporations,* reported in the Economic Planning Agency, Japanese Government, *Economic Survey of Japan 1980–81* (Tokyo: Economic Planning Agency, Japanese Government, 1981), p. 155. The 1980 survey included 1,031 manufacturing firms listed in Sections 1 and 2 of the Tokyo Stock Exchange and the top 1,000 firms in *Fortune's* list of mining and industrial firms. The scores reported were the mean value of each item, giving 3 points to those ranked first, 2 points to those ranked second, 1 point to those ranked third, and zero to those ranked lower.

control of the business, are obviously members of the community. Their management objective is the perpetuation of the firm as a communal body, and the pursuit of profits is merely the means for achieving this objective.[33]

This view was supported in a careful quantitative study by Iwao Nakatani, who compared econometrically 546 listed Japanese keiretsu firms with 173 listed independent firms, using control variables in a cross-section analysis to adjust for factors other than keiretsu/non-keiretsu that might influence performance.[34] Nakatani found that keiretsu firms had lower rates and lower variance of profit and growth than independents and suggested that this might reflect a tendency of management "to stabilize corporate profits at the cost of lowering the level of performance itself."[35] Such behavior would protect existing managers and workers. Nakatani also found that the average income received by employees in keiretsu firms is significantly higher than that of workers in independent firms. Some say that these higher wages merely reflect a high proportion of older male workers, yet Nakatani obtained his results after controlling for the age and male/female ratio of each firm.

The emphasis on security is not surprising. J.R. Hick's observation that "the best of all monopoly profits is a quiet life" must be one of the most quoted sentences in the economic literature. The anomaly is that the group firms are also regarded as aggressive competitors throughout the world. But, then, so are the independents, and Nakatani's finding that group firms are risk averse is true only relative to independent Japanese firms.

Neither is it surprising that firms with more market power pay their workers better, attributable either to paternalism or to the economic power of the union. There is no way to settle on one or the other as the explanation and perhaps no need to do so. Either way, the workers appear to be a primary recipient of corporate income.

What's in It for the Stockholders?

Stockholders, on the other hand, fare less well. Yet, the top ten stockholders (almost always manufacturing corporations and financial institutions) could vote to replace existing managers with others committed to giving them a larger distribution of corporation income and do not do so. Mutual obligations among managers can account for some of the passivity but surely not all. What, then, motivates the shareholders?

There are three distinct classes of stockholders, each with quite different interests: corporations, financial institutions, and individuals. Corporations represent the biggest puzzle, largely because of the complexity of Japanese corporate taxation. Intercorporate dividends are taxed at "an effective rate close to zero while realization of capital gains is taxed at 42 percent."[36] On the face of it, corporate stockholders should prefer dividends over capital gains, but another provision of the tax code states that "receiving dividends limits the right of the firm using tax deductibility of interest payments. Under this circumstance, the firm clearly prefers (unrealized) capital gains to dividends."[37] Thus, corporate stockholding is often viewed as a hedge against a financial crisis, when shares can be sold and capital gains offset against losses to avoid taxation.

Financial institutions, particularly banks, have a different set of interests because they are large lenders to the firms in which they own stock. Higher interest payments are more attractive than either dividends or capital gains since they are not shared with other stockholders. This is confirmed by Nakatani's finding that "the high debt-equity ratio of group firms can be regarded as a reflection of the main bank, which is often a major shareholder."[38] The bank, with its continually renewed fixed-interest loans, also prefers stable earnings. As is well known, Japanese large firms have a higher debt/equity ratio than U.S. firms, though the difference is not as great as the unadjusted accounting data indicate.[39]

Finally, small individual stockholders prefer dividends because a 10-percent tax credit makes this income tax free, while individuals with substantial holdings value capital gains since Japan has no capital-gains tax for individuals. In any case, from 1962 to 1977 the average annual return after taxes for stockowner dividends and capital gains was 17 percent, compared to a 6-percent return on one-year bank deposits.[40]

The large shareholders' acceptance of the status quo now becomes more explicable: long-term capital gains appear to be most advantageous for them, an objective usually achieved through corporate reinvestment and long-run profit maximization. And indeed, in 1979 Japanese corporations invested 87 percent of their total after-tax profits and depreciation charges, whereas U.S. corporations reinvested 77 percent.[41]

WHY THE KEIRETSU?

We have characterized the postwar keiretsu as a management protection society. While historically accurate, this definition still does not explain the keiretsu's perpetuation where expert observers confidently predicted it would wither away. The flourishing of the keiretsu suggests that it serves a risk-sharing function, what Nakatani calls "an implicit mutual insurance scheme in which member firms are insured and insurers at the same time."[42]

Such an insurance scheme requires payments from one keiretsu member to another. It also requires provisions to limit moral hazard (actions by the insured that increase risk), without which, mutual insurance would be a blank check for bad management.

The keiretsu bank appears to act as policeman, providing protection against moral hazard. The case of Mazda and its group bank, Sumitomo, offers an illustration. Mazda's difficulties began in 1973, when sales slumped and bank debt mushroomed. Sumitomo responded by placing eleven of its officers in top positions at Mazda and moving the CEO to an honorary position. As a Sumitomo executive said, "For now, we're an army of occupation."[43] Employment was reduced by attrition and early retirement, two-thirds of middle managers were reassigned, new car models were developed, and a quarter of the company stock was sold to the Ford Motor Company.

Sumitomo officials also took on the task of collecting funds to save Mazda. The Sumitomo bank itself provided additional loans, as did most of the sixty other Japanese banks with Mazda loans. Sumitomo also called on the nonfinancial keiretsu members for help. These bought 54 million dollars of stock, real estate, and stocks from Mazda's portfolio, as well as large numbers of Mazda cars for corporate use. As watchers of American television know, Mazda is alive and well.

From the viewpoint of management, the Sumitomo actions were comparable to those that often follow a hostile takeover in the United States. But there is a difference. The restructuring was triggered by Mazda's inability to service its debt, not simply the failure to maximize stockholder returns on corporate assets. Thus, for Japanese management, ouster follows doing badly, not from failing to do the best.

The keiretsu has other functions, the importance of which is difficult to evaluate. Caves and Uekusa have stressed that each keiretsu is a reciprocal buying club.[44] They argue that many products are priced above marginal cost, with the result that a purchase confers a benefit on the seller at no cost to the buyer since the price is simply the market price under imperfect competition. If firms in the same keiretsu engage in two-way trade, they will have higher profits than if each had distributed their purchases more widely.

Akira Goto provides still another definition of the keiretsu—an information club.[45] Information has peculiar economic properties; its economic value often depends on limiting its distribution. If everyone knows a good thing, the market price on that knowledge may be zero. Information is also an awkward item to sell—its value must be revealed to the buyer for him or her to evaluate its worth, after which there is no reason to purchase it. The keiretsu allows a mutual exchange of information that avoids this difficulty and still limits its distribution. As a corollary to the exchange of information, keiretsu members often make equity investments in one another's subsidiaries.

HOW DIFFERENT IS THE JAPANESE CORPORATION?

Even a casual survey of large corporations around the world uncovers features analogous to those in Japanese firms. Reliance on debt financing and on the bank as an active stockholder can be found in many Pacific and Western European countries, with the notable exception of the United Kingdom, which has banking traditions similar to those of the United States.

Western Europe requires high severance pay, which deters layoffs, but this derives from legislation rather than union contracts as in Japan. The placing of union representatives on various corporation boards (codetermination), also legally established in some Western European countries, most notably West Germany, corresponds to the consultation between enterprise unions and corporations that goes on in Japan. The group can be found in other Pacific countries, with that of South Korea following most closely the Japanese model. Korean groups, however, are held together by top holding companies, usually family owned—a striking resemblance to the prewar Japanese zaibatsu. Korea also shares some of the Japanese labor practices—semiannual bonuses, seniority wages, and lifetime employment, though none of these is as common or as well institutionalized as in Japan.

Yet, although these analogies suggest that it is a mistake to consider the Japanese corporation as the exception to a worldwide norm typified by the U.S. firm, much of the Japanese pattern still is unique.

IS THE JAPANESE CORPORATION SUPERIOR?

Recent American business literature frequently suggests that the Japanese corporation is superior to that of the United States, in terms of both economics and social responsibility. The test of an economic institution is how well it performs in a competitive market. By that standard, Japanese firms score high; their worldwide share has been rising sharply in most manufactured products. The characteristics of the Japanese corporation are one possible explanation for this success, but surely not the only one and probably not even the leading one.

Its ownership characteristics permit the Japanese firm to be a long-run rather than short-run profit maximizer. In direct competition, long-run profit maximizers will gain market share from short-run profit maximizers, all other factors being equal. The long-run profit maximizers will spend more on research and development and worker training, invest more in plant and equipment, and cultivate new markets more patiently.

The Japanese setting also promotes management security. That is usually held to be bad for economic performance, but one can argue the opposite. Security promotes loyalty, a long-run view, and even risk taking (since modest failure, at least, is not punished with dismissal). Furthermore, Japanese top management has affiliates, employees, and other keiretsu members, all looking over its shoulder and exerting pressure to perform well, and bad performance is punished.

As suggested earlier, developments in the world economy will test the Japanese corporation as an economic institution. Only then will what Ronald Dorr calls the "flexible rigidities" of Japan be severely stretched.[46] Even so, past performance suggests that the Japanese corporation will be able to cope with the new challenges.

Evaluating the Japanese corporation by the criteria of social responsibility is even more ambiguous. It receives acclaim for its lifetime commitment to employees, its seniority wages, and its semiannual bonuses. But these benefits are limited strictly to regular employees. Temporary workers, employees of affiliates, and, at the bottom, employees of the very small subcontractors of affiliates are treated as, and perhaps more, harshly than similar groups in the United States. There is no affirmative action; on the contrary, high school dropouts, nonconformists, and minorities are excluded from the ranks of regular employees. Women typically lose their regular employee status when they leave to have children.

Beyond the treatment of regular employees, there is not much difference between Japanese and U.S. corporations with respect to the most often cited aspects of social responsibility. Charitable contributions of the U.S. corporations are limited; those of Japanese corporations are even more so. In both countries, legal requirements largely determine corporate actions against pollution, and union pressures are responsible for concern over worker safety.

There is, then, no clear answer to the oft-asked question of whether the Japanese corporation is superior. Certain Japanese practices may be successfully emulated by the U.S. corporation. But it may be that one practice depends on many others to be effective, and only implementation of the entire set will replicate the Japanese result. For example, flexibility of job assignments works well in Japan because of the relatively low turnover. Some practices clearly require economy-wide adoption to succeed: The slow and undifferentiated promotion of young Japanese managers only works because all Japanese corporations follow that practice.

Most of the features of the Japanese corporation date only from the fifties. The theme of this volume is the changing nature of the U.S. corporation; the Japanese firm is also evolving. One can see signs that the Japanese corporation is becoming more like the American and that the American is becoming more like the Japanese. If there are now two distinct corporate systems, we cannot tell which represents the past and which the future.

NOTES

1. Rodney Clark, *The Japanese Company* (New Haven, Conn. Yale University Press, 1979), pp. 100–1. Clark provides an excellent description of the board's functions.
2. By law, Japanese boards also include one or more statutory auditors, full-time board members charged with checking the accuracy of financial statements as well as preventing fraud, tax cheating, and unreasonable expenditures. They lack significant power to perform more than these limited functions.
3. Tadanor Nishiyama, "The Structure of Managerial Control: Who Owns and Controls Japanese Business?" *Journal of Japanese Economic Studies* 11, no. 1 (Fall 1982): 33–77. See particularly table 1, pp. 51–54.
4. Eleanor Hadley, *Antitrust in Japan* (Princeton, N.J.: Princeton University Press, 1970), p. 2.
5. Ibid. Hadley argues this proposition most vigorously.
6. To confuse the pattern further, twenty-four companies belong to two or more keiretsu and two or more president's clubs. See Oriental Economist, *Kigyo Keiretsu Soran* (Tokyo: Oriental Economist, 1982). And to complicate the pattern still more, some keiretsu have subgroups and several different kinds of president's clubs.
7. Material used in this paragraph comes from Lisa Klein, "The Impact of Group Structure on the Strategy of the Japanese Firm" (Yale College senior essay, Yale University, 1987).
8. Oriental Economist, *Kigyo Keiretsu Soran*; Klein, "The Impact of Group Structure," p. 2.
9. In large firms, in 1983 workers in their fifties received wages averaging about twice those of workers eighteen and nineteen years old. See tables 4 and 6 in *Rodo Tokei Chasa Geppo 3*. The Japanese system is best described as a mixed age/seniority system. For example, newly hired workers who are twenty-five usually receive higher wages than beginning eighteen-year-olds but less than twenty-five-year-olds who joined at eighteen. (The hiring of older workers by large firms, most of whom

come from the lower paid small-firm sector, is one way large firms accommodate varying labor demand. In booms, many older workers —in their late twenties and thirties—are hired; in slow times, few.) The reader will note that the masculine pronoun is used in the text. Japanese labor practices apply to regular workers, who are mostly men.

10. Economic Planning Agency, Japanese Government, *Economic Survey of Japan, 1980–1986* (Tokyo: Economic Planning Agency, Japanese Government, 1986), p. 261.

11. Michael Smitka, "Japanese Labor Markets and Subcontracting" (paper presented at Japan Economic Seminar, Harvard University, April 18, 1987), p. 26.

12. Toshiaki Tachibanaki, "Labor Mobility and Job Tenure," in M. Aoki, ed. *The Economic Analysis of the Japanese Firm* (Amsterdam: North Holland, 1984), p. 82. Japanese male workers aged forty to forty-four, average 19.52 years of seniority; the comparable U.S. figure was 11.93 years. This data is for all industries and all firm sizes, so the average includes data for small and medium firms in which long tenure is less common, particularly in Japan.

13. Richard Freeman and Martin Weitzman, in a careful econometric study, found on average that 11 percent of the bonus payment is directly proportional to profits. Richard Freeman and Martin Weitzman, "Bonuses and Employment in Japan" (1987, Mimeographed).

14. Mashino Okuno, "Corporate Loyalty and Bonus Payments: An Analysis of Work Incentives in Japan," in M. Aoki, ed., *The Economic Analysis of the Japanese Firm* (Amsterdam: North Holland, 1984).

15. Job rotation is discussed in Kazua Koike, "Skill Formation in the U.S. and Japan: A Comparative Study," in M. Aoki, ed., *The Economic Analysis of the Japanese Firm* (Amsterdam: North Holland, 1984), p. 62. Koike points out, "The veteran workers always occupy positions next to beginners, looking after him and teaching him. The task of the veteran workers is, thus, not only to operate his own position, but to teach the beginner."

16. See Smitka, "Japanese Labor Markets," p. 29. Unions usually permit large proportions of temporary workers during seasonal peaks and periods of expansion in demand. Thus, at Toyota, temporary workers constituted 11 percent of the work force in 1974, a banner year, but fell to 2 percent subsequently.

17. See Merton J. Peck, Richard C. Levin, and Akira Goto, "Picking the Losers: Public Policy toward Declining Industries in Japan," *The Journal of Japanese Studies* 13, no. 1 (Winter 1987):79–124.

18. Clark, *The Japanese Company*, p. 116.

19. Ibid. p. 126.

20. Ibid. p. 176.

21. Masahiko Aoki, "Aspects of the Japanese Firm," in M. Aoki, ed., *The Economic Analysis of the Japanese Firm* (Amsterdam: North Holland, 1984), p. 27.

22. Smitka, "Japanese Labor Markets," p. 3.

23. The discussion in this section owes much to Michael Smitka's research on subcontracting in Japan for his forthcoming Yale doctoral dissertation.

24. Smitka, "Japanese Labor Markets," contains several detailed case studies of firms established to use housewives and retired people on a part-time basis.

25. Aoki, "Aspects of the Japanese Firm," pp. 28–29.

26. For data on sales in unrelated industries, see Clark, "The Japanese Company," pp. 51–52.

27. Merton J. Peck, with the collaboration of Shuji Tamura, "Technology," in Hugh Patrick and Henry Rosovsky, eds., *Asia's New Giant: How the Japanese Economy Works* (Washington, D.C.: The Brookings Institution, 1976), p. 555.

28. Christina Baird, "Power and Influence in the Japanese Group" (Yale College senior essay, Yale University, 1987), p. 25.

29. This view has been formalized by Masahiko Aoki, "A Model of the Firm as a Stockholder-Employee Cooperative Game," *American Economic Review* 70 (1980):600–10.

30. Indeed, Badaracco states, "In Japan, in fact, the blurring of corporate boundaries has reached its most ornate, almost rococo elaboration."

31. See Richard Caves and Masu Uekusa, "Industrial Organization," in Hugh Patrick and Henry Rosovsky, eds., *Asia's New Giant: How the Japanese Economy Works* (Washington, D.C.: The Brookings Institution, 1976), p. 478.

32. Economic Planning Agency, *Economic Survey of Japan*, Table II-I-6, p. 156.

33. T. Nishiyama, "The Structure of Managerial Control," p. 39.

34. Iwao Nakatani, "The Economic Role of Financial Corporate Grouping," in M. Aoki, ed., *The Economic Analysis of the Japanese Firm* (Amsterdam: North Holland, 1984), pp. 327–58.

35. Ibid., pp. 228–29.

36. Ibid., p. 248.

37. Ibid., p. 239.

38. Ibid., p. 248.

39. Aoki reports that the unadjusted debt equity ratio was 81.8 percent for corporations listed in the Tokyo Stock Exchange in 1981. With adjustments for the net of accounts payable and accounts receivable, for inflation accounting, for certain reserves, and for compensating balances held in lending banks, the debt equity falls to 61.6 percent, still high by U.S. standards. Aoki, "Aspects of the Japanese Firm," pp. 19–21.

40. M. Aoki, "Shareholder Non-unanimity on Investment Financing," in M. Aoki, ed. *The Economic Analysis of the Japanese Firm* (Amsterdam: North Holland, 1984), p. 198

41. Economic Planning Agency, Japanese Government, *Economic Survey of Japan, 1980–1981*, (Tokyo: Economic Planning Agency, Japanese Government, 1981), p. 156.

42. Nakatani, "The Economic Role of Financial Corporate Grouping," p. 229.

43. Robert B. Reich, "Bailout: A Comparative Study in Law and Industrial Structure," *Yale Journal of Regulation* 2 (1985): 179. Reich's article provides an excellent description of the financial rescue of Mazda.

44. Caves and Uekusa, "Industrial Organization," pp. 496–97.

45. Akira Goto, "An Economic Analysis of Firm Groups," *Keizai Kenkyu*, April 1978.

46. Ronald Dorr, *Flexible Rigidities: Industrial Policy and Structural Adjustment in the Japanese Economy, 1970–1980*, (Stanford, Cal.: Stanford University Press, 1986).

3 CORPORATE OWNERSHIP AND CONTROL

F. M. Scherer

During the nineteenth century, American business organization was revolution-ized. By 1801, fewer than 350 business corporations had been incorporated.[1] By 1900, when the Census Bureau first explored the question of ownership, 37,161 establishments in the manufacturing sector alone were owned by corporations. The move toward corporate organization was led by the great transportation enterprises. Manufacturing followed, with a marked acceleration of incorpora-tions during the 1880s and 1890s, while services and merchandising enterprises moved more slowly into the corporate era.

These dynamic differences have persisted into more recent periods. Table 3–1 shows the percentages of sales of three main forms of business organization—corporations, partnerships, and sole proprietorships—in key sectors. Even from 1958 to 1978, the trend toward incorporation is evident, approaching its limit only in manufacturing and the public utility industries. Agriculture and personal services remain a bastion of sole proprietorships. The partnership form continues to be important only in accounting and legal services, although the 1986 income tax reforms may initiate a reversion to more extensive partnership organization.[2]

Table 3–2 focuses more closely on manufacturing to show the shift in ownership forms during the twentieth century. The share of activity under the corporate mantle rose at an annual rate of 1.6 percent during the first two decades and at about 0.2 percent thereafter. Partnerships rapidly declined since World War II.

In 1982, more than 2.9 million business corporations filed U.S. income tax returns. Most were small, but 446,000 had receipts of $1 million or more. The roughly 50,000 corporations with receipts of $10 million or more accounted for three-fourths of all corporate receipts. Even among the larger corporations, the vast majority were privately held (i.e., without securities traded on public stock exchanges). In July 1986 the financial pages of the *New York Times* listed some 6,000 traded common and preferred stocks. The COMPUSTAT data base, which attempts to provide comprehensive coverage of publicly traded corporations,

Table 3–1. Percentages of Corporate Business Receipts in the Principal Industry Sectors (1958 and 1978).[a]

	Corporations		Partnerships		Sole Proprietorships	
	1958	1978	1958	1978	1958	1978
All industries	74.2	87.0	8.3	4.2	17.4	8.9
Agriculture, forestry, and fisheries	10.3	27.1	12.6	12.5	77.1	60.4
Mining	80.6	88.9	8.6	6.4	10.8	4.7
Construction	57.7	76.3	14.8	5.7	27.4	18.1
Manufacturing	95.8	98.8	2.4	0.6	1.9	0.7
Transportation	84.6	88.9	3.1	2.1	12.2	9.0
Communications, electricity, and sanitary utilities	99.1	99.3	0.3	0.5	0.6	0.2
Wholesale Trade	52.5	93.0	7.2	2.2	40.3	4.8
Retail Trade	54.1	79.9	13.1	4.1	32.8	16.0
Finance, insurance, and real estate	85.0	85.1	6.3	11.3	8.7	3.7
Services	37.4	63.5	18.8	13.7	43.7	22.8
Personal	35.5	50.4	17.0	6.8	47.5	42.8
Business	70.7	81.3	11.9	5.0	17.4	13.7
Physicians	n.a.	60.5	n.a.	11.4	n.a.	28.2
Legal	n.a.	22.7	n.a.	50.6	n.a.	26.7
Accounting	n.a.	14.4	n.a.	61.5	n.a.	24.1

a. Percentages are rounded and may not add up to 100.

Sources: U.S. Internal Revenue Service, *Statistics of Income*, "U.S. Business Tax Returns, 1958–59" (Washington, D.C.: U.S. Government Printing Office, 1961); idem, "Corporate Income Tax Returns, 1978–79" (Washington, D.C.: U.S. Government Printing Office, 1982); idem, "Sole Proprietorships, 1978" (Washington, D.C.: U.S. Government Printing Office, 1982).

contained 6,400 entries in 1985. Although publicly traded corporations tend to be among the largest, there are some billion-dollar-plus exceptions, such as textile producer Deering-Milliken, candy maker Mars, grain trader and processor Cargill, and greeting card specialist Hallmark, that remain private.

CORPORATE OWNERSHIP PATTERNS

The ownership of a corporation resides primarily in its stockholders. In 1985 the 1,541 companies with common and preferred stock traded on the New York Stock

Table 3–2. Percentage of Output Value Originated in Business Organizational Forms in the Manufacturing Sector (1900–1982).

Year	Corporations	Sole Proprietorships	Partnerships	Other[a]
1900	65.0	19.0	15.7	0.3
1905	73.7	11.5	14.4	0.4
1919	87.7	5.7	[6.6]	
1947[b]	91.9	2.9	4.5	0.7
1982[b]	98.0	0.6	0.5	0.9

a. Includes cooperatives and government-owned establishments.

b. Value added, rather than product sales, as in other years.

Sources: U.S. Department of Commerce and Labor, U.S. Bureau of the Census, *1905 Census of Manufactures* (Washington, D.C.: U.S. Government Printing Office, 1907), part 1, p. liv; National Industrial Conference Board, *A Graphic Analysis of the Census of Manufactures of the United States* (New York: National Industrial Conference Board, 1923), p. 111; and U.S. Department of Commerce, U.S. Bureau of the Census, *1982 Census of Manufactures: Type of Organization*, preliminary report, MC82-S-5 (Washington, D.C.: U.S. Government Printing Office, September 1985), p. 5–3.

Exchange had stock outstanding with a market value of $1.95 trillion.[3] The same companies had NYSE-listed bonds with a market value of $1.34 trillion, in addition to unknown quantities of privately placed obligations.

Broad Patterns

Although comparably defined statistics are lacking, it seems clear that there have been important changes over time in the ownership of U.S. corporations' common and preferred stock (see Table 3–3). The holdings of individuals have declined relative to those of domestic financial institutions and foreign investors. Critical to the increasing role of institutions have been the growing stock holdings of pension funds, from 2 percent in 1950 to 14.5 percent in 1979.

An alternate and more up-to-date view of the institutions' role is provided by Table 3–4. The median company had 44 percent of its shares in the hands of institutions such as pension funds, insurance companies, banks (presumably including trust portfolios), investment companies, and colleges. Larger corporations and/or those with relatively high stock values had significantly higher percentages of institutional ownership than companies with lower market values. The average corporation's stock, according to *Business Week*, was held by 166 different institutions.[4]

The Role of Individual Investors

Although the proportion of U.S. corporations' stock held directly by individuals has been falling, the ownership base among individual investors has broadened.

Table 3–3. Percentage Distribution of Common and Preferred Stock Holdings (1950–1979).

Type of Holder	1950	1960	1970	1979
Private noninsured pension funds	0.8	3.9	7.8	10.4
State and local retirement funds	a	0.1	0.9	3.1
Open-end investment companies	2.0	3.7	5.1	2.9
Other investment companies	a	1.3	0.7	0.2
Insurance companies	3.2	3.0	3.3	5.5
Trust funds	b	10.6	9.7	9.0
Mutual savings banks	0.1	0.2	0.3	0.4
Foundations	n.a.	3.2	2.6	3.4
Educational endowments	n.a.	1.0	0.9	0.9
Total institutional[c]	6.4[d]	26.7	30.9	35.0
Foreign investors	2.0	3.2	3.1	6.7
Domestic individuals	91.6[d]	70.1	66.0	58.3
Market value of stock (in billions of dollars)	146.0	421.2	854.8	1,188.6

a. Small.

b. Included in "domestic individuals" category.

c. Individual figures do not add up to total because of rounding errors and double-counted institutional holdings of investment company shares.

d. Not directly comparable with figures for other years.

Sources: U.S. Bureau of the Census, *Historical Statistics of the United States: Colonial Times to 1970* (Washington, D.C.: U.S. Government Printing Office, 1975). p. 987; U.S. Securities and Exchange Commission, *Annual Report 1973* (Washington, D.C.: U.S. Government Printing Office, 1973), p. 148; and idem, *Annual Report 1980* (Washington, D.C.: U.S. Government Printing Office, 1981), p. 117.

According to New York Stock Exchange surveys, stock ownership has generally risen since 1952, both absolutely and relative to the U.S. population, except during the 1970s, when many potential investors were apparently intimidated by the hyperactive conglomerate merger speculations that peaked in 1968 and collapsed thereafter.[5]

In one respect, the data on stock owners present an excessively roseate view of the extent to which "people's capitalism" has spread. Most individual stockholders own only small equity interests; a few, on the other hand, have very large holdings. The ownership of corporate stock is one of the most unequally distributed forms of personal wealth. Estimates by Lampman, Smith, and Franklin reproduced in Table 3–5 reveal that, over most of the twentieth century, the wealthiest 1 percent of all individuals have owned well over half the value of all personally held corporate stocks. Only state and local bonds—a favorite shelter from income taxes—and corporate bonds show higher concentration. From its

Table 3–4. Percentage Distribution of Institutional Common Stock Ownership Positions for the 1,000 Largest Corporations on *Business Week's* 1985 List.[a]

Institutional Ownership[b]	Top 100 Companies	Companies 101–500	Companies 501–1,000	All 1,000 Companies
0–9	0.0	1.0	7.4	4.1
10–19	1.0	4.5	10.2	7.0
20–29	6.0	7.8	18.6	13.0
30–39	14.0	15.3	18.8	16.9
40–49	26.0	20.8	19.4	20.6
50–59	24.0	19.3	14.6	17.4
60–69	22.0	22.0	7.8	14.9
70–79	4.0	7.8	1.8	4.4
80–89	2.0	1.5	0.4	1.0
90–100	1.0	0.2	0.8	0.6
Median	51	50	37	44

a. Percentages are rounded and may not add up to 100.

b. Institutional holdings include stocks held by banks, colleges, pension funds, insurance companies, and investment companies.

Source: "The 1,000 Largest U.S. Companies Ranked by Stockmarket Valuation," *Business Week*, April 18, 1986, pp. 62–119.

Table 3–5. Percentage of Personal Wealth Held in Various Forms by the Wealthiest One Percent of All Adult Wealth Holders.

	1922	1949	1972
Corporate stock	61.5	64.9	56.5
Bonds			
U.S. government	45.0	35.8 ⎫	
State and local government	88.0	77.0 ⎬	60.0
Other	69.2	78.0 ⎭	
Cash	n.a.	18.9	15.3
Real estate	18.0	10.5	15.3

Sources: Robert J. Lampman, *The Share of Top Wealth-Holders in National Wealth: 1922–56* (Princeton, N.J.: Princeton University Press, 1962), p. 209; and U.S. Bureau of the Census, *Statistical Abstract of the United States: 1979* (Washington, D.C.: U.S. Government Printing Office, 1979), p. 470 (from research by James D. Smith and Stephen D. Franklin).

survey of consumer finances, the Federal Reserve Board (FRB) has estimated that the top 2 percent of families (not individuals) ranked by income owned 50 percent of all personally held corporate stocks in 1983 and 71 percent of nontaxable municipal bonds and mutual funds but only 8 percent of the savings account balances and 20 percent of the real property.[6] The top 10 percent of income-earning families held 72 percent of the stocks by value and 86 percent of the nontaxable bonds.

Among less affluent stockholders, holdings are not only small, but also undiversified and hence relatively risky. Only 40 percent of all FRB-surveyed families with stock held shares in more than one company. Many single stock owners limit their ownership to the shares of their employers, which implies even greater risk. A 1971 survey analyzed by Blume and Friend revealed that nearly three-fourths of the portfolios valued at less then $10,000 contained only one or two stocks.[7] In contrast, 56.4 percent of the portfolios valued at more than $1 million included ten or more different companies' shares.

Stock Ownership by Workers

The data on individual stockholdings exclude shares held indirectly for workers covered by pension funds. Since pension-fund holdings have grown rapidly, while direct holdings by the wealthiest citizens have shown no clear trend, and since pension-fund beneficiaries number in the tens of millions, it is probably true that corporate ownership has, at least indirectly, become dispersed more widely. The top 10 percent of all families ranked by income received a third of all family income in 1982—much less than their share of stock- and bondholdings.[8] Since their income includes earnings on capital, the inequality of wage and salary earnings must be even less. It seems reasonable to suppose that the distribution of pension-fund benefits is more similar to that of wages and salaries than that of total income or securities holdings, although precise data are not available.

The ownership by employees of stock in the corporations for which they work—another facet of ''people's capitalism''—is undoubtedly one reason why small-lot stock ownership has become so widespread. There are three main types of worker ownership, each with distinct implications for participation and control: direct stock purchase; cooperative ownership, in which enterprises are totally owned by their profit-sharing workers, each of whom has a single vote on company business questions; and ESOPs, a special legal form of employee stock-ownership plan.

Direct employee stock-purchase plans are not new. A 1926 survey estimated conservatively that, under such plans, employees owned at least $700 million of their employers' shares, or about 1.5 percent of all listed corporations' stock value at the time.[9] Direct employee ownership under voluntary purchase plans presumably has increased both absolutely and relatively since then, but reliable data on the phenomenon have not been found. Although workers can vote their shares of stock, their combined holdings rarely constitute a major voting bloc.

Much more thoroughly studied are the ESOPs, sometimes called ''Kelso'' plans after their principal promoter, Louis Kelso.[10] Their formation has been encouraged through increasingly generous federal income-tax treatment beginning in 1974. In 1984 approximately 7,000 U.S. corporations had ESOPs, 10 to 15 percent of which involved majority employee ownership. Along with roughly 2,000 cooperatives and similar employee ownership arrangements, they affected an estimated 7 to 8 percent of the U.S. work force.[11]

The tax incentives for ESOP formation include the ability for corporations to deduct (within limits) against their income-tax liabilities the value of newly printed stock certificates distributed to the employees' stock trust and to deduct the principal value of repayments on loans made to purchase stock for the trust.[12] Because ESOP stock must be issued to a trust (operated by a management-appointed trustee) rather than directly to workers, it appears in Table 3–3 as institutionally held. Workers take direct possession of the stock in their ESOP accounts only when they retire or leave the company, and their rights to do so are vested gradually, with buildup to the fully vested point after an average of ten years. Full voting rights must be passed through the trust to workers only when the ESOP is in a publicly traded corporation (approximately 20 percent of all plans). Employee ownership in these companies typically falls far below the majority threshold.[13] About 15 percent of ESOP companies without publicly traded stock pass through full voting rights to the beneficiary workers. In many other cases, however, trustees are not bound to respect worker-owner preferences. This has led to problems. For example, a protracted work slowdown ensued when the board of Hyatt-Clark Industries, a 100-percent worker-owned ESOP company, rejected a union demand that profits be distributed to workers rather than invested in new machinery. In part as a consequence, Hyatt-Clark management entered a bankruptcy petition asking that the court revoke the union's contract and unilaterally set wage terms.[14]

As this example suggests, worker ownership does not ensure integration of management and workers or harmonization of their objectives. Nevertheless, when implemented effectively, it appears to affect both attitudes and performance. A survey of 2,804 ESOP participants in thirty-seven companies found that, although on average workers believed that their ownership did not increase their role in company decisionmaking, their job satisfaction was enhanced.[15] Employees' satisfaction and organizational commitment generally increased with the size of company contributions to the ESOP trust and the weight managers accorded to worker ownership as part of the company's culture.[16] In a more limited analysis, researchers at the Michigan Survey Research Center found that twenty-five companies with worker-ownership plans had greater average profitability than nonplan companies of similar size and industry orientation.[17] Profitability rose according to the fraction of company stock that workers owned.

The Role of Institutional Fund Managers

Even when employees share directly in ownership through an ESOP or pension-fund accumulation, voting rights and (except under ESOPs) decisions to buy, retain, or sell shares of a particular company are often made by a trustee or fund manager—most commonly, an official of a bank, insurance company, or other financial intermediary. Voting rights are also exercised by the managers of mutual funds and, less frequently, by the custodians of personal trust funds and institutional endowment funds. U.S. commercial banks, unlike their banking counterparts in the nations of Western Continental Europe and Japan and insurance companies, legally may maintain sizable stock positions for their own investment accounts only temporarily, but, as fund managers for others, they occupy a prominent stock-voting position.

For the *Fortune* 500 industrials of 1981, Thomas R. Dye attempted to identify "strategic ownership positions," defined as those with 1 percent or more of a company's outstanding common shares and listed among the company's top five shareholders.[18] Of the 2,156 positions identified, 860 were held by financial holding firms (such as trust companies, mutual funds, and employee-stock trust managers), 486 were held by banks, 122 by pension funds (including strong representation by CREF, the principal retirement equity fund of university faculty), and 101 by insurance companies. Altogether, 73 percent of the strategic ownership positions were traced to financial intermediaries.

The degree to which owners' control responsibilities are exercised by these financial intermediaries is not known with precision. However, several general observations can be made.

One aspect of control is voting on mergers, compensation plans, directoral appointments, and other matters put before stockholders on annual or special proxy solicitations. Mutual-fund managers and insurance companies characteristically exercise full voting rights with respect to their investment portfolios. A 1969 survey revealed that fifty pension-fund managers had full voting authority over 73 percent of the common stock in their portfolios.[19] They have perhaps the least discretion over personal trust holdings—voting independently in less than 50 percent of the cases, according to Edward Herman.[20] Overall, four major banks had sole voting rights in 1974 for 64 percent of the stockholdings over which they had buy-and-sell discretion.[21] A Securities and Exchange Commission survey of twenty-eight banks (out of a larger sample of fifty-eight) that had voted against management at least once over a thirty-three-month period tallied a total of 351 votes against management.[22]

Financial intermediaries have even more discretion in exercising the "Wall Street Rule"—selling portfolio shares of companies with whose performance they are displeased. In recent years, their power has been enhanced by the increased frequency of tender-offer takeover attempts, for the decision of intermediaries to hold or sell often determines the outcome of a contest for corporate control.[23]

Least quantifiable is the power financial intermediaries wield through face-to-face interaction with operating company management, either through representation on boards of directors or through less formal contacts. Herman found that 162 of the 200 largest U.S. nonfinancial corporations in 1975 had at least one financial intermediary official on their boards of directors; altogether, the 200 corporations' boards had 345 bank and insurance company representations.[24] Herman argues that these influences are relatively unimportant except when corporations are in "serious financial difficulty"; David Kotz, however, perceives a much more pervasive and powerful control role.[25] The only point on which widespread agreement seems to exist is that the control power of financial institutions has been less in the 1970s and 1980s than it was around the turn of the century, when J.P. Morgan, George F. Baker of New York's First National Bank, and a few other interlocked financial leaders intervened aggressively in shaping individual company policies and entire industry structures.[26]

Management Buyouts

The broad trend in business-enterprise ownership since 1900 has been toward increased use of the corporate form, widespread participation in corporate ownership through the trading of securities on organized exchanges, and a decline in the prominence of corporations owned preponderantly by their managers. There have been important exceptions to this pattern—notably, the millions of small nontraded corporations as well as the relatively few privately owned corporate giants. Recently, a new countertrend has materialized: a greatly increased tendency for corporations or parts thereof to go private, often through buyouts organized by their incumbent managements and financed through borrowings sufficiently heavily leveraged to give management a dominant equity ownership position.

W.T. Grimm & Co., compilers of statistics on corporate merger and sell-off activity, report management buyout transactions in two categories—"unit buyouts," in which only part of a corporation is sold to its management, and "going private transactions," in which a whole company leaves the publicly traded arena. For the two categories combined, the average annual dollar growth rate from 1979 through 1985 was 63 percent. A $29.1 billion consideration paid in 1985 transactions amounted to 1.5 percent of the value of all common stocks listed in that year on the New York Stock Exchange.[27]

There is evidence that going private leads to significant behavioral changes, especially when a business unit moves from being a subsidiary of a large conglomerate corporation to being a self-standing enterprise "owned" by its managers.[28] Overhead staffs are cut, product lines are pruned to their most profitable core, less expensive office space is occupied, inventory and accounts-receivable control is tightened, and much else. Risk also increases, partly because of high debt leveraging and partly because the new entity's fortunes hinge upon conditions in a single, undiversified line of business. Whether the efficiency gains following recent management buyouts reflect pervasive incentive effects or merely anomalous fringe behavior—such as the weeding out of exceptional divisions for which conglomerate parents' managerial skills were especially ill suited—remains to be seen. The evidence of efficiency-enhancing behavioral changes is much weaker, if not lacking altogether, for whole-company buyouts, which cautions that the phenomenon may not be universal.[29]

THE BEHAVIORAL CONSEQUENCES OF OWNERSHIP STRUCTURE

Since the publication in 1932 of an enormously influential book by Adolf Berle and Gardiner Means, if not before (e.g., in Adam Smith's tirade against English crown corporations), it has become clear to scholars, policymakers, and the thinking public that the ownership structure of corporations could have serious behavioral consequences.[30]

Berle and Means advanced three major theses:

1. Sizable public corporations were carrying out a large and growing share of the nation's business;

2. The stock ownership of public corporations was becoming increasingly dispersed and divorced from the control functions exercised by managers holding, at most, minor ownership stakes; and

3. This separation of ownership and control could lead to the operation of corporations to advance management interests at the cost of owner goals.

Berle and Means were correct in their assertion that the corporation had become the dominant organizational form of business in America. They were not demonstrably mistaken in their estimate that, between 1909 and 1929, the share of all nonfinancial corporation activity traceable to the 200 largest enterprises had been rising fairly steadily.[31] For present purposes, it is of little consequence that subsequent events failed to validate their warning that if past growth rates continued, all U.S. corporate activity would be controlled by the largest 200 corporations at some time between 1962 and 1972.[32]

Drawing upon a case study of John D. Rockefeller's difficulties in maintaining control of the Indiana Standard Oil Company, Berle and Means set a 20-percent ownership share of voting stock by some "compact" group as the dividing line between minority ownership control and the abrogation of control to management.[33] Applying this criterion, they found 88 of the largest 200 nonfinancial corporations to be management controlled. Only 22 were privately owned or controlled by a majority ownership group.[34] Replicating the Berle and Means methodology but using a lower 10-percent ownership share as the threshold, Robert Larner found that 161 of the 200 largest nonfinancial corporations had come to be management controlled by 1963. Larner concluded that the "managerial revolution" identified by Berle and Means was "close to complete."[35]

These inferences have been challenged by Phillip Burch, Edward Herman, Thomas Dye, and others for ignoring the power positions of financial intermediaries and the possibility that family or other interest groups might exercise effective control with an ownership share well below a 10- or 20-percent threshold.[36] Reworking the source data under an assumption that control could be exercised with a family stock position of 4 to 5 percent accompanied by extended representation on the board of directors, Burch concluded that in 1965 only 41 percent of the 300 leading industrial corporations and 28 percent of the top 50 merchandising corporations were "probably management controlled."[37]

Evidently, how much autonomous power one believes nonowner managers wield depends upon fine quantitative distinctions over which reasonable observers can disagree. Wherever the line between owner and manager control is drawn, however, its relevance depends upon how differences in the locus and extent of control affect behavior. On this point, too, a lively debate has emerged.

Berle and Means were modest in their statement of how behavior might change. Owner goals were clear to them: maximum profits compatible with "reasonable" risk; an appropriate distribution of those profits to shareholders; and free marketability of the company's securities at a "fair price." "The interests of control," they conceded, "are not so easily discovered." Owners' and managers' interests might be parallel in many instances. But they might also diverge, Berle and Means speculated, as inside managers profit at the stockholders' expense from sham transactions, insider trading, and stock market manipulation. Or, in the quest to enlarge their own power and prestige, managers might reinvest too much of an enterprise's profits in expansion, or offer excessively generous wages and working conditions, or improve product quality beyond the point of maximum profitability.[38] Not mentioned explicitly by Berle and Means, but no less plausible, might be a tendency for managers to overspend on luxurious offices, abundant staffs, corporate jets, and the other perquisites of control. Or they might simply avoid risks and unpleasantness and opt for "the quiet life."[39]

The Constraints on Managerial Discretion

One seminal contribution extending the Berle and Means thesis was by Michael Jensen and William Meckling.[40] They first transformed the discourse by changing the semantics—from the "separation of ownership and control" of Berle and Means, with its ominous negative ring, to the much better sounding challenge of securing the optimal relationship between principals (stockholders) and agents (managers). Second, accepting the view of Berle and Means that the requisites of large-scale and low-cost (i.e., risk-hedged) capital raising made the modern corporate ownership structure inevitable, they insisted that it was equally inevitable that some "agency costs" would be incurred. These agency costs included expenditures by the principals to monitor agent behavior, "bonding" expenditures by the agent to convince principals that it would serve them faithfully, and "residual losses" owing to (optimal) divergences between principals' objectives and agent decisions. To fret about such costs, they argued, was to commit the "Nirvana fallacy" of assuming that markets can be made to work at zero resource cost. Third, Jensen and Meckling identified several factors that keep agency costs in the modern corporation within tolerable bounds: for example, competition among would-be managers to accept performance contracts correlating their rewards with the degree to which principals' welfare is advanced; the possibility for owners to sell out their interests to others who would manage the firm themselves or, at least, monitor its managers more effectively; and (most originally) the incentive of managers to "bond" themselves by borrowing from banks or other well-organized interests who would monitor company performance sufficiently carefully to ensure a close approximation to profit maximization.

Eugene Fama carried the principal-agent argument even further.[41] Contrary to the view of both Berle and Means and their critics, who attach almost mystical significance to ownership, Fama argued that risk capital is an input like any other input (including management's) and that "control over a firm's decisions is not necessarily the province of security owners." In his view, management's behavior is controlled instead through the competition among managers to be the "boss of bosses" and through managers' recognition that, by maximizing profits, they build their reputations and thus can expect higher future compensation in the "ex post settling up" that occurs in the market for managerial services both inside and outside their companies.

The Takeover Mechanism

Fama considered his solution to the corporate principal-agent problem less expensive and, hence, preferable to the tender-offer alternative stressed by other scholars. Under the tender-offer approach, corporations whose nonowner managers perform poorly will be taken over by companies (or investment groups), who will fire or discipline the errant incumbent managers and reinstate profit-maximizing policies.[42] However, with the great increase in tender-offer takeovers (and perhaps the commensurately increased need for an apologetic that explains them), the takeover theory has gained ascendance over alternative theories in nominating a mechanism, or, at least, the most important last-resort mechanism, for constraining managers to serve stockholder interests.

Still, the takeover theory is not free from criticism. Some question whether takeovers truly tend to enhance profits or efficiency, as the theory assumes.[43] Louis Lowenstein raises a more fundamental objection.[44] For modern business enterprises to thrive, they need capital that will stay invested over the long lives of plant, equipment, and good will. Investors, however, want to be able to liquidate their investments on short notice. Extending a point made by Berle and Means and implicitly accepted by Jensen, Meckling, and Fama, Lowenstein argues that the modern corporation and its associated capital markets reconcile these needs admirably. From the managers' perspective, capital inflows are as permanent as sensible real investment opportunities and their cash-flow returns warrant, while the individual stockholder can secure liquidity by selling or buying shares on an active securities market. This system served well for the better part of a century, Lowenstein concludes, but the emergence in the 1960s and 1970s of effective takeover mechanisms altered the balance radically. Investors gained the option of reneging on their commitments, taking (or conveying) actual control of the investments previously sunk in an enterprise and reorienting them in new, perhaps quite different, directions. The consequence, Lowenstein fears, may be an altered corporate culture in which long-term resource commitments—the sine qua non for achieving real economic gains—become less secure and less subject to the pursuit of confident, steady-handed policies.[45] If such farsighted commitments are more difficult to make, economic growth will be retarded.

Further Perplexities

In sum, theoretical thought on the ownership and control of the modern corporation is in a state of turmoil. There is lack of agreement on how seriously the goals of owners and managers diverge. It is not clear a priori how small the ownership share of leading stockholders (or financial intermediaries) must be before managers begin to enjoy substantial discretion to pursue their own goals. Nor is it agreed what incentive mechanisms reconcile owner and manager goals most effectively or even whether certain prominent mechanisms might be harmful from the standpoint of broader economywide objectives.

Nor do the problems end there. Rightly or wrongly, most of the literature on corporate control assumes that managers should choose operating and investment policies that serve owner objectives. But who are the owners? What if they have heterogeneous goals not easily reconciled among themselves?

The close family-owned and -operated corporation is often assumed to be the classic form that reconciles most directly ownership and management goals. But the mythology of the family corporation ignores the problem of internally diverging preferences concerning managerial salaries, reinvestment versus dividend payout, the employment of in-laws, the availability of company cars, and much else.[46] In fact, a voluminous set of legal precedents strains to disentangle the complex knots created by quarreling family corporation stockholders.[47] I recall from my youth that few things struck more consternation into the heart of my father, president of a corporation whose stockholders were the eight children of his founder-father, as the warning, ''Aunt Helen's coming to town.''

In answer to the question, Who is the owner? no one has clear pride of place over the individual who founded a corporation and retains a significant share of its outstanding stock. Yet some research reveals a likely conflict between such owner-managers' preferences and those of other stockholders. It shows that the unanticipated death of founder-executives, unlike the death of nonfounder-executives (with much lower stock-ownership positions), triggered a statistically significant increase in company stock prices.[48] Similarly, others argue that when insider executives, founders or not, control a significant fraction of company shares, they are able to block takeover attempts and hence may be free to indulge objectives that conflict with outside shareholders' desire for maximum profits.[49]

Thus, not only is it unclear how concentrated ownership positions must be to ensure that management serves as a faithful agent of owner interests, but questions remain as to which owner interests management should serve, given likely conflicts among the preferences of diverse ownership groups.

OWNERSHIP STRUCTURE AND PERFORMANCE

Since theory provides few unambiguous clues, economists have turned to statistical studies to learn whether ownership structure affects corporate perform-ance, and, if so, how. There have been two main and one still-undeveloped research foci: the determinants of managerial compensation, the influence of alternate ownership forms on profitability, and the impact of bank and other institutional holdings.

Managerial Compensation

As soon as one asks how corporate ownership affects management compensation, one is forced to recognize that, even in very large and diffusely held corporations, stock ownership per se can be an important contributor to top managers' wealth. To be sure, managers may own only a tiny fraction of the outstanding shares of their employer, but a small share of a large sum can amount to significant wealth for an individual. Studying fifty leading U.S. manufacturing corporations, Wilbur Lewellen found that dividends, capital gains on company stockholdings, and changes in the value of stock options averaged 136 percent of fixed dollar compensation (salary plus bonus) for those companies' top three executives from

1940 to 1963.[50] More recent confirming evidence is provided by Kevin Murphy, who investigated the compensation and stockholdings of 461 corporate executives (59 percent of them below the chairman or presidential level).[51] On average, their 1983 stockholdings were $4.7 million per capita—thirteen times annual salary plus bonus. In terms of common stock returns for shareholders generally from 1964 to 1981, moving from the lowest decile to the top quintile increased the average value of the managers' own stockholdings by some $5 million. The typical top executive, then, could hardly be unconscious of how his or her own wealth depends upon company fortunes. What remains unclear is whether this linkage might have been significantly weaker in certain ownership structures—for example, in companies lacking identifiable outside control groups, for which William McEachern found inside managerial stockholdings to be appreciably below average.[52]

Numerous scholars have investigated whether executives' salaries and bonuses are correlated systematically with their companies' profitability, which would reinforce the inference that manager and owner interests are parallel. The research varies widely in quality, so no comprehensive survey is warranted here.[53] One problem is that greater corporate size undoubtedly calls for superior managerial skills, so a positive association between size and compensation is expected, but the exact form of the relationship is unclear. A related problem is that levels of sales and assets and levels of profits are highly correlated, making it difficult to isolate effects without a carefully specified econometric model. Close statistical "fit" and some theory suggest a nonlinear size-compensation relationship of double logarithmic form.[54] When the size effect is so controlled, the weight of evidence indicates that higher or rising profits imply higher compensation, although the regulated electric power and telephone companies may be an exception.[55] Dennis Mueller's unusually rich analysis showed no effect when profitability was measured as the reported return on assets toward which 499 U.S. manufacturing companies gravitated from 1950 to 1972, but top five executives' compensation was associated positively and strongly with the profitability returns predicted for the companies, had they taken full advantage of their market opportunities.[56] Using stock-price changes rather than reported profits as his indicator of how well managers served shareholders, Murphy found that for 461 executives from 1964 to 1981 annual percentage changes in compensation were correlated positively and significantly with stock-price changes. Managers who led companies with stock-price declines of 30 percent or more saw their pay decrease by 1.2 percent per year on average; those in companies whose stock increased in value by 30 percent or more averaged pay gains of 8.7 percent.[57]

A strict interpretation of Berle and Means might insist that, even after differences in company size and profitability are taken into account, executives of management-controlled corporations are compensated more handsomely than executives of corporations with a strong independent ownership group. Only a few studies have tested this hypothesis. Using data roughly contemporaneous with the

Berle and Means book, George Stigler and Claire Friedland found no significant relationship between executive compensation and a dichotomous Berle and Means control-form variable, taking company asset values into account as well.[58] Applying a more elaborate model to data on forty-eight companies in three industries, McEachern discovered that management compensation was correlated more closely with profitability in corporations controlled by an outside owner group than in companies controlled either by an inside owner-manager group or by inside managers alone.[59] Analyzing sixty-eight large U.S. corporations in 1980, a recession year, Rexford Santerre and Stephen Neun found chief executive officer salary-plus-bonus payments to be *negatively* correlated with the concentration of stock ownership, measured by a Herfindahl index, controlling also for company size and profit rates.[60] On the other hand, for a small British sample, John Cubbin and Graham Hall found managerial compensation to be significantly *higher*, company size and profitability held constant, in companies whose board of directors members held 5 percent or more of outstanding shares and for which no equivalent outside ownership group was identified. They also observed that managers of companies active in making mergers and (especially) hostile takeovers were compensated more generously.[61]

The compensation studies reveal definite linkages between managers' and stockholders' economic fortunes. If there are significant agency problems on the compensation front, they are subtle, and pinning them down more completely will require better data, better-focused models, and more powerful statistical methods than those employed to date.

Ownership Structure and Profitability

Management compensation is only one of the many things that can be affected by how the corporation principal-agent problem is solved. When the whole array of effects is taken into account, what remains is the bottom line—profitability.

Many statistical studies have attempted to determine how profitability varies with ownership structure. Their results are highly varied and often contradictory, apparently because of differences in the scope and timing of the sample, how the corporate control variables have been defined, and what other profit-influencing variables have been included.[62] A serious failure has been a lack of tests for the sensitivity of results to other measurement and model-specification assumptions. If any pattern is discernible in the findings, it is that management-controlled companies tend to be somewhat less profitable than corporations with a concentrated outside ownership group, as Berle and Means might have predicted. But it is unclear whether companies controlled by managers with a sizable ownership stake, who are hence particularly secure in their tenure, have chosen to trade off profits for other amenities more or less than controlling managers with little personal equity stake who face no well-coalesced outside ownership group.

Five recent works illustrate the range of results and the reasons for continuing puzzlement. For samples of sixty-eight to ninety-two corporations with data available from the 1920s and 1930s, Stigler and Friedland regressed the logarithm of profits (with constants added to suppress negative values) on the logarithm of assets and a variable distinguishing management-controlled corporations, as determined by Berle and Means, from owner-controlled entities. Management-controlled companies were consistently less profitable, but the difference was statistically significant only for 1937–38 data.[63] For a study of 499 U.S. corporations, Mueller estimated an unusually elaborate model in which the dependent variable was the *predicted* return on assets toward which profits gravitated over the long run of twenty-two years.[64] In addition to variables measuring the proportion of common shares held by the top five managers and (separately) identifiable outside ownership groups, he took into account company market share, 1972 size, diversification, industry concentration, industry advertising, and the industry's record of patented invention. Corporations with a strong inside owner group proved to be significantly less profitable, while the existence of a strong outside owner group made no difference. Harold Demsetz and Kenneth Lehn analyzed 511 U.S. corporations' net profit as a percentage of stockholders' equity, controlling also for stock-price risk, capital intensity, advertising intensity, research-and-development expenditures, size, and status as a public utility or financial intermediary.[65] Variables measuring the predicted or actual percentage of common stock controlled by the five or twenty largest shareholders (with no distinction between outside and inside holdings) had trivial and statistically insignificant coefficient values. The results of Mueller, a confirmed "managerialist," and Demsetz, who has long argued that ownership structure does not matter, differ so sharply that they recall an earlier Demsetz observation that among economists, "believing is seeing."[66] An alternative possibility is that nonlinearities underlie the differences in results. When Randall Morck and his coauthors replicated the Demsetz analysis using 1980 data for 371 *Fortune* 500 corporations, they obtained a negative linear relationship between profitability and the proportion of company stock held by members of the board of directors. But when they allowed the relationship to be nonlinear, they found maximum profitability or stock-market valuation to be achieved when directors held 5 to 20 percent of the company's shares. Both lower and higher inside shareholdings coincided with lower profitability.[67] Finally, James Bothwell subtracted from the average profit/sales ratios of 150 U.S. industrial corporations from 1960 to 1967 a risk premium estimated using Capital Asset Pricing Model techniques.[68] He then found that, in industries with "high" and "substantial" barriers to competitive entry, managerially controlled companies had significantly lower profitability than owner-controlled companies. Without the risk adjustment, the differences relating to control form faded to insignificance, suggesting that companies without a strong ownership group fritter away what otherwise would be supranormal profits by accepting (or having forced upon them) high market risk.

Financial Institution Control

The state of the theoretical art on how ownership structure affects profitability has advanced to the point of richly elaborated confusion. The literature on how financial intermediary holdings affect managerial performance is more primitive. There is much qualitative discussion of possibilities but little quantitative analysis.

John Cable tested hypotheses on how bank ownership, trusteeship, and lending positions affect industrial company profitability in Germany and Japan, where the role of the banks as direct long-term capital sources is much stronger than in the United States. For West Germany, he found the profitability of forty-eight industrial enterprises to increase with the concentration of common-stock voting control among financial institutions, with the degree that companies financed their operations by bank loans as compared to other debt, and also with the concentration of nonbank ownership interests.[69] His interpretation does not stress management monitoring and bonding effects, but rather the role of bank involvement in perfecting what would otherwise be quite imperfect capital markets (at least, given German institutions). His results for eighty-nine Japanese firms reveal a positive (but statistically insignificant) influence of main keiretsu bank-loan shares on profitability and, in contrast to the German study, a negative impact of bank-loan reliance generally.[70]

David Kotz analyzed the tendency of 147 U.S. manufacturing companies to make mergers as a function of diverse bank-holding positions.[71] Enterprises whose bankers occupied strong control positions by virtue of heavy lending and seats on the board of directors were found to be significantly more prone to mergers. Bank holdings of stock (usually in trust) had no perceptible effect— perhaps because trust activities have little clout within bank power structures compared to that of the larger, more profitable lending and investment departments.[72]

Through whatever control position they maintain by managing securities portfolios, financial intermediaries may influence operating company management behavior, not only by face-to-face suasion, but also by the signals they send in the form of buy-and-sell decisions. Two quantitative facets of the intermediaries' behavior are of special interest.

First, there is an appreciable subset of institutional investors whose decisions appear consonant with fad or "bubble" models of investment. At the micro level, some fund managers base their decisions on word-of-mouth from other market participants, place considerable emphasis on observed security price trends, add to their portfolios gradually as a stock's price rises, and sell abruptly when the price movement reverses.[73] In the aggregate, pension-fund managers have tended to increase the share of their portfolios devoted to common stocks as equity market prices were generally rising and to sell only after the market turned unfavorable.[74] Thus, they come close to following the small-investor maxim, "buy high, sell low,'' and must have sent a message to operating corporation managers that they were fickle and not investing for the long run.

Second, institutional investors, including pension-fund managers, are often under considerable pressure ''to perform.'' Many, therefore, especially those not committed to a market-matching ''index'' approach, ''churn'' their portfolios at a high rate, selling when some new development provides the opportunity to make a quick capital gain that will enhance their quarterly performance records. This behavior, combined with the rising proportion of all corporate stocks held by fund managers, has led to, among other effects, a substantial increase in stock turnover rates. The average New York Stock Exchange share is now traded every two years—three times the rate in the 1950s.[75] And for the stockholdings accounted for by institutions—roughly half of all shares—the turnover rate is undoubtedly much higher.

Again, the message to operating corporations is that the average institutional buyer is in for the short run, not the long. How the message is read and transformed into operating policy by industrial corporations is not known. Certainly, in an era when unenthusiastic investors and depressed prices can lead to takeover, operating managers ignore fund managers' preferences at their peril. The crucial question is whether they reshape their investment and product-pricing decisions to enhance short-run profits at the expense of longer term growth. The business press contains numerous allegations that they do.[76] However, it is difficult to distinguish alarmism from actual behavioral changes. Only two conclusions can be drawn: first, that we really do not know what the effects are, but, second, that if institutional investors' preferences do induce a shortening of operators' decision-making horizons, the cost in terms of eventually eroded industrial strength could be great. Indeed, of the many unsettled questions concerning corporate ownership structures and how they matter, this is probably the most important.

CONCLUSION

Over the past century, the corporation has come to be the dominant organizational form for conducting business. Corporate control through ownership by individual families has declined over time, although it has by no means disappeared. Control by financial intermediaries declined after the first decade of the twentieth century and may have experienced some resurgence during the past two decades. Unfortunately, we have little conclusive knowledge about how much discretion these developments have left nonowner managers or how, if at all, managers' behavior is changed in exercising that discretion. Nor do we know how corporate behavior is altered by pressure, direct or indirect, from outside ownership groups. Competition and natural selection may ensure, as some ''Chicagoans'' hold, that the surviving ownership structures will be those efficiently adapted to the mandates of the marketplace—or, as Marxists argue, those best serving the interests of a concentrated capitalist class. Ideology assuages the discomforts of ignorance. Greater intellectual unease is the lot of those like myself who, following Berle and Means, believe that ownership structure can make a difference but are uncertain what difference it makes.

NOTES

The author is indebted to Saleha Jilani for valuable research assistance and to John Meyer for critical comments.

1. Oscar Handlin and Mary F. Handlin, "Origins of the American Business Corporation," *Journal of Economic History* 5 (May 1945):4.
2. Barnaby Jo Feder, "Tax Bill May Spur Rush To Form Partnerships," *New York Times*, October 20, 1986, p. D1.
3. New York Stock Exchange, *Fact Book: 1986* (New York: New York Stock Exchange, 1986) pp. 78–79. New York Stock Exchange companies accounted for approximately 47 percent of all business corporations' sales in 1982.
4. "The 1,000 Largest U.S. Companies Ranked by Stock-Market Valuation," *Business Week*, April 18, 1986, p. 119.
5. New York Stock Exchange, *Fact Book: 1984* (New York: New York Stock Exchange, 1984), p. 54; ibid., *Fact Book: 1986*, p. 56; and idem, *Shareownership: 1981* (New York: New York Stock Exchange, 1981), p. 1. A more cynical explanation of the high 1970 and 1985 participation levels is that individual investors tend to buy at the peak and sell at the trough.
6. Robert B. Avery et al., "Survey of Consumer Finances, 1983," *Federal Reserve Bulletin* (September 1984):687–89. These results do not indicate that the concentration of individual stockholdings has declined, since the survey ranks stockholders by current income rather than wealth and focuses on families rather than individuals.
7. Marshall E. Blume and Irwin Friend, *The Changing Role of the Individual Investor: A Twentieth Century Fund Report* (New York: Wiley, 1978), pp. 47–49.
8. Avery et al., "Survey of Consumer Finances," p. 681.
9. Robert E. Foerster and Else H. Dietel, *Employee Stock Ownership in the United States* (Princeton, N.J.: Princeton University Industrial Relations Section, 1926), p. 62.
10. See Louis O. Kelso and Mortimer J. Adler, *The Capitalist Manifesto* (New York: Random House, 1958).
11. Corey Rosen, Katherine J. Klein, and Karen Young, *Employee Ownership in America* (Lexington, Mass.: Lexington Books, 1986), pp. 16, 43.
12. Most of the information in this paragraph is drawn from Rosen et al., *Employee Ownership in America*. Other valuable sources include Christopher E. Gunn, *Workers' Self-Management in the United States* (Ithaca, N.Y.: Cornell University Press, 1984); Irwin Ross, "What Happens When the Employees Buy the Company," *Fortune*, June 2, 1980, pp. 108–11; James O'Toole, "The Uneven Record of Employee Ownership," *Harvard Business Review* 57 (November–December 1979):185–97; Keith Bradley and Alan Gelb, "Employee Buyouts of Troubled Companies," *Harvard Business Review* 65 (September–October

1985):121–30; John Hoerr, "ESOPs: Revolution or Ripoff?" *Business Week*, April 5, 1985, pp. 94–108; Raymond Russell, Arthur Hochner, and Stewart Perry, "Participation, Influence, and Worker Ownership," *Industrial Relations* 18 (Fall 1979):330–41; and Tove Hammer and Robert N. Stern, "Employee Ownership: Implications for the Organizational Distribution of Power," *Academy of Management Journal* 23 (March 1980):78–100.

13. For the seven publicly traded companies in the sample in Rosen et al., *Employee Ownership in America*, p. 136, average employee ownership was 14 percent.

14. "The Question for Unions: Who's in Charge Here?" *Business Week*, April 15, 1985, p. 106; John Hoerr, "Power-Sharing Between Management and Labor: It's Slow Going," *Business Week*, February 17, 1986, p. 37. Earlier and more optimistic Hyatt-Clark accounts are found in William Serrin, "In Experiment in Jersey, Workers Buy a Factory," *New York Times*, April 27, 1982, sec. II, p. 1; and Rosen et al., *Employee Ownership in America*, pp. 153–56.

15. Rosen et al., *Employee Ownership in America*, pp. 89–92. See also Hammer and Stern, "Employee Ownership," pp. 96–97, where the results of a study of one worker-owned firm showed that the more workers had invested, the more inclined they were to leave decisionmaking to specially skilled managers.

16. Rosen et al., *Employee Ownership in America*, pp. 109–37.

17. Michael Conte and Arnold S. Tannenbaum, "Employee-owned Companies: Is the Difference Measurable?" *Monthly Labor Review* 101 (July 1978):23–28. A more complete survey appears in their monograph, *Employee Ownership* (Ann Arbor: University of Michigan Institute for Social Research, 1981).

18. Thomas R. Dye, "Who Owns America: Strategic Ownership Positions in Industrial Corporations," *Social Science Quarterly* 64 (December 1983):865–67.

19. David M. Kotz, *Bank Control of Large Corporations in the United States* (Berkeley: University of California Press, 1978), p. 68, quoting a Securities and Exchange Commission survey.

20. Edward S. Herman, *Corporate Control, Corporate Power* (New York: Cambridge University Press, 1981), p. 131.

21. Ibid., pp. 137–38.

22. Cited in Kotz, *Bank Control*, p. 126.

23. The role of arbitrageurs here is particularly important, although the arbs' rise to prominence is so new, and their stockholdings so transitory, that their position is undoubtedly quite small in any cross section of institutional holdings. Among other things, arbitrageurs often buy stock unloaded by pension funds and individual owners anxious to take quick advantage of the price increases triggered by a tender-offer announcement.

24. Herman, *Corporate Control*, pp. 130–31.

25. Compare Kotz, *Bank Control*, pp. 60–71, 119–30; and Herman, *Corporate Control*, pp. 121–61.

26. Herman, *Corporate Control*, pp. 118–20, 157–60; and Kotz, *Bank Control*, pp. 28–41, 51–60. See also David Bunting and Mark S. Mizruchi, "The Transfer of Control in Large Corporations: 1905–1919," *Journal of Economic Issues* 16 (December 1982):985–1003; and Beth Mintz and Michael Schwartz, *The Power Structure of American Business* (Chicago: University of Chicago Press; 1985).

27. W. T. Grimm & Co., *Mergerstat Review: 1985* (Chicago: W. T. Grimm, 1986), pp. 105, 117–18.

28. See David J. Ravenscraft and F. M. Scherer, *Mergers, Sell-Offs, and Economic Efficiency* (Washington: The Brookings Institution, 1987), especially chapter 5; and, on the parallel British experience, Mike Wright and John Coyne, *Management Buy-Outs* (London: Croom Helm, 1985).

29. See Louis Lowenstein, "Management Buyouts," *Columbia Law Review* 85 (May 1985):730–67.

30. Adolf A. Berle, Jr., and Gardiner C. Means, *The Modern Corporation and Private Property* (Chicago: Commerce Clearing House, 1932). *The Journal of Law and Economics* 26 (June 1983) is devoted entirely to an exploration of the antecedents of the Berle and Means thesis, the reasons for its influence, and its weaknesses.

31. Berle and Means, *The Modern Corporation*, pp. 36–37.

32. Ibid., pp. 40–41.

33. Ibid., pp. 82–83.

34. Ibid., p. 94.

35. Robert J. Larner, *Management Control and the Large Corporation* (Cambridge, Mass.: Dunellen, 1970), p. 22.

36. Philip H. Burch, Jr., *The Managerial Revolution Reassessed* (Lexington, Mass.: D.C. Heath, 1972); Dye, "Who Owns America"; and Herman, *Corporate Control*, pp. 54–65. For an unpersuasive neo-Marxist restatement of the problem, see Christos N. Pitelis and Roger Sugden, "The Separation of Ownership and Control in the Theory of the Firm," *International Journal of Industrial Organization* 4 (March 1986):69–86.

37. Burch, *The Managerial Revolution Reassessed*, pp. 68, 96.

38. Berle and Means, *The Modern Corporation*, pp. 121–24. In an apparent elaboration of the expansion thesis, Berle and Means argue on page 350 that more might be learned from studying the motives of Alexander the Great, seeking new worlds to conquer, than by considering the petty tradesmen of Adam Smith's time.

39. Since the publication of the Berle and Means book, the possibilities have been elaborated on richly. See, for example, Robin Marris, "A Model of the 'Managerial' Enterprise," *Quarterly Journal of Economics* 77 (May 1963):185–209; Oliver E. Williamson, *The Economics of Discretionary Behavior* (Englewood Cliffs, N.J.: Prentice-Hall; 1964); R. J. Monsen and Anthony Downs, "A Theory of Large Managerial Firms," *Journal of Political Economy* 73 (June 1965):221–36; and Dennis C. Mueller, "A Theory of Conglomerate Mergers," *Quarterly Journal of Economics* 84 (November 1969): 643–59.

40. Michael C. Jensen and William H. Meckling, "Theory of the Firm: Managerial Behavior, Agency Costs, and Ownership Structure," *Journal of Financial Economics* 3 (October 1976):305–60.

41. Eugene F. Fama, "Agency Problems and the Theory of the Firm," *Journal of Political Economy* 88 (April 1980):288–307. See also the two papers coauthored by Fama and Michael Jensen, "Separation of Ownership and Control" and "Agency Problems and Residual Claims," *Journal of Law and Economics* 26 (June 1983):301–50.

42. Pioneering exponents of this view were Marris, "A Model of the 'Managerial' Enterprise"; and Henry G. Manne, "Mergers and the Market for Corporate Control," *Journal of Political Economy* 73 (April 1965):110–20.

43. See F. M. Scherer, "Takeovers: Present and Future Dangers," *The Brookings Review* 4 (Winter/Spring 1986):15–20; and Edward S. Herman and Louis Lowen-

stein, "The Efficiency Effects of Hostile Takeovers," in John Coffee, Jr., Louis Lowenstein, and Susan Rose-Ackerman, eds., *Knights, Raiders and Targets* (New York: Oxford University Press, 1988).

44. Louis Lowenstein, "Pruning Deadwood in Hostile Takeovers: A Proposal for Legislation," *Columbia Law Review* 83 (March 1983):259–68.

45. Ibid., pp. 262, 310.

46. The neglect parallels the omission in the theory of consumption taught every economics major of how members of a family combine their often disparate preferences in choosing how to spend their collective income.

47. See Frank H. Easterbrook and Daniel R. Fischel, "Close Corporations and Agency Costs," *Stanford Law Review* 38 (January 1986):271–301.

48. W. Bruce Johnson, Robert P. Magee, Nandu Nagarian, and Harry Newman, "An Analysis of the Stock Price Reaction to Sudden Executive Deaths," *Journal of Accounting and Economics* 7 (April 1985):151–74.

49. Randall Morck, Andrei Shleifer, and Robert Vishny, "Management Ownership and Corporate Performance: An Empirical Analysis," working paper no. 2055 (Cambridge, Mass.: National Bureau of Economic Research, October 1986). See also Andrei Shleifer and Robert Vishny, "Large Shareholders and Corporate Control," *Journal of Political Economy* 94 (June 1986):461–88.

50. Wilbur G. Lewellen, *The Ownership Income of Management* (New York: Columbia University Press, 1971), pp. 79–103.

51. Kevin J. Murphy, "Corporate Performance and Managerial Remuneration: An Empirical Analysis," *Journal of Accounting and Economics* 7 (April 1985):26–27.

52. William A. McEachern, *Managerial Control and Performance* (Lexington, Mass.: D.C. Heath, 1975), pp. 82–83.

53. For a survey of the literature up to 1978, see F. M. Scherer, *Industrial Market Structure and Economic Performance*, 2nd ed. (Boston: Houghton Mifflin, 1980), pp. 35–37.

54. For a theoretical examination, see Herbert A. Simon, "The Compensation of Executives," *Sociometry* 20 (March 1957):32–35.

55. See Mark Hirschey and James Pappas, "Regulatory and Life Cycle Influences on Managerial Incentives," *Southern Economic Journal* 48 (October 1981):327–34. See also W. J. Boyes and Don E. Schlagenhauf, "Managerial Incentives and the Specification of Functional Forms," *Southern Economic Journal* 45 (April 1979):1225–32.

56. Dennis C. Mueller, *Profits in the Long Run* (New York: Cambridge University Press, 1986), pp. 157–61.

57. Murphy, "Corporate Performance and Managerial Remuneration," p. 26.

58. George J. Stigler and Claire Friedland, "The Literature of Economics: The Case of Berle and Means," *Journal of Law and Economics* 26 (June 1983):248–54.

59. McEachern, *Managerial Control and Performance*, pp. 77–84.

60. Rexford E. Santerre and Stephen P. Neun, "Stock Dispersion and Executive Compensation," *Review of Economics and Statistics* 68 (November 1986):685–87.

61. John Cubbin and Graham Hall, "Directors' Remuneration in the Theory of the Firm," *European Economic Review* 20 (January 1983):345–46. In *Profits in the Long Run*, pp. 159–61, Mueller observed a similar pattern for his much larger U.S. sample, but the inside and outside stockholder control coefficients were not statistically significant.

62.   For a survey of the literature, see Scherer, *Industrial Market Structure*, pp. 39–40.
63.   Stigler and Friedland, "The Literature of Economics," pp. 254–58. Some of the results—for example, the values of the estimated asset slope and elasticity terms—suggest serious statistical problems.
64.   Mueller, *Profits in the Long Run*, pp. 149–57.
65.   Harold Demsetz and Kenneth Lehn, "The Structure of Corporate Ownership: Causes and Consequences," *Journal of Political Economy* 93 (December 1985):1155–77.
66.   Harold Demsetz, "Two Systems of Belief About Monopoly," in Harvey J. Goldschmid et al., eds., *Industrial Concentration: The New Learning* (Boston: Little Brown, 1974), p. 164.
67.   Morck et al., "Management Ownership and Corporate Performance," pp. 6–12.
68.   James L. Bothwell, "Profitability, Risk, and the Separation of Ownership from Control," *Journal of Industrial Economics* 28 (March 1980):303–11.
69.   John Cable, "Capital Market Information and Industrial Performance: The Role of West German Banks," *Economic Journal* 95 (March 1985):118–32.
70.   John Cable and Hirohiko Yasuki, "Internal Organisation, Business Groups and Corporate Performance," *International Journal of Industrial Organization* 3 (December 1985): pp. 401–20. For partly confirming and partly conflicting results suggesting that Japanese banks capture some of their industrial affiliates' rents by levying high interest charges, see Richard E. Caves and Masu Uekusa, *Industrial Organization in Japan* (Washington, D.C.: The Brookings Institution, 1976), pp. 72–87.
71.   David M. Kotz, "Bank Influence over the Merger Activity of Large Manufacturing Companies" (Public Interest Economics Foundation, Washington, D.C., October 1980, Mimeographed), pp. 39–66.
72.   See the review of Kotz's earlier book by Robert J. C. Lussier, *Southern Economic Journal* 46 (January 1980):977–78.
73.   See John Pound and Robert J. Shiller, "Survey Evidence on Diffusion of Interest Among Institutional Investors," working paper no. 1851 (Cambridge, Mass.: National Bureau of Economic Research, 1985); and idem, "Speculative Behavior of Institutional Investors," working paper no. 14 (New Haven, Conn.: Yale University School of Organization and Management, June 1986).
74.   See Patrick J. Regan, "Inflation and the Pension Fund Asset Mix," *Financial Analysts Journal* 36 (March/April 1980):16–17, 80.
75.   New York Stock Exchange, *Fact Book: 1957* (New York: New York Stock Exchange, 1957), pp. 18–19; idem, *Fact Book: 1986*, p. 69.
76.   See Robert H. Hayes and William J. Abernathy, "Managing Our Way to Economic Decline," *Harvard Business Review* 58 (July–August 1980):67–77; "Will Money Managers Wreck the Economy?" *Business Week*, August 13, 1984, pp. 86–89; John Perham, "What's Wrong with Management?" *Dun's Business Month*, April 1982, pp. 48–52; and "The Casino Society," *Business Week*, September 16, 1985, pp. 78–90, 144.

4 CHANGING FORMS OF THE CORPORATION

Joseph L. Badaracco, Jr.

The form, or forms, of American companies may be undergoing a sea change with potentially dramatic effects. The transformation could make U.S. companies more competitive or less so. It could reshape our thinking about the workings of markets, the tasks of business managers and public officials, and the political role of firms. The new forms could even alter basic concepts of the corporation.

The nature and extent of this transformation are difficult to determine. The new forms rearrange familiar organizational building blocks, such as joint ventures, in protean, sometimes bewildering patterns. Changes are taking place on the boundaries of firms, rather than at their core, where analysts and observers have, for decades, sought and found them. Finally, it is unclear whether the forces driving the changes will wax or wane. One thing is certain, however: Just as DNA combines into innumerable life forms, so more and more U.S. firms are choosing new partners, designing new relationships, and thereby spawning an extraordinary diversity of organizational forms.

Much thinking about firms presupposes that boundaries of some sort separate them from their markets or, more broadly, their environments. Arm's-length, explicitly contractual, market-based relations with other organizations define a firm's boundaries, within which managers exercise authority and deploy assets that the firm owns or controls. But recently, in myriad ways, managers have been blurring these boundaries with networks of cooperative arrangements with other companies, labor unions, universities, and government bodies.

Perhaps the clearest and most important example of this phenomenon is the case of General Motors. Beginning in the early 1980s, GM commanded worldwide attention by implementing a seemingly radical organizational strategy involving new relationships with labor unions, other companies, and government bodies. By 1987 GM had formed a joint venture with Toyota, its most formidable Japanese adversary, and had bought shares in two other Japanese car firms, Suzuki and Isuzu. It set up five joint ventures with Daewoo, a Korean conglomerate, and another with Fanuc, the world's dominant robotics firm. Other linkups tied it to

Nissan and Hitachi. GM had also bought shares in five small companies specializing in factory automation and announced a partnership with Volvo to make and sell trucks. In addition, it made two large acquisitions, Hughes Aircraft and Electronic Data Systems, which it did not treat as conventional mergers but, instead, tried to establish as semiautonomous units. Finally, through several pathbreaking agreements with the United Auto Workers, GM heralded a new era of cooperation with labor, and its executives expressed hope that more cooperation with government agencies could replace the adversarial clashes—over safety, emissions, price controls, and fuel economy—of the past fifteen years.

These new relationships, which have altered and blurred the firm's boundaries, adumbrate a "new" GM, described in the elusive phrase of its president as an "agglomerate company." Peter Drucker said that GM was creating "the multinational of tomorrow," a business "comprised of autonomous partners, linked in a confederation rather than through common ownership."

Many other American companies have entered into relationships that hover in a conceptual and managerial limbo somewhere between the familiar alternatives of arm's-length market relations and outright merger. Not surprisingly, numerous smaller firms facing global competition have banded together to resist giant competitors or to share the risks of new technology. But large and powerful firms—GM's counterparts—have also surrounded their managerial hierarchies with networks of alliances. By 1986 General Electric had more than 100 cooperative ventures with other firms. IBM, which had long prized and defended fiercely its autonomy, joined forces with Rolm, Intel, Merrill Lynch, Aetna Life and Casualty, MCI, and COMSAT. AT&T's new partners include Olivetti in Italy, Philips in the Netherlands, and NTT, Toshiba, and Ricoh in Japan. Entire industries—automobiles, biotechnology, pharmaceuticals, and robotics—have become overlaid with intricate cooperative lattices.

If such developments continue, the results will be profound. Firms might evolve into complex networks, a far cry from the archetypal hierarchies directed and controlled by executives. Increasingly, competition would occur not in markets, but within the interstices of these networks. And executives might find their work transformed dramatically as they spend more and more time negotiating with and accommodating the managers of other bodies, public and private, whose destinies are intertwined with theirs.

This chapter describes, explains, and assesses the multitude of organizational forms now reshaping the boundaries of U.S. companies. The chapter draws upon examples from many industries and countries, but it concentrates on GM. This firm, dominating what has probably been the most important industry of the twentieth century, has engaged in almost every form of complicated interorganizational relationship. Its efforts to manage its boundaries have raised and clarified the issues confronting the many other firms now pursuing such ventures.

HOW FIRMS CREATE NETWORKS

Albert Einstein said, "Everything should be made as simple as possible, but not simpler." This is the spirit in which the recent changes in American companies must be examined. A firm may choose to pursue any activity, with any sort of partner, through any form of interorganizational relationship, although as this chapter will show, economics make certain types of cooperation more likely in certain industries, while law, culture, and government policy load the dice in favor of different national patterns. However, the basic decisions through which managers have brought about changes fall into three simple categories. The first is the choice of a partner. A firm may choose to collaborate with one of its suppliers or buyers, a competing firm, a labor union, a university, or a government body.

The second entails deciding which activities a cooperative endeavor will involve. Any business decision or activity can be performed in collaboration: All of the classic business functions—marketing, manufacturing, research and development, and finance—can be managed with a partner, and decisions about pricing, capacity, product lines, and even strategy can be shared.

The third decision relates to the form of the relationship. Here, managers choose from a spectrum of possibilities. At one extreme are long, detailed, contractual agreements specifying the rights and responsibilities of the partners. Joint-venture agreements, licensing contracts, and minority equity ownership (in which a firm buys a substantial fraction, though less than a majority, of another firm's shares) all usually involve elaborate specifications of duties. At the other end of the spectrum lie informal, open-ended, flexible arrangements, often based on long-standing relationships and mutual understanding and trust. Tacit rules of the game that shape the behavior of firms in certain industries or regions also fall into this category.

The options open to firms through the manipulation of these three elements are very wide. For example, firms sometimes decide to work with more than one partner on a single activity. A prominent case is the Microelectronics and Computer Technology Corporation in Austin, Texas, founded in 1982. Twenty-one member firms—including Digital Equipment, RCA, and Kodak—each paid up to $1 million to become members and continue to pay as much as several million dollars a year to support a staff of over 400 researchers doing advanced research in areas such as artificial intelligence and computer architectures. A firm and a partner may also join forces in several activities. For example, in the early 1920s GM teetered near insolvency, and Du Pont bailed it out by buying roughly a quarter of GM's shares. This arrangement provided critical financing, as well as an infusion of management talent. (Pierre Du Pont became GM's chairman, and other Du Pont executives brought to GM their sophisticated accounting and financial techniques.) Du Pont also strengthened its position as a supplier of paints and finishes to GM. In this case, collaboration spanned the functional areas of finance, supply, and control and also encompassed executive decisionmaking.[2]

More complexity arises when two firms, engaged in a single activity, commingle different forms of cooperative relationships. A joint venture begins when two parties trust each other sufficiently to agree to collaborate on an activity; but, at the beginning, each usually guards its interests with a formal, detailed contract. As time passes, however, the partners may build a relationship based on mutual trust and understanding. Employees may develop informal relationships, norms, and sometimes even loyalties to each other that outweigh their ties to their parent firms. In the end, a joint venture can become a minisociety that overlays or supersedes the formal, contractual arrangements that created it.

By enlisting many partners simultaneously to work on a variety of activities through a variety of relationships, a firm creates an even more complex organization. IBM's Japanese subsidiary tried for decades to avoid cooperative arrangements with Japanese firms. Then, in the early 1980s, IBM Japan established two multipartner joint ventures to develop telecommunications networks, bought one-third ownership of another leasing company, created a network of authorized IBM dealers, and entered into long-term agreements to buy printers, keyboards, and cathode-ray tubes from its most powerful Japanese competitors, such as Hitachi. In just a few years, the clean, classic hierarchical lines of IBM's Japanese subsidiary were blurred by a complicated network of relationships with Japanese partners.[3]

In Japan, in fact, the blurring of corporate boundaries has reached its most ornate, almost rococo elaboration. Roughly a quarter of all Japanese industrial assets belong to firms that are members of economic groups called keiretsu, the offspring of the zaibatsu, the giant concerns that dominated the Japanese economy until after World War II.[4] Each keiretsu comprises dozens of member firms—the largest, Mitsubishi, has 101—and each member may itself have hundreds of affiliates, which it may own completely or in part. Some affiliates make and sell the same products as others; some supply others with raw materials; some are sales companies that handle other affiliates' products. These firms may have joint ventures with each other; their boards of directors may interlock; their presidents meet regularly with each other; in times of difficulty, they may aid each other through favorable credit terms or purchasing decisions. Many keiretsu firms have cooperative relationships with their labor unions. And most have collaborated in various ways with the Japanese government, whose instruments of industrial policy range from outright protection and subsidy to the subtlest administrative guidance, all of which blend and blur the separate efforts of state and firms. Finally, unlike a large, diversified American firm and unlike the zaibatsu, the keiretsu have no headquarters or central office. (For this reason, the keiretsu were nicknamed "headless zaibatsu.") This absence of a central coordinating hierarchy accentuates the fundamental character of the keiretsu: loose, complex networks that link their member firms through all varieties of relationships, with every type of partner, and on virtually every type of business decision and function.

Yet one need not look overseas to find examples of elaborate networks. Nor are complex networks solely the handiwork of giant firms. For example, Advent International is a Boston-based network of fourteen independent venture-capital firms around the world. Its chairman sits on the boards of all its member firms, actively supervising their deal making, and computers link all of them to Advent's U.S. headquarters. One of Advent's largest investments is in a consortium of European microchip makers, European Silicon Structures, whose members have design and manufacturing facilities in six European countries. In essence, a network of small firms has linked itself to another network of small firms.[5] In this and countless other cases, extraordinary corporate forms are the progeny of choices among partners, activities, and relationships.

THE BOUNDARIES OF THE FIRM

Even though the metaphor of blurred boundaries furnishes a clear, simple, and suggestive definition of the central characteristic common to a multitude of complicated organizational forms, it may seem slightly odd to suggest that firms actually possess boundaries. Property has boundaries, as do nations; even the human body has a boundary—the skin. But what constitutes the boundaries of a company?

The concept of sharp boundaries is rooted in the neoclassical economists' view of firms in purely competitive markets, in which a firm is "an island of planned coordination in a sea of market relations."[6] Within the firm, transactions are governed by the firm's administrative hierarchy; outside the firm, they are governed by market exchanges.[7] Such a firm is an imaginary but nevertheless familiar creature. It is a small, atomistic unit; its executives are impersonal calculating devices that superintend the efficient transformation of inputs into outputs. The relations among all these little units take place at arm's length: In the economists' phrase, there are no nonmarket interdependencies among them. If consumer preferences and technology are stable, equilibrium reigns, and resources—people, information, technology, capital, and so forth—remain within the boundaries of each firm that owns them, under the authority of its managers. If preferences or technology change, resources migrate—in theory, instantly and costlessly—to more efficient uses. But after they migrate, they are once again inside another firm, where they remain, in placid equilibrium, until another change disturbs them.[8]

The notion of sharp boundaries is not simply an academic abstraction. In the United States, it has become a bedrock idea about business and management, an assumption so powerful that Alfred Sloan described it as one of the two basic principles underlying his pathbreaking 1920 plan for reorganizing GM. In *My Years With General Motors* Sloan writes:

> The responsibility of the chief executive of each operation shall in no way be limited. Each such organization headed by its chief executive shall be complete in every necessary function and able to exercise its full initiative and logical development.[9]

Countless business executives found they could run their companies better following Sloan's advice.

Hierarchical control enabled executives in capital-intensive industries to run huge, worldwide operations that exploited advantages of scale, experience, and high-volume throughput. Moreover, the control did not have to be highly centralized and bureaucratic: In large, diversified firms, senior managers delegated authority to several lower levels of general managers and managed through coordinated decentralization, not autocracy. Finally, hierarchical control enabled senior executives to shape the culture of their organizations. Firms are social bodies, communities of individuals whose work together creates shared norms and values and common beliefs and behavior. Through hiring policies, promotions, formal and informal rewards, personal example, and other means, senior executives can mold the human character of the organizations over which they have formal authority and thereby make their firms even more competitive.

With laws favoring freestanding, competing firms, Americans heeded Adam Smith's universally cited warning about the dangers of collusion when members of the same trade gather together, even for "merriment and diversion." Sloan's principle was consistent with an abiding strain in American thinking which holds that society should keep its major institutions at arm's length from each other, with their boundaries clearly marked off, thereby avoiding tacit, behind-the-scenes, self-serving deal making or aggregations of power that could imperil political or economic liberty.

Implicit in neoclassical economics and the concept of sharp boundaries is the notion that each company ultimately has one boss. For example, even though GM is one of the largest and most complex organizations on earth, all lines of authority within GM ultimately trace back to its chair and then to its board of directors. In principle, GM's chair can issue a fiat to the Delco Moraine division telling its managers to make more brakes; Toyota's chair can issue a similar order to any of the operations within Toyota Motor. But neither can issue a unilateral directive that will change the operations at the GM-Toyota joint venture in California. Strategic decisionmaking at this operation is the responsibility of a board of directors representing both parents. Toyota executives assigned to the joint venture control its day-to-day operations, but they are responsible to this joint board.

Shared ownership or jointly operated facilities can occur in a relationship in which one organization wholly dominates the other. When there is an extreme imbalance of power, decisionmaking may take the form that Winston Churchill parodied in this description of his expectations of his wartime cabinet: ''All I ask is agreement with my wishes, after reasonable discussion.'' For example, most of Toyota's suppliers are legally independent companies, but in practice, some of them are simply cogs in the Toyota system. They deliver components to Toyota's assembly lines on a schedule and in quantities determined every hour by Toyota's central scheduling. Toyota buys nearly all of their output, regularly inspects their books to see whether their profits are too high or too low, and may dispatch its own executives to assist in improving the supplier's operations.[10] An organization whose decisionmaking is dominated by another has, in effect, been taken over. It is a captive. Such a firm rests *within* the boundaries of another organization, regardless of its legal status.

Blurred boundaries, in contrast, overlay or even replace market relationships with organizational ones, often creating close, even intimate connections between separate organizations. Genuine sharing of authority takes place. Firms are neither fully independent nor is one wholly dependent upon the other. They do not lose their legal identities; they retain their own culture and management structure and can pursue their own strategies. But they do reduce their autonomy, share decisionmaking, interconnect their organization structures, manage jointly some activities or operations, and open their company cultures to outside influences. Alfred Sloan's principle—that an operation is best managed if it has one boss, one hierarchy and (implicitly) one culture—gives way.

FIRMS' BOUNDARIES IN THE PAST

Corporations that blur their boundaries are not changing to a new corporate form but instead returning to old patterns of doing business. The history of commerce, until the Industrial Revolution in Britain, is essentially a chronicle of indefinite and permeable boundaries around business organizations. Modern joint ventures, such as the GM-Toyota effort, can trace their lineage through the British trading companies of the fifteenth and sixteenth centuries and, ultimately, to Phoenician and Egyptian merchants, who organized joint ventures to pool their resources and limit the risks of overseas trading. Against the broad sweep of the history of commerce and business organization, companies with sharp boundaries—that is, clearly defined zones of ownership and control amid seas of market relations— are the novel phenomenon.

In the centuries before the Industrial Revolution, the boundaries around business activities were blurred by relationships with many institutions: families, since the household was a basic economic unit; villages and manors, the organizing units of agriculture; guilds, which regulated the relations of masters, journeymen, and apprentices; and towns and their customs, which shaped and regulated the behavior of guilds and their workers. Long before the Industrial Revolution, the Japanese merchant class was tied closely to territorial lords, who supervised, taxed, and directed their activities. In both France and Prussia, the governments made heavy investments in small firms that produced weapons, and the Prussian monarchy was the kingdom's largest producer of iron and coal.

Only roughly 200 years ago, in Great Britain, did a self-regulating market begin to appear separating large numbers of economic units. But, even in Britain, market capitalism of independent competing units as described by Adam Smith did not spring full-blown into existence. Rather, economic units slowly sharpened their boundaries as they emerged from the cocoons of social, political, and corporate influences that had enveloped economic activity for millennia.[11]

Britain's rapid industrialization and growing economic might frightened the French, Prussian, and, later, German governments, who responded by promoting and directing economic activity through subsidies, state ownership, cartels, protection, and administrative guidance—all of which obscured the boundaries between the states and firms. Japan followed a similar pattern. After Admiral Perry's "barbarians" had humbled the proud nation, its industrial policies pursued the imperative, "rich nation, strong army." The blurring of business boundaries remained extensive in Japan and Europe in the twentieth century. Mobilization for wars, recovery from devastating losses, the rise of national planning in Britain and France, the nationalization of industry after the Second World War, and Japanese industrial policy brought about extensive interpenetration of public and private sectors.

RECENT CHANGES IN FIRMS' BOUNDARIES

Sharp boundaries around firms are temporal exceptions and not the eternal rule; yet, blurred boundaries are new for certain large, powerful American firms with vast resources and long traditions of independence. Both GM and IBM are clear examples.

After World War II, GM developed the highest degree of vertical integration among the "Big Three" auto makers. It secured effective control over many of its suppliers by purchasing large fractions of their output, renegotiating contracts annually, arranging alternative suppliers for the same parts, and often by making some of the parts itself. GM's huge, internally generated cash flow secured its independence from financial markets. During the early 1980s, for example, GM's cash flow for the next decade—before acquisitions and capital expenditure—appeared likely to exceed $100 billion. Spending just 5 percent of this staggering sum, $5 billion, enabled GM to purchase Hughes Aircraft, in what was, at the time, the largest non-oil acquisition in history.

IBM's preference for independent action was epitomized during the early 1960s by its internal development of the 360 series computers. Despite the colossal financial and technological risks involved in this project, IBM did not seek partners. IBM's later decision to create relationships with Intel, MCI, Rolm, and others was a startling departure from its postwar strategy: In the previous thirty years, it had made only a few minor acquisitions and engaged in only a handful of joint projects.[12] The same pattern appears in IBM's overseas activities. Like many other multinationals, IBM was often compelled to use local partners because of government requirements and unfamiliarity with local markets in its early years. But IBM resisted pressure to collaborate. It chose to withdraw from India rather than sell a minority interest in its Indian concern to local partners. Only the coercive powers of the Japanese state compelled IBM, during the late 1960s and 1970s, to share some of its technology—which proved to be patents on the verge of obsolescence—with Japanese firms. It was not until the 1980s that IBM abandoned its policy of avoiding joint projects with other companies.[13]

Cooperative arrangements are also new in a second sense: During the early 1980s they became much more common in certain service and manufacturing industries. Several recent studies have revealed this pattern. One, for example, documenting a rise in the number of domestic U.S. joint ventures, showed the greatest increases occurring in service industries, such as advertising, financial services, communications systems and services, and data-base development and management. The next largest cluster of expanding cooperation appeared among manufacturers of electrical equipment, consumer electronics, computer peripherals, software, robots, electrical components, and aerospace technology. In some of these sectors, more domestic joint ventures were announced in a single year of the early 1980s than in the previous fifteen or twenty years.[14] In Europe, cooperative agreements may have increased nearly tenfold between 1980 and 1985. International joint ventures involving U.S. firms and overseas partners have nearly doubled since 1978.[15]

Finally, cooperative relationships proliferated in functional areas where they had not been common. Most of the industries mentioned above are R-and-D dependent or even R-and-D intensive. Technical cooperation and joint research and development were the fastest growing subcategories of cooperative arrangements among European firms between 1980 and 1985, and a similar trend appears in international joint ventures involving U.S. firms.[16] This last is notable because, during the 1960s and 1970s, U.S. firms that relied heavily on R-and-D tended to form wholly owned subsidiaries for their overseas business rather than use joint ventures.[17] The extensive cooperation among universities, their faculties, and private companies in biotechnology has recently been dubbed "the university-industrial complex."[18]

Another functional area in which cooperative arrangements have spread is human-resource management. Here, the blurring of traditional boundaries has taken the form of new, participatory arrangements between companies and their managers on one side and workers and their unions on the other. For example, GM announced in 1983 that it would create the Saturn Division, its first new car division since 1918. The UAW participated in planning the Saturn project from its earliest stages—the first time in history that the union had participated directly in GM corporate planning. The UAW was also to become a "full partner" in Saturn's decisionmaking. Saturn would abandon GM's traditional managerial hierarchy and replace it with a five-tier organization, running from a top-level strategic advisory committee down to work groups, in which the UAW would be represented at every level. Furthermore, the relationships between the two intermeshed parties, the GM managers at Saturn and their UAW counterparts, were not governed by a traditional, arm's-length labor contract minutely specifying rights, obligations, and grievance procedures. The Saturn contract did not even have an expiration date; instead, it was described as a "living document" whose terms could be renegotiated at any time.[19]

The Saturn experiment reflected a broad trend in American industry, especially among manufacturing firms, toward expanding the role of nonmanagement employees in decisionmaking. Beginning in the early 1970s as a movement to improve the "quality of work life," it involves restructuring plants, redesigning jobs and incentive programs, and creating new task forces and production teams to encourage greater rank-and-file participation in decisions. Quality circles—small groups of employees, usually from the same unit, who meet regularly to analyze and seek solutions to the problems of their unit—have proliferated rapidly. The first quality circles were inaugurated by Lockheed in 1974, reportedly because a group of Lockheed managers who visited Japan in 1973 were astonished to find that shop-floor workers often helped to solve problems that had baffled engineers. By 1977 about fifty U.S. companies had quality circles. Five years later, over 1,500 companies had established more than 12,000 quality circles. Interest was so great that a professional organization, the International Association of Quality Circles, had been created with 6,400 members in eighty-five regional chapters.[20]

Finance is the third functional area in which a variety of boundary-blurring relations have flourished. This trend, most pronounced in smaller firms, is reflected partly in the burgeoning venture-capital industry. Venture-capital firms are active, long-term investors that buy shares in embryonic companies and often assist their managers. In the four years following the cut in capital-gains taxes in 1978, venture-capital commitments quadrupled to $18 billion. The bulk of this financing has flowed into the technology-intensive industries—computers, software, electronics—in which joint ventures have become much more common.[21] Another index of financial interrelationships has been the rapid rise in the early 1980s of investments by large firms in small ones.[22] Many of these new financial arrangements are intended to support joint R-and-D efforts. The larger firm wants an open window on the small firm's technology, often including the right of first refusal on new developments. The large firm's funds secure these opportunities, and, in return, the small firm can accelerate its development work.

WHY FIRMS ALTER THEIR BOUNDARIES

In some cases, once firms have made certain decisions, they have no choice but to implement them in cooperation with a partner. For example, American firms that decided to expand into the Japanese market found many obstacles preventing them from creating wholly owned subsidiaries. First of all, until the mid-1970s, Japanese law prohibited overseas firms from acquiring majority ownership of Japanese firms. Hence, when GM, Ford, and Chrysler decided to establish bases in Japan in the early 1970s, each of them did so by taking minority equity positions in Japanese firms. But even after this law changed, other difficulties remained. Japanese law still requires that a company's directors agree unanimously to a merger, and Japanese directors are nearly all career employees, whose interests could suffer in a merger. Moreover, Japanese are less likely than Americans to sell their firms: Managers and employees regard a company as a community, not as a piece of property. Finally, in recent years, the appreciation of the yen and the booming Japanese stock market have raised the prices of Japanese companies to extremely high levels. Because of these factors, U.S. firms usually could not make an acquisition to gain a subsidiary.

Building up a subsidiary in Japan, an alternative to acquisition, is also extremely difficult. Land is very expensive; in many parts of Tokyo, it is simply unavailable at any price. Furthermore, the Japanese distribution system is enormously complex, enmeshing commercial transactions in long-standing webs of personal and company relationships. This creates serious marketing problems for a new subsidiary. Finally, a brand new subsidiary must be staffed, but outstanding Japanese graduates generally want to join established Japanese firms, and midcareer Japanese executives have rarely (until quite recently) been willing to leave their firms. Only a handful of American and European firms have been able to surmount these difficulties and achieve strong, independent positions in Japanese markets. As a result, partnerships—usually some form of joint venture— have been the most common path of entry into Japan for overseas firms.

When a firm has a choice, three very different avenues are often open. One is to acquire another firm. Another is to create a boundary-blurring relationship. The third is to rely upon arm's-length market relationships. Similar alternatives exist when American firms consider their relationships with labor unions, government agencies, and university bodies. Of course, a firm cannot acquire any of these organizations, but it does have a choice between the two other alternatives. The old relationship between the UAW and the Big Three auto makers is typical of a distant, highly contractual and specific formal association. GM's new relationship with the UAW at its Saturn subsidiary and at the NUMMI joint venture with Toyota provides an example of a closer, more flexible and intimate relationship.

Thus, a basic question arises: Why, when they have a choice, have many American firms recently chosen to create close boundary-blurring relationships? There is no simple, airtight answer to this question. Too many disparate factors have influenced the ways in which U.S. executives have recently managed and modified the boundaries of their firms. As a result, it is more illuminating to look for interpretations. Each provides an alternative map of the same territory—the complex, varied, shifting terrain on the periphery of firms. In combination, they suggest a full explanation.

Economics

An economic perspective on boundary-blurring activity proceeds on a project-by-project or activity-by-activity basis. It compares the revenues, costs, and risks of handling a project or activity through arm's-length contractual relations, through direct managerial control, or through cooperation with another organization.

The costs of the alternatives include both standard accounting costs and transaction costs—which are incurred in negotiating, monitoring, and managing the risks of each alternative. Transaction cost received little attention until recently, when the writings of Oliver Williamson and others brought them to the fore. Economic analysis can indicate which option is likely to yield the highest benefits at the lowest cost and risk. For example, joint ventures and consortia have been common for decades in the chemical and energy industries. Chemical plants often have scale economies that can be captured only by building one huge facility rather than several smaller ones. Similarily, one large pipeline from a gas field will cost less than several smaller ones. Sometimes, firms choose to own and operate their own pipelines or chemical plants—if they have enough capital, if they are large enough to make the investment safely, and if they can run the facility at or near full capacity and thereby capture the scale economies.

When firms cannot afford the cost or risks of owning their own facilities, they must rely on one of the two remaining options: the market or some form of collaboration. The market option sometimes proves defective: No firm, acting alone, may be willing to build a large-scale facility and sell its output to others. And even if one firm does so, others may be wary of relying on it—it could exploit its monopoly position by charging very high prices, and other firms might be unsure about the reliability of a supplier they do not control.

By relying on a joint venture, firms can reduce these three problems. They can make sure the facility is built and, as joint owners, can influence pricing and supply decisions directly. Of course, negotiating with partners, having two bosses instead of one for an operation, and renegotiating relations among partners when markets or technology changes can be time-consuming and frustrating. There are also perils: For example, an unscrupulous party might try to gain leverage over its partners by taking advantage of its ownership of joint assets. This creates the additional costs of monitoring one's partners. All of these factors—monitoring costs, frustration, negotiation, and risk of opportunistic behavior—are among the costs and risks of joint activity. But for many chemical and energy firms, these costs and risks appeared lower than those of building and owning their own facilities or relying on contracts with suppliers in the marketplace: Hence, they cooperated.

This economic perspective helps to explain the rise in boundary-blurring activity and its growing role in technology-based industries and the financing of firms and projects—especially in an era of global competition. It now costs roughly $4 billion to produce a new automobile model and $5 billion to create a new jet aircraft. Each new generation of mainframe computers has required more R-and-D, while the life expectancy of these mainframes has fallen dramatically—to just four years, by some estimates. Firms join forces to share the cost and reduce the risk of developing products that obsolesce quickly. In addition, when the life span of a costly new technology is short, a firm needs a distribution channel through which to market its product quickly and cheaply; otherwise, it can't recoup its investment and earn a profit. But, sometimes, firms cannot afford the time, effort, and risk of piecing together a distribution system through a multiplicity of contracts with individual distributors all around the world. Hence, they form relationships with firms that already have distribution systems and thereby gain the global reach they need to exploit product developments quickly and widely.

A similar economic logic has produced the common pattern of cooperative arrangements discussed earlier, in which a large firm supplies marketing expertise and distribution power, while a small firm offers a promising technology that is not yet ready to be commercialized. By working together, the two firms can shape the final development of the technology in a way that will improve its marketability.[23] At the same time, each firm can concentrate on what it does best. Firms and university research laboratories join forces for similar reasons.

Many markets are now intensely competitive, so American firms rely increasingly on Asian partners to supply components and products. The American firms often want these items customized; they want assured supply; and they may want to share in the profits of the supplier. To do so, they often form joint arrangements in which ownership and control are shared. Finally, intense competition reduces profits, limiting the ability and willingness of individual firms to develop future technologies and strengthening the rationale for joint research and development. Economic factors have also pushed firms into new relationships with governments and labor. Trade policies affect the profits of firms and industries directly, and productivity arrangements with workers can reduce a firm's costs.

An economic analysis of whether a market relationship, direct ownership, or any of a multitude of possible cooperative relations will yield the lowest costs is complex and uncertain. Before a major investment in new technological development, the analysis of cost and risk is riddled with educated guesses and relies on sketches of best-case, worst-case scenarios. In the end, the best efforts to quantify often give way to judgment. This reliance on judgment opens the door to a second set of considerations that can lead managers to blur their firms' boundaries.

Administrative Experience

The paradigmatic version of hierarchical control is suggested by a conventional organization pyramid, at the apex of which reposes the chief executive, to whom functional areas like marketing, manufacturing, and finance report. Problems, information, and questions flow upward; decisions flow back down. In Alfred Chandler's phrase, the visible hand of management replaces the invisible hand of the market.

In practice, of course, this simple approach has been modified, sometimes radically, as firms have grown larger, more complex, and more diversified. Decentralized hierarchical bureaucracies are a permanent feature of modern economic life, and their advantages are diverse and well known. But several waves of skepticism about classical hierarchical control spread among American managers during the last decade or so.

First of all, giant, ostensibly invincible American firms in autos, steel, and electronics lost highly publicized, global competitive battles during the 1970s. The victors were often smaller, nimbler, and more entrepreneurial firms marked by high levels of commitment among employees and managers, looser controls, and greater flexibility. Studies of Japanese management and best-selling books such as *In Search of Excellence* suggested alternatives to conventional top-down, rule-oriented, routinized management and organization. The twin themes of entrepreneurship and "small is beautiful" became guides to outstanding management.

Disenchantment also set in because many managers found that their ability to exercise power and control within a well-defended core had waned substantially. Layers of middle management sometimes resisted directives from above and impeded the flow of information from below. Work forces grew intractable in many large firms, a problem epitomized by General Motors' Lordstown plant, which became a nightmare of absenteeism, resentment, and drug abuse. GM's labor contracts—based on hierarchical control by management, extreme specialization of worker's tasks, and elaborate rules specifying rights and procedures—expanded to hundreds of pages and were fully comprehensible by only a handful of people. Finally, during the 1960s and 1970s the boundaries around many large firms failed to defend any sphere of managerial autonomy. Government policies for safety, emissions, affirmative action, and price controls gave government bodies authority over decisions that executives had long regarded as their prerogative. During the 1980s scores of large hierarchies also proved to be vulnerable to attacks by financial entrepreneurs who sought to seize them and break them up.

Frustration also grew during the 1970s, as many firms that actively had pursued mergers and acquisitions were disappointed in their efforts. Even the most sophisticated planning and management techniques failed to improve the performance of businesses that were acquired and then integrated within the hierarchy of the acquiring firm. The problem was especially acute when small firms were acquired: Their management often became impatient with the slower pace and bureaucratic routines of larger firms and eventually departed.

But executives who were frustrated with deficiencies of hierarchical control did not rush to close down their corporate offices and break their large hierarchies into small autonomous units. They did not escape into the embrace of unfettered market relationships. This is no surprise. Managers' ambivalence about markets is well known and deep rooted. Markets do offer choice, flexibility, and the chance to reduce costs by choosing among suppliers; markets open ranges of opportunities for managers to pursue; they offer managers the satisfaction and rewards of winning a genuine competitive struggle. But when competition intensifies, markets can also severely constrain managerial discretion. And market competition can become excessive, especially in cyclical capital-intensive industries prone to overcapacity. During the 1970s the volatility of markets for money and raw materials discouraged managers from throwing themselves upon the mercies of arm's-length market transactions.

Finally, as managers became more concerned about technology, arm's-length market transactions and other formal arrangements proved to be poor means to encourage cooperation between organizations. If a company wants to learn about another's technology, it generally needs ways to permit personnel, equipment, ideas, and sometimes even organizational culture to flow across its boundaries. Such transfers of skills require trust reinforced by joint commitment—a far more intricate relationship than simply dropping hardware on a loading dock in exchange for cash. Markets are devices for trading and for simple, fast communication via the price mechanism; the supposition is that firms will read the messages sent by the pricing mechanism and then respond internally, within their own boundaries. When firms found that their own technical or financial resources left them unable to respond as quickly or as fully as they wanted, they sought to learn from other organizations through complex, intimate, working relationships—just as GM has done with Toyota, Fanuc, and others.

Strategic Interests

Concepts of power, self-interest, and hegemony that are used to explain international relations can also be applied to firms.[24] Like states, firms, will seek to preserve their own sovereignty and autonomy. They will act self-interestedly in pursuit of their own vital interests. In a world of shifting, competitive centers of power, firms and their executives, like nations, seek to control their own destinies.

A strategic interpretation of the management of boundaries may be summarized quite simply: Managers will seek to control the resources that are critical to their company's vital, long-term objectives. These resources—human, technological, manufacturing, financial—form the core of a firm. If managers lose control over them, they seek to recapture them; if intrusions into the core are unavoidable, they are circumscribed as sharply as possible. An attendant benefit of such efforts is that they help managers secure and enhance their positions.

Above all, the strategic perspective regards boundary-blurring, authority-sharing activities cautiously. The preferred choice is to control key operations and decisions, rather than to entangle them in complicated dealings with outside organizations. Sometimes, however, economic analysis or frustrating administrative experience will lead a firm to share vital activities or authority with another organization. In these situations, the strategic perspective suggests that a firm's managers should seek hegemony, managing their relations with other companies, labor unions, or government agencies with the aim of securing power. A firm need not be a giant like GM to prefer hegemonic relationships with other organizations. Small firms, vulnerable because of their size, will often take care to protect their autonomy, avoiding reliance on single suppliers or single, powerful customers, either of which can imperil their independence.

Sometimes, however, other bodies are very powerful, and a firm cannot be the senior partner in a relationship. Then, it may seek a detente in which each of the two powers has its own clear and stable zone of authority and respects the core activities of the other. Or the firm and another organization may share authority. In either case, a firm must be vigilant. Changes in markets, technology, or other factors could disturb the balance, creating opportunities to gain or lose power.

A more difficult situation arises when a weak firm cannot prevent others from intruding into its core activities. Such a firm, at best, can expect to be a junior partner in a relationship. This is not necessarily a calamity, for hegemonic relationships are not necessarily exploitative. The relationship can still produce better results than either side would have attained alone. At worst, however, a firm may suffer the economic equivalent of harsh colonization. It becomes a unit in the operations of another organization, regardless of its legal status, and its executives, regardless of their titles, are subordinates of the managers of the dominant organization.

The perspective of strategic interests places the postwar history of GM, as well as the GM partnerships of the 1980s, in a dramatically different light. GM's efforts to limit its dependence on its new relationships and to control their impact on its organization mirror the experience of many companies with cooperative endeavors.

By the late 1950s the firm was a dominating monolithic body. It had achieved detente with its two large American competitors, Ford and Chrysler; a policy of mutually assured destruction discouraged price competition, catastrophic in the highly capital-intensive auto industry. The UAW, whose strikes had disrupted GM's core activities in the mid-1940s, had finally agreed to an arrangement in which GM retained control over the workplace in exchange for high wages and benefits. GM's gigantic cash flows rendered it independent of financial markets, and it was able to dominate its suppliers.

By the early 1970s much of this had changed. Government authorities had intruded upon many vital decisions, piercing the sphere of managerial control. The rise of Japanese auto firms undermined GM's domination of the world auto industry. How did GM react? First, it sought vigorously to protect its internal decisionmaking from the regulatory efforts of the U.S. government and responded to the Japanese challenge by developing its own fuel-efficient, smaller cars. Even in the 1980s, when GM forged many new relationships with other organizations, its abiding interest in maintaining its sovereignty continues. GM's Asian joint ventures account for less than 10 percent of its car supply. By having a portfolio of Asian suppliers and by creating the option of in-house manufacture of high-quality smaller cars in its Saturn subsidiary, GM avoids becoming too dependent on any one partner and may be able to play its partners off against each other. When GM wanted to acquire technology it considered crucial, it bought Electronic Data Services and Hughes Aircraft in transactions whose magnitude dwarfed all of its cooperative arrangements with other firms.

Even GM's widely heralded shift to a more participatory cooperative relationship with labor must be scrutinized from the strategic perspective of power and control. There is no question that GM has offered its workers and their unions the chance to participate much more extensively in workplace decisions. The results—in terms of labor harmony and productivity—have been extraordinary at the GM-Toyota joint venture. At the same time, however, GM has made it clear, through its Asian joint ventures, that it can reduce its reliance on American workers for cars or components; its Saturn division, which will rely heavily on robots, sends a message that GM can produce cars in America, relying on far fewer U.S. workers. The joint venture with Toyota softens this message by signaling that if the UAW is willing to abandon many of its hard-fought gains—such as job classifications, complex grievance procedures, and virtually automatic pay boosts—GM and the union may reach a new accommodation. To stress only the new and important participatory elements of GM's relationship with the UAW is an oversimplication. Greater cooperation has arisen against the background of a shift in power away from the UAW and toward GM. Indeed, the movement towards greater participation for workers and unions over the last ten years has been paralleled by another, perhaps even more widespread effort to limit their power through overseas sourcing, givebacks, and manufacturing strategies that expand facilities in nonunion states.

Few studies of collaborative endeavors by U.S. firms examine their duration. Yet abundant anecdotal evidence testifies to the instability of many boundary-blurring relationships. For example, Siemens AG's computer partnerships with RCA ended abruptly when RCA changed its strategy and abandoned the computer manufacture business. IBM's partnership with Mitel, a Canadian manufacturer of telephone exchange equipment, collapsed because Mitel could not conform to IBM testing procedures and demands for changes in technology. Power struggles, discordant company cultures, senior executive inattention, misjudgments about the skills or commitments of one's partners, and a host of mundane managerial problems can all subvert cooperative relationships. A study by one large consulting firm concluded that only a third of such ventures proved to be long-term successes.[25]

Nor is it clear that firms take major strategic risks willingly when they create collaborative arrangements. The studies and articles hailing a new era of cooperation concentrate exclusively on the frequency with which joint ventures, licensing agreements, and similar arrangements are announced, yet rarely examine the strategic importance of these joint activities. While cooperative research and development have recently increased dramatically in the United States, such arrangements account for only 3 percent of the $50 billion that American firms spend on research and development each year.[26] Even in Japan, the widely publicized joint efforts in computer technology involve only a slender fraction of all R-and-D spending by Japanese computer firms. Moreover, vital questions remain unanswered: Do Japanese computer firms assign their best scientists to these joint activities, and do they disclose their most sophisticated, proprietary ideas in these forums?[27]

These varied pieces of evidence all suggest the importance of taking a strategic perspective on the new relationships that firms have been forming. Even in Japan, where a host of factors encourage collaboration among government agencies, firms, and unions, a similar pattern may be emerging. Some of the most successful, dynamic, and aggressive Japanese firms—among them, Sony, Matshushita, and Toyota—are not members of keiretsu but are instead (within the Japanese context) relatively autonomous, each controlling its own network of satellite suppliers. Furthermore, as these firms have grown stronger in recent decades, they have chosen increasingly independent courses. As a young firm, Toyota depended heavily on resources and funding from banks, but its cash flow has been so great recently that it has paid off virtually all of its debt and accumulated such substantial liquid resources that Japanese informally refer to the company as "the Toyota Bank."

IMPLICATIONS AND CONSEQUENCES

Will economic and administrative factors lead more firms to create networks of relationships? Or will cautious strategies of autonomy and hegemony impede these efforts? If important markets continue to globalize, if technological advances occur in more and more companies around the world, if the life spans of products diminish, and if overcapacity and intensifying competition pare margins further, then complex intraorganizational networks will become more common. What would be the implications of this development?

For managers, the proliferation and elaboration of networks would accelerate an already established shift toward a political view of the work of general managers. The classic notion of a manager rested heavily upon direct, personal authority and control. Many small firms, and some large ones, are still run by managers cast from the classic mold of direct, hands-on personal leadership. But as U.S. firms divisionalized in the 1950s and 1960s and diversified their range of products, businesses, and technologies, the work of managers often moved from direct decisionmaking and control to balancing interests and shaping negotiations among decentralized centers of power and expertise within their firms. Instead of leading by direct involvement and fiat, executives worked to establish the context in which others would make decisions.[28]

But if company boundaries continue to blur, power, expertise, and authority will not simply be decentralized—they will be dispersed, and the authority and responsibility of executives, already weakened, may erode even more. Consider, for example, a company that enters a cooperative long-term relationship with a supplier. The company's purchasing department no longer performs the relatively simple task of negotiating short-term, price-based contracts that meet its precise specifications. Instead, purchasing encompasses efforts to learn about suppliers' capabilities, aid in improving them, coordinate contacts between design personnel in the firm and their counterparts at the supplier, and perhaps even finance inventory and equipment at the supplier. The purchasing department will grow in size and surely grow in expertise and responsibility, and important decisions may well be shared with the suppliers.[29] Senior executives will no longer face only the classic challenges of power and authority within their firms; control over important activities and decisions will be shared with others outside the firm's boundaries.

When managerial authority is both dispersed and decentralized through elaborate networks of relationships, firms may become cumbersome and even more vulnerable to attacks from competitors. A well-worn administrator's adage holds that when everyone is responsible for something, no one is responsible for it. As Napoleon put it, "one bad general does better than two good ones."

Consider, for example, the broad and murky question of U.S. international competitiveness. Will the many new linkups between firms and the new participatory arrangements between labor and management help U.S. firms and industries become more competitive? The economic advantages of such arrangements are often crystal clear, and some firms simply could not survive on any other terms. But two caveats are in order. First of all, the administrative costs of managing complex networks of relationships that disperse authority and power may prove to be high. It is quite possible that firms entangled in alliances with many other partners will find that they decide and act more slowly because of the negotiations and renegotiations, and ensuing contests for power and authority, that occur as these relationships are adapted to changing markets and technologies. Each point of contact along a blurred boundary is a potential source of conflict as well as cooperation. When government is a partner, destabilizing changes may originate from many different constituencies. Further points of conflict arise as relationships with one set of partners spill over into relationships with others. For example, GM's decisions about outsourcing and subcontracting have now moved to high positions on the UAW's bargaining agenda. As a result, two sets of intrinsically complicated relationships—one with suppliers and another with labor—are now intermeshed.

Second, a firm's boundaries are dynamic. Some American firms entering attractive relationships in which Asian firms acted as junior partners making low-cost components have later observed a slow shift to parity, as the Asian firm gained skill, engineering expertise, and knowledge of North American markets, and then awakened to a new relationship in which the American firm was the subordinate party. If one assumes benevolence and good will among partners, such scenarios are unlikely. But if one assumes, as the strategic perspective does, that the parties will seize opportunities to enhance their own self-interest, then many arrangements that begin with a cautious, well-intended weakening of a firm's boundaries may end with its core activities jeopardized, constrained, or dominated by its erstwhile partner. The manifest short-term economic benefits of cooperation may be outweighed by the subtler, organizational complications of managing complex networks and the strategic vulnerability that these networks may create.

Basic ideas about the nature of a firm could even be altered. A new paradigm could arise, based upon the two contradictory elements that have recently spread through many U.S. firms: The blurring of boundaries around firms and the introduction of market or market-like arrangements within firms. For example, GM recently reorganized its five car divisions into two super groups, one for larger and one for smaller cars. In principle, each super group would have all of the resources of an independent car company and be run as a free-standing business.

The supergroups are free to go outside GM to find lower cost or higher quality suppliers. GM has also told its internal divisions that produce parts and components to seek outside markets. The creation of quasi-autonomous super groups and the erosion of long-established administrative relationships among GM's internal supply divisions and its assembly divisions are both market-like solvents that loosen components of the internal hierarchy that have been tightly coupled for decades. To the extent this internal decoupling takes place, the interior regions of a firm become less hierarchical. Instead, they come to resemble networks.

In another example, when GM acquired Hughes Aircraft and Electronic Data Services, it created two special classes of stock—so-called H shares for Hughes and E shares for EDS—whose value depends upon the performance of Hughes and EDS, not GM. The interests of the owners of E and H shares could differ from those of owners of GM common shares. At EDS, where many employees owned E shares, the ground was thus laid for clashes on decisions, such as the pricing of EDS services to units of GM, that were essentially zero-sum games in which one side's gain was the other's loss. According to the conventional view of a firm as a hierarchy, this arrangement was a mistake. But if a firm is viewed as a network of partially coupled, partially independent units—and if the conflicts created were intended to shake up a complacent, insulated organization while maintaining the aggressive entrepreneurial spirit of a unit like EDS and holding on to its best employees—the creation of E and H shares follows the same logic as the creation of quasi-autonomous supergroups and outside procurement options. They are all ways of loosening old hierarchical structures and introducing networklike arrangements inside firms.

As more firms introduce market relations within their boundaries while blurring their boundaries by replacing market relations with organizational ones, it becomes much more difficult and perhaps much less useful to think in terms of activities taking place either inside or outside of firms, of decisions being made either by firms or by markets, or of assets being owned by one firm or another. At the extreme, firms become almost evanescent—or, in the phrase of two scholars, little more than "legal fictions, which serve as a nexus for a set of contracting relationships among individuals."[30]

These changing forms, if they proliferate, will almost certainly require changes in public policies as well as in popular perceptions. Decisions about antitrust, for example, will need to apply a far finer and more sophisticated lens to examine the competitive effects of boundary-blurring activity. GM's joint venture with Toyota raised many of the issues that these changing forms introduce. When the two companies announced their venture, the general reaction was surprise, even astonishment. Two entrenched adversaries were planning to cooperate with each other; moreover, the two most powerful firms in the auto industry were proposing collaboration—an arrangement that would have been virtually unthinkable just ten years earlier. Even though the FTC and the Justice Department had become more tolerant of joint efforts among competitors, the GM-Toyota venture received intense scrutiny. The FTC reviewed the antitrust issues in one of the largest efforts in its history. The House of Representatives held hearings on the proposal that were later published under the title, *Future of the Automobile Industry*.[31]

The vexed issue at the heart of this controversy turned on whether the venture's potential benefits to consumers, through the increased efficiency of the participating firms, would surpass the potential harms derived from reduced competition. In the past, the U.S. government has approached this question by following a principle called the "rule of reason." In this approach, the government assesses the structure, intent, and likely competitive effects of a joint venture and decides if it will restrain trade unlawfully. This case-by-case approach has provided few guidelines for considering joint efforts; it requires time-consuming, costly proceedings, and decisions often depend on inevitably speculative judgments about the future. If joint ventures become even more common, the government's ability to assess and occasionally to reshape joint ventures will be severely handicapped by its limited resources. Decisions vital to the competitiveness of U.S. firms could sink deep into a bog of litigation. A more sophisticated approach would set intermediate guidelines that would give companies, courts, and government agencies clearer indications of what sort of cooperative arrangements are likely to prove acceptable under U.S. antitrust laws.[32]

Finally, the new forms of the corporation are likely to render issues of corporate social accountability far more troubling. When authority is shared across the boundaries of organizations, so is accountability. In a classical, simple world of atomistic firms run by managers and directly responsible to shareholders, accountability was clear. The old model of social responsibility, in simplified form, presupposed sharp boundaries and hierarchical firms. Governments wrote laws, and executives were responsible for their firms' compliance. The laws were legitimate because they were the outcome of open pluralistic contention among many independent bodies within society. But where does the buck stop within a network of shared authority?

It will be necessary to transform our thinking about the political role of firms. A new model of social responsibility and legitimacy would recognize that firms are not separate economic units but social and political complexes linked to many other bodies in society, including agencies of government, with interests and decisions that represent and balance the needs of many constituencies.

If firms' decisions and operations are intricately intermeshed, they can claim plausibly that they speak and act, not just for the financial interests of their shareholders, but for the broader interests of other groups in society. Moreover, firms are likely to have more political clout. They will be able to enlist the support of their networks of allies for whatever public policies they advocate. Inevitably, some groups will be left out of these alliances—those that do not make economic contributions to the network—so the overall balance of political interest may shift further toward the larger, more economically powerful, and more cohesively organized elements of society.

GM President Charles Wilson, at the congressional hearings on his nomination to become secretary of defense under President Eisenhower, declared, "What's good for the country is good for General Motors, and what is good for General Motors is good for the country." It is hardly certain, three decades later, that this proclamation can be dismissed as the overly enthusiastic and narrow view of a prototypical organization man. Today, Wilson's bald statement reads as an attack on conventional assumptions about the political role of firms, the legitimacy of their actions, and their power, assumptions that must indeed be reconsidered— along with our thinking about the work of business managers, the nature of the firm, antitrust policy, and competitiveness—if networks of authority-sharing relationships continue to blur the boundaries of firms.

NOTES

1. Peter F. Drucker, "The Shape of Industry to Come," *Industry Week* 21 (January 11, 1982): 55; see also Anne B. Fisher, "GM's Unlikely Revolutionist," *Fortune*, March 19, 1984, p. 106–12.

2. Alfred D. Chandler, Jr., and Stephen Salsbury, *Pierre S. Du Pont and the Making of the Modern Corporation* (New York: Harper & Row, 1971), pp. 435–65, 572–84.

3. K. Komahashi, "IBM Japan Launches Counterattack," *The Oriental Economist*, September 1983, pp. 14–18.

4. Yoshikazu Miyazaki, "Big Corporations and Business Groups in Postwar Japan," *Developing Economics*, 14 (December 1976):383–87.

5. Anthony Ramirez, "Foreign Affairs of a Venture Capitalist," *Fortune*, February 2, 1987, pp. 84–88.

6. G. B. Richardson, "The Organization of Industry," *The Economic Journal* 82, (September 1972):883.

7. The distinction between markets and hierarchies has been a central theme in the work of Oliver E. Williamson. The distinction forms the title of his book, *Markets and Hierarchies* (New York: The Free Press, 1975), and is further developed in *The Economic Institutions of Capitalism: Firms, Markets, Relational Contracting* (New York: The Free Press, 1985).

8. Of course, the real world is messier. But price theory, the economics of industrial organization, and the theory of the firm are clear. For example, William G. Shepherd writes, "the firm is an organization, with its own independent life, form, and powers of decision." See William G. Shepherd, *The Economics of Industrial Organization* (Englewood Cliffs, N.J.: Prentice-Hall, 1985), p. 101. George Stigler writes that one of the main conditions of competition is that firms "are assumed to act independently." See George J. Stigler, *The Organization of Industry* (Homewood, Ill.: Irwin, 1968), p. 6.

9. Alfred P. Sloan, Jr., *My Years With General Motors* (Garden City, N.Y.: Doubleday, 1972), p. 57.

10.   Toyota was investigated by Japan's Fair Trade Commission and censured for its treatment of some of its suppliers. See Y. Monden, *The Toyota Production System* (Atlanta, Ga.: Industrial Engineering and Management Press, 1983), ch. 3.

11.   Karl Polanyi, *The Great Transformation* (Boston: Beacon Press, 1965), pp. 48–55, 68–75, and pp. 150–55.

12.   Robert Sobel, *IBM vs. Japan* (New York: Stein and Day, 1986), p. 191.

13.   Ibid, p. 155–56.

14.   Kathryn Rudie Harrigan, *Strategies for Joint Ventures* (Lexington, Mass.: D. C. Heath, 1985), pp. 7–12.

15.   Karen J. Hladik, "International Joint Ventures" (Ph.D. dissertation, Harvard Business School, 1984), p. 56.

16.   Ibid., p. 64.

17.   John M. Stopford and Louis T. Wells, Jr., *Managing the Multinational Enterprise* (New York: Basic Books, 1972), p. 108.

18.   Martin Kenney, *Biotechnology: The University-Industrial Complex* (New Haven, Conn.: Yale University Press, 1987).

19.   Marilyn Edid, "How Power Will Be Balanced on Saturn's Shop Floor," *Business Week*, August 5, 1985, pp. 65–66.

20.   William C. Freund and Eugene Epstein, *People and Productivity* (Homewood, Ill.: Dow Jones-Irwin, 1984), pp. 128–29; Y. K. Shetty and Vernon M. Buehler, eds., *Productivity and Quality through People* (Westport, Conn.: Quorum Books, 1985), p. 261; Roger W. Berger and David L. Shores, eds., *Quality Circles* (New York: Marcel Dekker, 1986), p. 56; Richard B. Kopelman, *Managing Productivity in Organizations* (New York: McGraw-Hill, 1986), p. 131.

21.   Stanley E. Pratt and Jane K. Morris, *Guide to Venture Capital Sources* (Wellesley Hills, Mass.: Venture Economics, 1986), p. 8; Lindsay Jones, ed., *Trends in Venture Capital* (Wellesley Hills, Mass.: Venture Economics, 1986), p. 33.

22.   Norm Alster, "Electronics Firms Find Strength in Numbers," *Electronic Business* 12, no. 5 (March 1, 1986):102–4, 106, 108 (part 1 of a three-part series on partnership).

23.   James D. Hlavacek, Brian H. Dovey, and John J. Biondo, "Tie Small Business Technology to Marketing Power," *Harvard Business Review* 55, (January–February 1977):106–16.

24.   See, for example, Robert O. Keohane, *After Hegemony* (Princeton, N.J.: Princeton University Press, 1984), pp. 5–48; and Robert G. Gilpin, "The Richness of the Tradition of Political Realism," in Robert O. Keohane, ed., *Neorealism and Its Critics* (New York: Columbia University Press, 1986), pp. 301–21.

25.   The study was by McKinsey and Company, Inc., New York, New York. See also Norm Alster, "Dealbusters: Why Partnerships Fail," *Electronic Business* 12, no. 7 (April 1, 1986):70–75 (part 2 of a three-part series on partnerships).

26.   Andrew Pollack, "United to Create Products," *New York Times*, January 14, 1986, p. D-7.

27.   James C. Abegglen and George Stalk, Jr., *Kaisha, The Japanese Corporation* (New York: Basic Books, 1985), p. 139.

28.   The theory that executives in complex firms manage the context in which others make particular decisions is developed in Joseph L. Bower, *Managing the Resource*

Allocation Process (Homewood, Ill.: Irwin, 1972). See also David A. Lax and James K. Sebenius, *The Manager as Negotiator* (New York: The Free Press, 1986).

29. Roy D. Shapiro, "Toward Effective Supplier Management: International Comparisons," working paper no. 9-785-062 (Boston, Mass.: Division of Research, Harvard Business School, 1985).

30. Michael C. Jensen and William H. Meckling, "Theory of the Firm: Managerial Behavior, Agency Costs, and Ownership Structure," *Journal of Financial Economics* 3 (October 1976): 310.

31. *Future of the Automobile Industry: Hearings before the Subcommittee on Commerce, Transportation, and Tourism of the Committee on Energy and Commerce, House of Representatives* (Washington, D. C.: U.S. Government Printing Office, 1984).

32. Joseph F. Brodley, "Joint Ventures and Antitrust Policy," *Harvard Law Review* 95, no. 7 (May 1982,):1523–90.

5 SOCIAL ORGANIZATION OF THE CORPORATION

James S. Coleman

The modern corporation can be seen as a new actor in society, endowed with rights by charter and by the common law's recognition of it as a "fictional person." This new conception of an actor as a legal entity abstracted from any physical person has come to be complemented by an idea of the actor's structure, composed of elements or "positions" equally as abstract. This is classical formal organization, a form that has attracted numerous theorists. Max Weber, writing in the late nineteenth century, developed the concept of "rational authority" as a structure of positions, filled according to merit, compensated with a money wage, and directed toward a purpose or goal determined by the ultimate authority in the organization.

This notion of an abstract actor containing within it abstract positions was a social invention of the first magnitude. The demographic explosion of this form— corporation—began in the second half of the nineteenth century; its emergence as a major locus of power has come about in the twentieth. It has, quite simply, transformed the structure of society.

Yet the theory of the functioning of formal organizations has a fundamental flaw: It recognizes only the single "goal of the corporation" as an actor, failing to include the interests and resources at each position in the corporation's structure. These interests and resources constitute a separate system of action within the corporation, not merely a set of agents dutifully implementing the central purpose of the corporation.

The theory of formal organizations has taken its cue from Max Weber, who contrasted rational authority with traditional forms based on custom, norms, and blood ties and with the transitory authority characteristic of charismatic leaders. This new, rational, explicitly purposive form of organization was sufficiently different from traditional organization that overlooking the purposes of the individuals who filled its positions was a natural error to make.

And it continues. Its legacy can be found in much organization theory, which takes the Weberian bureaucratic model as a starting point and looks for deviations from that model. It can also be found in the identification of the theory of formal organization with a theory of managerial decisionmaking.[1] This conception of the formal organization as one in which authoritative direction emanates from the top and is obeyed and transmitted downward at each successive level is difficult to overcome.

It should be clear, however, that as long as positions in the formal organization are filled by real persons, those persons will have interests or goals that may differ from the purposes of the organization and have resources (some that they bring with them and some that come with their positions in the organization) that can be used to further their interests.

All of this has not gone completely unrecognized, either in theory or in practice. One theoretical statement was that of an Italian sociologist writing in 1915:

> By a universally applicable social law, every organ of the collectivity, brought into existence through the need for the division of labor, creates for itself, as soon as it becomes consolidated, interests peculiar to itself. The existence of these special interests involves a necessary conflict with the interests of the collectivity.[2]

In general, however, the theory of organizational functioning has been led by practice as the modern corporation has evolved. Consequently, in this chapter, I will describe some of the variations in practice, emphasizing more recent developments to provide a sense of how this special system of action within the corporation functions. Toward the end of the chapter, I will attempt to characterize more generally the new conceptual basis for the organization implied by these changes in practice.

FORMAL ORGANIZATION AND MODES OF MAINTAINING VIABILITY

Oliver Williamson, among others, has compared the functioning of market organization and hierarchical organization of economic activities.[3] One aspect of the difference between markets and hierarchies is the modes of viability that they require.

As a system of action, a market requires "reciprocal viability." With money as a medium of exchange, the constraint of the "double coincidence of wants" in a barter market is removed; but for a market transaction to be carried out, there must be two positive accounts, one for each party.[4] Each exchange is a self-contained relation between a pair; any imbalances must be made up within that relation.

In modern authority structures, the corporation acts as a third party in relations between positions, eliminating the need for reciprocal viability between them. A secretary-clerk's obligations to a supervisor need not be balanced exactly by the supervisor's obligations to the secretary-clerk; the discrepancy is made up by the corporation. What is necessary is what I will call "independent viability." A structure in which both parties in each relation must benefit is transformed into a structure with a third party that balances debits and credits. In a structure of n persons in relation, an exchange system contains $n(n-1)/2$ potential relations, each of which must be reciprocally viable if a transaction is to take place. When the corporation serves as a third party, there need be only n viable relations, each being profitable to the firm and to the employee.

The difference between reciprocal and independent viability grows with the size of the structure. A complete network among four persons requires mutual benefit in 6 relations, or 12 positive accounts; in a formal organization of the same size, 4 mutually beneficial relations are required (between the organization and each of the 4), or 8 positive accounts. The difference between reciprocal and independent viability amounts to only 4 accounts. However, in a market of twenty-five persons, 300 (25x24/2) mutually beneficial relations are necessary, 600 positive accounts altogether. In a formal organization, this is reduced to 25 relations, with a total of 50 positive accounts. This "balance of inducements and contributions" is exactly what Chester Barnard specified as necessary for the firm. Each employee must feel that the inducements are of greater value than what must be given up to stay at the firm, and, in turn, the firm must consider the employee's contributions to be of greater value than what it must give the employee as inducements.[5]

The number of accounts showing a positive balance may be decreased even further. Since the corporation is an actor in each relation, it can make up its losses in some relations with gains in others. Under "global viability," the employees' side of the equation remains the same, but the corporation need only show a profit on the total of all accounts to maintain viability. In an organization of twenty-five positions, only twenty-six positive balances are necessary, one for each employee and a global account for the corporation.

The Primary Danger of Global Viability

Global viability constitutes a danger to any organization, including corporations. If especially profitable relations (that is, especially valuable contributors) fail to provide excess value, then the whole system can become nonviable. If this excess value is produced by some employees because of their individual characteristics and if there is a market for the services of individuals who provide excess value, these individuals will receive better offers from other organizations and may leave their current employer, which will then become nonviable.[6]

The solution arrived at in economic theory is to reintroduce independent viability.[7] In such a case, the corporation is assumed to be capable of adjusting each employee's compensation to equal the value of that employee's marginal contribution. Each individual earns a market wage, ensuring that there will be no better offer from elsewhere, unless another employer can get more value from the employee's services. Furthermore, the market wage shows the employee's marginal contribution in the activity that can make the most valuable use of these services.

But this solution is seldom feasible in practice. Because of the interdependence of activities, it is often difficult to isolate the marginal contribution of each employee. And because of collective bargaining and other social constraints, the firm does not have the power to pay individual employees their marginal products.

A number of devices have evolved within organizations to solve the problem of viability in other ways. A brief examination of three of these follows.

Divisional Viability.   In the 1930s General Motors and DuPont developed a management practice now widespread in large business firms: the creation of divisions that must each justify their products through "make or buy" decisions of the firm.[8] The central innovation was the partial introduction of the market into the firm by using the outside market to gauge the competitive viability of divisions within the firm. An extension of this has been the introduction of internal transfer pricing within the firm, with each division "selling" its services or products to other parts of the firm. If a way can be found to establish a market price for each product or service, this practice allows the firm to measure a division's contribution and compare it to that division's costs, providing the possibility of replacing global viability with "divisional viability," that is, global viability for each separate division.

Sometimes, transfer pricing is merely an accounting device to measure a division's performance; in other cases, divisions' budgets are determined in part by their shadow profits or losses. Obviously, only the latter constitutes a movement away from global to divisional viability.

Within a division, the same practice can be used to determine departmental contributions and thus departmental viability. In principle, internal pricing can be extended all the way to the level of the individual. For some jobs in some firms, this is done by paying a portion of wages in bonuses, the size of which depends on an evaluation of each individual's contribution. Carried far enough, this is equivalent to independent viability, realized through compensation equal to the employee's marginal contribution.

One serious weakness of divisional viability lies in the difficulty of setting appropriate transfer prices for goods and services for which there is no external market price to serve as a benchmark.[9] A second appears to be the lack of incentive, except in central management, which wants to measure the performance of various units of the firm, for establishing and maintaining an internal set of accounts. Unless the transfers are more than mere accounting devices and full divisional viability is realized through divisions receiving a share of the profit or loss they bring the firm as a whole, individual units will have little reason to embrace the system.

Forward Policing.   The classical means of attempting to ensure viability has been through the exercise of authority over the actions of employees. In such a system, the feedback loop through which viability is determined goes from the final product back to the starting point of the process, at the highest authority. Based on this feedback, modifications are introduced to increase viability, with authority continuing to be exercised downward.

I call this "forward policing" because actions at time t produce outputs for actions at time $t + 1$ throughout the sequence of the production process. Thus, policing follows a forward course.

Backward Policing.   Around 1980 the general manager of the Pontiac Division of General Motors studied the production process at Honda to learn why the quality control on their automobiles was so high. He learned that Honda employed a form of backward policing: Each unit in the process of producing and shipping the automobiles had the right to reject its inputs and was held strictly accountable for its outputs by the unit next in line, which in turn had the right to reject out-of-specification inputs, even if this meant shutting down the line. The unit supplying the unacceptable parts would be held accountable for any downtime.

Each unit had an inspector, not at the end of its stage in the process, but at the beginning. Another property of the system, which appeared to be a consequence of this reallocation of rights, was that there was a much lower ratio of supervisors (forward policing) to operators. A third aspect of the system, again an apparent consequence of the reallocation of rights, was that operators themselves, who would be held accountable for the quality of the product, also acted as inspectors, of both inputs and outputs.

Each unit at each stage in the process had a set of rights similar to those held by the final customer for Honda's product. The policing thus operated backward, from the final product back to the first stages of the production process. The long feedback loop from the final customer was broken into a large number of very short loops. Most fundamentally, the shift from forward to backward policing involves nothing more—or less—than a reallocation of rights and accountability in the organization.

Further Consequences of Global Viability

If the transactions between each employee and the corporate actor are independently viable, as when wages and benefits equal marginal productivity, each of these internal transactions is self-policing. If the contribution declines, the wage declines; if it increases, so does the wage. If the wage is below the marginal contribution and competing employers will pay the marginal wage, the employee can move to the competitor.

With global viability, if the organization is to maintain viability, either or both of two devices is necessary: There must be detailed constitutional specification of the obligations of the occupant of each position; or there must be extensive policing to ensure that correct actions are taken. Even if the first of these devices is employed, only the second will guarantee that the proper actions are taken. And if only the second is employed, detailed prescriptions of what actions are correct must become part of the policing. But if a means can be found to move back to independent viability, the corporation is relieved of these two tasks. In the case of Honda, backward policing comes close to bringing about that move.

Although backward policing appears to be a satisfactory means of shifting from global to independent viability in some forms of productive activity, such as that found in the automobile industry, it is unclear how widely applicable it is. What does appear to be widely applicable, however, is the reallocation of rights found in backward policing. In the employment transaction, the employee-to-be gives up rights of control over actions in the realm covered by the employment contract. The reallocation of rights that allows backward policing returns a portion of those rights to their original owners, in exchange for the right of the corporation to make compensation contingent on productivity. Another portion of the rights, the right to reject the product of the employee's action, is given to the employee who must use this product.

CONSTITUTIONS IN CORPORATIONS, IMPLICIT AND EXPLICIT

The different allocation of rights and their reciprocal obligations in forward and backward policing forces recognition of the fact that, in every organization, there exists such an allocation, which may be called the "constitution" of the organization, whether explicitly stated or implicitly recognized as the legitimate order. Alongside any formal allocation of rights, the informal allocation that determines what is legitimate can be called the "informal constitution" of the organization.

Some rights and obligations are associated with relations between positions in the organization, as in the case of backward versus forward policing. Others concern relations between employees—occupants of the positions—and the corporation, such as rights of collective bargaining. But it is not possible to separate fully the two sets of rights. The conception of the corporation that allows this separation no longer holds. This evolution can be seen by reference to the classical legal concept of agency, where the agent's skills and services are employed in the principal's interest.

Because of the evolution of the corporation, this concept is now either inappropriate or, at least, subject to considerable revision. In it, the interests of the agent can be segregated from those of the principal by means of appropriate compensation (including compensation based on performance), and the functioning of the organization, like that of a machine, can be described in terms of the functions of each of the parts in relation to the others (the obligations and expectations associated with positions). But the evolution of corporations has come to intertwine and combine so fully the interests of the corporation and those of the persons who work in it that such a separation becomes increasingly difficult.

The modern corporation is less a machine with interdependent parts or agents than a system of action comparable to an unconstrained market. It is, however, a special sort of market, in which the organization defines rights, provides resources, and structures reward systems. Hierarchical authority remains as a last resort, but one that represents a failure in the structuring of incentives. Far from all organizational practice has evolved to this stage, just as much organizational theory continues to follow Max Weber's conception of bureaucratic authority. Yet it is clear that both the Weberian theory of bureaucracy and the practice that mirrors it are earlier, and less successful, stages in the evolution of purposive social organization. It is also clear that they are conceptually deficient in their failure to recognize formal organization as a system of action in which each actor has interests and attempts to implement them.

I will examine the character of constitution formation—formal and informal— in modern corporations by way of two examples, which illustrate, in differing ways, the evolution of organizational form beyond that of hierarchical authority and Weberian bureaucracy.

Quality of Work Life Programs

A number of American firms have initiated programs patterned after Japanese "quality circles." Sometimes termed "Quality of Work Life" (QWL) programs, they involve extensive restructuring of the organization of a manufacturing plant. The supervisor's activities are largely replaced by the collective decisions of a work team comprising about seven to fifteen persons engaged in interdependent activities (e.g., a section of an assembly line or a group of stamping machines). A team elects a chair, decides first how it will conduct its business, and then meets regularly, ordinarily once a week during work hours. Actions range from modifying the work structure to resolving interpersonal problems among members of the team.

A peculiar pattern characterizes QWL programs that are initiated when a plant first opens. For several months, a small group, made up of people from management (usually including the future plant manager), representatives from the production line (including union leaders in unionized plants), and a QWL advisor, meets full-time to work out the organization of the new plant. A major accomplishment of this group is the production of a statement expressing the "operating philosophy" of the plant, which is subsequently framed and hung on a wall. Surprisingly, the operating philosophies of different QWL plants are quite similar and appear to an outside observer to consist mostly of platitudes. One might question the purpose of this intensive preparation that produces nothing that could not have been borrowed directly from another plant.

The answer, I believe, is that this process leads to the creation of an informal constitution, a set of rights and obligations supported both by the core of production-line workers and the core of management. (Typically, the remaining managerial and work force is hired and trained by this group or a group drawn from it. A fundamental question posed to prospective employees is whether they agree with the operating philosophy and form of organization of the plant.) The nature of the informal constitution, that is, the structure of rights and obligations, derives largely from suggestions of the QWL advisor, who serves as a channel of information from other QWL programs. But the lengthy and intense collective effort that produces the operating philosophy represents a period during which members of the core group are building their own commitment to the constitution. Their commitment appears necessary to elicit the commitment of the rest of the work force, which, in turn, is essential to ensure that the allocation of rights provided by the constitution will be enforced by all members of the plant. The preproduction meetings by the core group, together with the elaborate procedures to induct new people into membership, are all systems that help bring about the legitimacy of the authority system under which all will work.

We may ask why such lengthy induction-and-commitment processes were not used (and possibly not useful) in earlier periods. The answer lies in the character of the two authority systems. In the classical hierarchical form of authority that has characterized industrial production, legitimacy of authority was intrinsic to the labor contract. Employees gave rights of control over their actions to the employer and received a money wage as compensation. Authority was either exercised directly or delegated by the employer to an intermediate agent.

When collective bargaining was introduced, the transaction took a different form, and its terms (such as the processing of grievances) changed, with some rights being reallocated to the collective body of workers made into a corporate actor through the formation of the union. The principal change, however, was that a smaller set of rights of control were transferred to the employer by the employee.

In QWL-organized plants, authority is diffused, with a large portion held and exercised collectively by the team. This implies that members must accept the collective authority of their peers and also exercise authority collectively. The allocation of rights in such an organization includes an allocation to the team as a corporate actor, and the members of the team must accept that allocation and exercise the rights. Thus, the allocation of rights that was accomplished in a single employment contract in the classical labor market is now much more complex. Acceptance of this allocation of rights presupposes an understanding of this more complex structure. Because the functioning of the system depends more on the acceptance and exercise of the rights by all workers, a period of indoctrination is valuable to increase commitment to the constitution.

Mitbestimmung in German Corporations

In 1976 the existing "Mitbestimmung" or codetermination law in Germany was extended to give new rights to workers.[10] An example of a general movement toward "industrial democracy" in Western societies, particularly in Western Europe, the law reflects a modified conception of the corporation, just as does the QWL movement.

The law makes extensive changes at both the level of the board and of the workplace. It fixes the size of the board of directors at twenty for large firms and specifies that ten must be representatives of stockholders and ten representatives of employees. It also details the procedure by which employees' representatives will be selected and defines the role of the board in the corporation, including the type of information to be made available to board members, the minimum frequency of meeting, and the kinds of decisions that must not be made without their approval.

At the level of the workplace, the law requires the creation of workers' councils, with procedures for the election of representatives and with specific powers, such as those concerning grievances of workers. Workers' councils have some powers that previously had been prerogatives of management, exercised through supervision. The workers' councils, as well as the newly constituted board of directors, greatly increase workers' power in the organization.

RESTRUCTURING INCENTIVES IN THE CORPORATION

The QWL programs in the United States, based on Japanese models, and European codetermination both constitute changes in the implicit constitution of the corporation and give additional rights to production workers. Codetermination, however, does not challenge the conception of the corporation as consisting of a managerial class and a class of workers; it establishes, in fact, a political structure emphasizing that division and the distinct interests on each side. It does not alter the structure of authority through which work is carried out but, instead, introduces a formal voice of labor within that authority structure. Codetermination is more compatible with a system of forward policing than with a system of backward policing.

QWL programs, on the other hand, and, even more, the Japanese patterns on which they are based, deemphasize the division between management and labor. More compatible with backward policing, they are founded on a conception of common interests throughout the corporation and utilize consensual decision-making for production decisions. Authority is exercised collectively, through group norms, rather than hierarchically.

These two different ways of redistributing rights appear to stem from the ways in which the corporation emerged from feudalism in Japan and in Europe. The Japanese corporation is derived more closely from the feudal estate, without the intervening history of enlightenment philosophy, with its emphasis on individualism, and revolutions that destroyed the vestiges of feudalism in eighteenth- and nineteenth-century Europe. Corporate paternalism in Japan is the residue of the feudal lord's responsibility for all in his demesne. For example, in Japan, the corporation is responsible for a number of the welfare activities that are state responsibilities in Europe.

In America, with no history of feudalism but an immigrant population of European descent, the corporation has inherited Europe's conceptual basis, though with muted class divisions. Potentially, the American corporation would seem to be hospitable to either of these reallocations of rights, although it may be revealing that neither had its origins in America. But another reallocation of rights that did begin in the United States appears to reflect its historical origins.

Ownership Rights to Innovations

In capitalist corporations, the standard employment agreement for persons engaged in activities that might result in patents includes the assignment of patent rights to the corporation. It also places restrictions on the employee's rights to employment or consultation by competing firms for a period following employment. The agreement for such employees of state-owned enterprises is similar, containing a provision that patent rights will be assigned to government.

The terms of faculty appointments at most universities in the United States are entirely different, probably because the origins of the university predate the modern corporation and the conception of the employment relation that is intrinsic to it. Ownership rights to ideas and innovations that originate in universities are vested in the person rather than the institution, except where a contract with a government, corporation, or other source of research funds specifies otherwise. This has led to what may be termed "professorial spin-offs," in which faculty members who have developed a set of ideas as part of their university research form a corporation to carry the ideas to commercial realization. Or university faculty members, working on their own time, may make use of a company's laboratories and facilities under a contractual arrangement in which the ownership of ideas is regarded as being shared by the person and the corporation. This has occurred not only in the physical sciences (where it is especially evident in electronics), but also extensively in the biological sciences (where firms for genetic engineering have been formed by groups of faculty members, sometimes in a joint venture with existing corporations) and even in the social sciences (especially in the development of data bases in law and economics and statistical software).

In some corporations, the principle that ownership rights to ideas and innovations lie with the corporation has begun to erode. One corporation where this change came early was the 3M Company in Minneapolis. Donald Schon describes the development:

> They got Scotch tape out and it seemed to work and they sold a lot of it and then along came research with magnetic tape. They said, ''We know how to make tape. We'll make magnetic tape.''
>
> They had an invention along with this: the invention was that the man who developed the idea would go off and take a piece of the business and become in effect a semi-autonomous firm based around the product which he had developed. The company then kept profit and loss control over that division, but in no other way attempted to manage that man.
>
> And pretty soon what you had was a constellation of forty semi-autonomous firms surrounding a bank and a development facility. And if you asked what business MMM was in you could not say as long as you remained on the substantive product level. They are a company that makes money out of exploiting and commercializing entities that come from development. And the entities that come from development are organically related to one another and bear what Wittgenstein would call family resemblances to one another which reflects that organic process. But there's no Aristotelian basis for saying what the firm is, that is to say there is no set of characteristics which all and only products of that firm possess.[12]

The innovations in ownership rights to ideas and the potential variations in structure are especially great in the personal-computer software and hardware industry. In this industry, ideas are especially easily transportable. The production process itself requires little capital and few persons to implement an idea, so a person or a subgroup may resign from a firm and start a separate company without great difficulty. There are also many small firms in the industry, among which an extensive flow of persons (carrying ideas) can occur. Spin-offs of the sort described by Schon have been one response to this flow. Another has been to give partial ownership of the firm to an employee with an especially important idea.

Such organizational innovations are rarely found in certain industries, such as the automobile industry and other heavy industry. Their near absence, however, may have less to do with the nature of the product than with the traditions of these corporations, which were born before such ideas were widespread.

As in the case of the shift of rights to replace forward policing with backward policing, this change in ownership rights to innovations appears to have extensive consequences for the corporation as a system of action. Empirical observation suggests that a major effect is an increased rate of innovation. In the United States, university laboratories seem to be a much richer spawning ground for ideas than are corporation or government laboratories. Industries where there is extensive theft of ideas from firms by those who had the ideas (by resigning and forming a start-up firm or a new unit with special rights in another firm) have very high rates of innovation. For example, the rate of innovation in the computer industry has exploded since the invention of mini- and microcomputers (both of which began when innovators broke away from larger firms).

In another illustration, it is generally agreed that a major cause of IBM's extraordinary dominance of the infant microcomputer industry was that the IBM personal computer had an open architecture, that is, empty slots for hardware add-ons and an operating system developed by a third party. A small army of individuals and start-up firms began to construct and sell hardware and software that would fit the specifications of this open system. Within a very short time, the IBM specifications became the standard. In effect, the open architecture strategy expanded the set of persons working to enhance IBM's product far beyond the confines of the firm itself. (This was aided by the fact that Apple, a chief competitor, introduced a microcomputer that used closed architecture.)

The dangers of openness are apparent in this example, for the strategy facilitated the introduction of low-priced compatibles, designed to free ride on the specifications so firmly established by IBM's success. The matter is complex, as is determining the best strategy for a corporation to exploit innovations. It is clear, however, that neither the rate of innovation nor the corporation's best interests are maximized by closure that wholly prevents actors outside the corporation from exploiting the innovations.

Another observation suggests a more subtle inhibition to the exploitation of ideas. In many corporate research and development divisions, there exists the "NIH syndrome": a lack of motivation, interest, and effort applied to ideas "Not Invented Here" that originated either elsewhere in the firm or outside the firm. An investigation into an idea that originated elsewhere often seems to result in a catalog of the reasons why the idea will not be useful.

The prevalence of the NIH syndrome suggests another motivation that leads to a differential rate in innovation depending on the location of ownership rights. Persons have an interest in seeing an idea fail if it belongs to another and they cannot benefit from its exploitation. This appears to arise even in the absence of rights of ownership: By demonstrating the defects in another's idea, one justifies not having had the idea oneself; by demonstrating its potential, one is relatively worse off, because the other's status is elevated.

However, shared ownership rights between a corporation and the innovating person or group carry their own hazards. The potential divisiveness that such an allocation of rights can create is particularly deleterious to organizational functioning. If ideas become the partial property of their originator, they are less likely to be shared openly and worked on jointly. Disputes about ownership of ideas may arise within a unit of the organization, furthering the divisiveness. This problem can be reduced or eliminated, however, by appropriate allocation of ownership rights—for example, not in an individual, but in a group that works in a given area.

Altogether, we may describe the shift of ownership rights to the actor or group that innovates as a partial reuniting of the "split atom of private property," the separation of ownership and control that Berle and Means described as the major innovation of the modern joint-stock corporation.[13] But it reunites them in a different way than might have been envisaged by theorists of the corporation like Berle and Means, by vesting the rights to benefit from the action in the agents, rather than returning control to those who hold ownership rights (or, as Berle and Means proposed, giving control to "the community").

Modifying ownership rights affects motivation by changing interests. Changes in interests cannot be accounted for in rational choice theory; interests must be taken as given. However, interests may be changed easily, merely by altering the constraints on what is possible for an actor. Actors usually increase their satisfaction by gaining control of those goods or events in which they have an interest, often through exchange. Here, actors' satisfaction can be increased by giving them an interest in something over which they have control. Of course, this does not create an interest out of thin air; rather, interest arises because something in which actors already have an interest (money, prestige, or fame in this case) is made dependent on what they already control, that is, their ideas or innovations. The change in structure that gives an actor who has an idea interests in the innovation is achieved either by making money income (or something else in which the actor has an interest) directly contingent on the innovation or by making income contingent on the success of the product that results from the innovation.

Reward Structures Linking Interests to Actions

Ownership rights are only one means by which the interests of an actor may be made contingent on the initiation and development of innovations, and money is not the only thing of intrinsic interest on which these actions may be made to depend. Nor is a restructuring that creates this contingency always sufficient to bring about the actions that will lead to an improved corporate product. A change that gives the innovator some control over further development of the innovation may be important. In the organizational innovations described earlier, the innovator's partial control of the innovation's development appears to be important to success.

There are many successful examples of such organizational innovations, some of them striking because of the departure they represent for the corporation. An example shows some of the consequences when an organization fails to develop such a structure. An automobile manufacturer has an advanced product engineering division, responsible for innovations that, it is hoped, will come to be incorporated in new product designs by the divisions responsible for manufacturing and marketing the corporation's automobiles. In the 1970s this division had developed a cambering principle that was applicable to a range of vehicles including scooters, motorcycles, and small three-wheeled vehicles. The head of the advanced product engineering division was greatly taken with this principle and wanted to see it incorporated in products. The division developed the principle in a number of test vehicles, spending a great deal of attention, interest, and time on it. The division head attempted in vain to sell the idea of developing and marketing such vehicles to both the corporation and the automobile divisions. The decision not to do so may have been correct for the corporation and the divisions. But the failure to vest partial ownership rights in the developers and to create a spin-off outside the corporation resulted in the partial diversion of the division from other developments that would have been of interest to the automobile divisions as long as the division head was enraptured by the idea. More generally, this structure, in which new design ideas were developed in a unit that was not organizationally within a division that would carry the innovation through development, manufacture, and marketing, meant that design innovations seldom moved beyond the boundaries of the specialized division.

Breaking the Power of Norms

As in any system of action involving real persons, formal authority, consisting of regulations, laws, and explicit rules, is supplemented by informal norms. Peter Blau demonstrated this graphically for a government agency, and other well-known research, such as the Hawthorne experiments, show how informal norms affect production levels.[14] Some of these norms are beneficial to the overall purposes of the organization; others are not. How these norms can be made to serve the interests of the corporation is a difficult question, and I will not address it here. I will, instead, give one concrete illustration of a norm that was harmful to an organization and describe one organizational device that is sometimes used to break the power of a norm.

Some norms take the form of not questioning certain beliefs that are locally regarded as "facts." For example, the engineers in one American automobile company in the late 1970s "knew" that there were no significant advantages to overhead cam engines; but, for the engines the company was designing at the time, that was not a correct technical assessment. A pervasive technical culture prevented certain questions from being raised anew as conditions changed. All organizations are subject to such cultural norms; they are characteristic of every collectivity engaged in a common endeavor, arising from too-great pressures toward agreement.[15]

Certain organizational devices can prevent such norms from obscuring technically superior solutions. One is a procedure that may be termed "structured dissent," though variations of it are known by other names in different organizations. Structured dissent operates something like this: When a policy decision is to be made and there are several possibly viable alternatives, each alternative is assigned to a staff member, who must argue its merits in writing, orally, or both. The relevant official or committee then makes the decision after a presentation of these position papers, or briefs.

Structured dissent has been used by U.S. presidents confronted with policy decisions; NASA uses a similar procedure called "nonadvocacy policy review." The procedure, through the arbitrary assignments of alternatives, breaks the normative constraint against taking a position that is internally unpopular but may be the most viable. It reshapes the incentive structure to motivate staff members to show the best points of their assigned alternatives.

CHANGES IN THE CONCEPT OF THE CORPORATION

Max Weber's conception of rational authority, the legal conception of principal and agent, the economic work in principal-agent theory, and most organization theory in sociology have one element in common: They see the corporation as an extension of a single purpose, with an owner or set of owners (or principals) who bring together "factors of production" or "agents" or "office-holders" to implement this purpose. Employees, having no interest in the purpose of the owners, agree to fill the positions, become the agents, and constitute one of the factors of production, in exchange for compensation. They also acquire certain rights, mainly associated with the specific commodity—labor—that they bring to the marketplace.

The decline of shareholders' interest in the corporation except as a source of return on capital, QWL programs and the quality circles in the Japanese corporation on which they are patterned, the codetermination law of 1976 in Germany and the movement toward industrial democracy that it reflects, the trend toward vesting partial rights to innovations in their inventors, the use of company songs, company dress, and other symbolic actions to increase employees' identification with the firm—all of these developments challenge the traditional conception of the corporation. Whether the change is in the conception of rights or in the conception of interests, the distinction between owner as principal and employee as agent appears less sharp than in the past. Modes of governance are moving away from authority exercised by a superordinate toward discipline imposed by the structure of incentives.

As described earlier, the organization is best conceived as a system of action. The occupants of positions are the actors; their positions, the incentive structures, and their personal aims interact to determine their interests and to provide them with the resources to realize those interests. The difference between this and any other system of action is that the positions, rights, and incentive structures arise from the constitution of the organization, which is created, directly or indirectly, by those who bring the organization into being. This does not occur in the absence of constraints. Sometimes, as in the case of codetermination, these constraints even dictate specific elements of the constitution.

There is, however, the question of whether the rights to establish the organization's constitution are appropriately held. This is a step backward toward an infinite regress; but, in this case, the step lands squarely in the allocation of rights in civil law: It is the legal structure of the larger society that determines the allocation of rights in constructing the corporation's constitution.

We may ask, however, whether anything might be said more generally about appropriate allocations of rights in the constitutions of corporations. Two extreme cases may help to fix ideas in answering this. One is the start-up company created by one or two persons with an idea for an innovation and a source of venture capital, that is, a person or corporate actor with money to invest. Stock in the firm is divided between the persons with ideas and the venture capitalist. A number of persons are hired to aid in the implementation of the ideas. The company may or may not be successful, depending on a variety of factors, some internal to the company, some not under its control. The other extreme is a large, long-established corporation with many employees and stock widely dispersed among a set of stockholders who hold it because it offers a higher rate of return than other possible investments, or because it is safer than most, or for a variety of other reasons.

It seems unlikely that the same set of legal rights or the same conception of organization is appropriate in the two cases. If we consider only the criterion of survival (without attempting to settle the question of whether this is the only appropriate criterion), it is likely that organizational survival will be maximized by a different division of rights between owners and employees in each case. In the first, survival (which is in the interests of stockholders and employees alike) is much more contingent on the actions of the owners (the entrepreneurs pursuing the development of their idea and the venture capitalist providing additional capital at crucial points). In the second case, survival depends much more on the actions of employees.

Yet there is no single point marking where a partial reallocation of rights from owners to employees is natural, although much civil law affecting corporations recognizes some difference of this sort. Just as one cannot pinpoint when a tadpole becomes a frog, one cannot specify when a corporation's success depends less on the actions of its owners than on those of its employees or agents.

THE CORPORATION AND THE SOCIETY

This chapter has been confined thus far to an examination of the internal social organization of the corporation. But numerous additional questions concern the corporation as an element in the larger social system. I will examine only one of those questions here, an issue that is central to the functioning of society: the corporation's effect on child rearing.

Throughout history, the family has been the institution responsible for child rearing. Until this century, the family, or another social unit directly derived from it, was also the principal unit of economic production, which involved, in most cases, subsistence production of food and clothing within the family or labor in settings that had families as their basic units, such as the local community.

The modern corporation has changed all that, as a result of the different conceptual base from which it springs and the extraordinary prosperity that it has brought. First men, and now women, have been drawn away from the household to the corporation. In 1810, 87 percent of men were employed in agriculture, that is, in or near the household, and most of the remaining 13 percent were undoubtedly working in a setting socially proximate to the family. By 1900 the 87 percent had dropped to 42 percent; and by 1980 it was less than 5 percent. As for women, in 1810 almost none were in the employed labor force; nearly all were in the home. By 1900 the percentage in the home was 79 percent; by 1980 this had declined to 48 percent. Thus, the exodus of men from production in the household to production some distance beyond it began in the nineteenth century; women followed men out of the household into the corporation about a hundred years later.[16] These statistics indicate the movement of economically productive activity from the household to the corporation.

The raising of children has always been a coproduction with other activities; now, much of the time that adults once had to raise their children is spent in locations remote from them, behind the closed doors of a plant or office. Not only the family, but also the neighborhood, including the voluntary associations that sometimes thrive there, depend on the time and activity of these same adults.

If employment in the corporation is the primary means of distributing income in modern society, we see that the movement of productive activity from the family to the corporation has also redistributed income away from children. This redistribution occurs, not only because many children begin life without a connection to the corporation (e.g., children of welfare mothers), but also because of an increase in households termed "DINKS" (an acronym for "Double Income No Kids"), where income has no way to reach children. In confirmation of this, Samuel Preston reports that in 1970 persons over sixty-five made up the highest proportion of the population below the poverty line; by 1980 it was children under five who were highest.[17]

The corporation has replaced the family as the central institution around which modern society is constructed. But the substitution is not complete, for the corporation lacks one property necessary to the continuation of society: It has no place for the next generation. This might be remedied, either through modifications of the corporation or through the assumption by other institutions of some of the functions the family can no longer perform. But until such changes occur, it must be acknowledged that a society in which the corporation has replaced the family as the central institution is not naturally hospitable to children. Some legal changes and corporation-initiated actions have already altered this social structure to make it somewhat less inimical to children. One innovation, recognizing the centrality of the corporation, involves moving some of the social functions of child rearing into it. Company day-care centers are perhaps the most interesting development, because they bring children into the same corporate body as their parents. Company schools could constitute an equally interesting innovation, if the disincentive created by free public schools could be overcome.

Other accommodations adjust corporate demands to child-rearing demands. These include flextime, which is now widespread, the repartitioning of work to create more part-time jobs, and maternity leaves. Spatially distributed organizations, too, could allow much work to be done in the home, and, already, some unions have reduced their opposition to this alternative.

There are other changes that do nothing to increase the compatibility of the corporation with child rearing but merely take child-rearing activities out of the family. One is an increased comprehensiveness of the schools, which take responsibility for a wider range of child-rearing functions and a larger fraction of the child's time. Another is the existence of specialized child-care facilities. As with some of the accommodations by the corporation discussed above, changes in these directions have already occurred.

If the corporation remains the central institution of modern society and no comprehensive solutions are found to the problems described in this section we may find that we have lost the means to carry out one of the activities most crucial to survival: the process of getting from one generation to the next, through raising and socializing children.

NOTES

1. See, for example, R. M. Cyert and J. G. March, *A Behavioral Theory of the Firm* (Englewood Cliffs, N.J.: Prentice-Hall, 1963).
2. Robert Michels, *Political Parties* (1915; reprint, New York: The Free Press, 1949), p. 389.
3. Oliver E. Williamson, *Markets and Hierarchies* (New York: The Free Press, 1975).
4. F. Y. Edgeworth, *Mathematical Psychics; An Essay on the Application of Mathematics to the Moral Sciences* (1881; reprint, New York: A. M. Kelly, 1967).
5. Chester Barnard, *The Functions of the Executive* (Cambridge: Harvard University Press, 1938).
6. The family is subject to this as well. In the United States around 1970, when most households were supported by the husband-father, many families found themselves suddenly without an income as men were attracted away by a change in market conditions: a large influx of young unmarried women, a result of the baby boom of the late forties and early fifties.
7. John R. Hicks, *The Theory of Wages* (London: Macmillan, 1932).

8. Alfred D. Chandler, Jr., and Stephen Salsbury, *Pierre S. Du Pont and the Making of the Modern Corporation* (New York: Harper & Row, 1971).

9. For a discussion of the problem, see Robert Eccles and Harrison White, "Firm and Market Interfaces of Profit Center Control," in S. Lindenberg, J. Coleman, and S. Nowak, eds., *Approaches to Social Theory* (New York: Russell Sage, 1986), pp. 203–20.

10. See the Federal Minister of Labour and Social Affairs, *Codetermination in the Federal Republic of Germany* (Geneva: International Labour Organisation, 1976).

11. See James S. Coleman, "The University and Society's New Demands Upon It," in Carl Kaysen, ed., *Content and Context: Essays on College Education* (New York: McGraw-Hill, 1973), pp. 359–99.

12. Donald A. Schon, Reith Lectures (London: British Broadcasting Corporation, 1970).

13. Adolf A. Berle, Jr., and Gardiner C. Means, *The Modern Corporation and Private Property* (New York: Macmillan, 1934).

14. Peter Blau, *The Dynamics of Bureaucracy* (Chicago: University of Chicago Press, 1955); F. J. Roethlisberger and W. J. Dickson, *Management and the Worker* (Cambridge: Harvard University Press, 1959).

15. Group decisionmaking can also lead to inferior decisions in certain types of problems. Irving Janis discusses this phenomenon through examples such as the Kennedy decision to invade Cuba at the Bay of Pigs, which was arguably an incorrect policy decision given the information then available. See Irving Janis, *Victims of Groupthink: A Psychological Study of Foreign-Policy Decisions and Fiascos* (Boston: Houghton Mifflin, 1972).

16. Sources for these statistics may be found in J. Coleman, "Families and Schools," *Educational Researcher* 16, no. 5 (1987):32–38.

17. Samuel Preston, "Children and the Elderly," *Scientific American* 251, no. 6 (1984):44–49.

6 CORPORATIONS AND THE WORK FORCE

Harvey Brooks and Michael Maccoby

What makes companies competitive so that they can create wealth and provide employment? What stimulates the fullest development of human skills and character and strengthens democratic values in the surrounding society? These questions relate to different criteria—one economic/technical and the other social/human—that can be used to evaluate work relationships. Of course, the degree to which these two criteria are mutually compatible or, conversely, the degree to which trade-offs must be made between them raises serious issues.

The oldest model of the corporation was derived from the traditional military organization in which democratic principles and organizational efficiency were seen as mutually exclusive. At the present time, however, economic/technical and social/human criteria may be less incompatible. For example, in companies that use advanced technology to deliver customized products and services, effectiveness apparently requires more delegation of responsibility and authority to workers. Conflict is more likely to occur in less advanced companies requiring less skilled workers. We believe that in such situations society must be prepared to intervene collectively to impose minimum social/human standards on the relationship between the corporation and its work force. Otherwise, a lower level of humane and democratic standards will tend to prevail. This would weaken society as a whole by undermining standards of justice and setting the stage for destructive conflict.

A second conflict between economic/technical and social/human criteria may arise from the demand made on American corporations to conform to a social agenda committed to furthering equality among races and gender. It is unknown whether affirmative action will strengthen or weaken American industry relative to competitors, like the Japanese, with more homogeneous work forces. American management, more than that of any of its competitors, must integrate a value-diverse work force. For example, the large-scale entry of women with children into the work force pressures corporations to allow flexible arrangements and to limit overtime.[1] Dual wage earners may not offer the degree of dedicated commitment gained in the past from the sole male wage earner with a family supporting his career.

Sweden appears to have adapted to the gender issue without losing competitiveness. With levels of participation by women in the work force even higher than those of the United States, national policy supports extensive child care and grants liberal leaves for parents. However, neither in Sweden nor in any other European or Asian country are many women to be found in top management positions.

An assumption underlying much of our discussion is that the United States, especially in companies using advanced technology, better human/social norms, particularly in terms of less hierarchy and more participation, will lead to improved competitive performance. This assumption remains to be tested fully by experience in the new global economy, and we will not address the details of its implementation here.

Our discussion deals primarily with the large, multiplant corporation, with little reference to the small businesses that currently employ a sizable percentage of the U.S. work force. This may be a serious limitation. However, while the problems of impersonal bureaucracy and rigid work rules and organizational relationships are less applicable to small firms, insecure employment and unilateral decision-making by management may often be more acute, though tempered by the closer personal relationships between managers and employees that can inhibit arbitrariness. This limitation in our treatment can be justified further if one argues that the relationships in large corporations tend to establish the norms of all economic relations in society.

HISTORY

At the beginning of the Industrial Revolution, in the 1830s, Alexis de Tocqueville warned America about the growth of large manufacturing companies and the division of labor, predicting that a new and powerful class of industrial owners would undermine equality and democracy. Independent small farmers and businessmen, with general knowledge of politics and the economy and confidence in their own judgment, would become dependent wage earners with narrowed vision and understanding. He wrote that the "workman unceasingly and exclusively engaged in the fabrication of one thing . . . loses the general facility of applying his mind; . . . in proportion as the workman improves, the man is degraded."[2]

At the beginning of the twentieth century, Tocqueville's prophecies seemed to be coming true. Large-scale American industry was based on mass production of standardized products; jobs were simplified, and tasks fragmented. Workers' rights were strictly limited. The authority exercised over employees by managers as representatives of the owners was, in theory, absolute, limited only by the benevolence and good will of the manager or by the degree to which he perceived it to be in his own enlightened self-interest to treat his employees fairly and with respect. In the courts, the corporation was treated as a legal person, with relatively few societal restraints on the uses of its property.[3]

Why did Americans imbued with values of individual liberty and insistent upon rights that limit the power of government accept authoritarian relations in the workplace? In part, this was because so many workers were immigrants from rural Europe or the American South, where obedience to authority was traditional and accepted. Moreover, workers and the public recognized the corporation's ability to create wealth, to raise the standard of living for all. There was also some degree of protection by unions, which were able to bargain for rights as well as for economic benefits through their power to enforce demands by striking.

In most large companies, however, the unions could achieve little until late in the 1930s, when government stepped in to sanction legally the right of employees to form unions and to impose an obligation on employers to bargain collectively in good faith. In 1935 the Wagner Act formalized and institutionalized collective bargaining. It also encouraged the growth of large industrywide unions, which gained power relative to the older unions organized according to crafts and skills. Through seniority and work rules, union members also gained a measure of job security and protection from the arbitrary exercise of authority that protected their jobs from being changed unilaterally by management. Management, too, supported such rules because they increased the predictability of labor and reduced conflict. Over time, however, the proliferation of detailed job classifications diminished management's ability to adapt the work organization to the changes in technology and product mix demanded by increasingly volatile markets, although the degree of rigidity differed widely from industry to industry, being more severe, for example, in steel and autos than in the more technically dynamic telephone industry.

In the collective-bargaining contract, unions negotiated limitations to the unilateral power of the corporation over its employees, the extent of which depended entirely on the relative bargaining power of the unions and management. Specific rights of employees, other than the right to join unions and to choose without coercion or improper influence by employers those who were to represent them in the collective-bargaining process, were nowhere embodied in law. The only obligation imposed on the corporation was to bargain in good faith with union representatives elected in accordance with carefully defined procedural rules enforced by the National Labor Relations Board. The issues open to bargaining were narrowly delimited in law; otherwise, the power of management remained largely unimpeded. It was assumed that the interests of management and the union were inherently in conflict and, hence, their relations intrinsically adversarial. Indeed, as interpreted by the Supreme Court, the Taft-Hartley Act of 1946 was considered to limit union organizing to hourly workers, excluding supervisors and middle managers—anyone, in fact, who was expected to exercise managerial discretion and not just follow instructions.[4] This arrangement worked fairly well as long as competition was mainly among domestic oligopolies subject to similar rules and the dominant mode of production was highly rationalized mass production within large bureaucratic structures.

THE LEGACY OF TAYLORISM

The dominant organizational paradigm of "scientific management" was pioneered in the early twentieth century by Frederick Taylor and others.[5] The legacy of the Tayloristic or "technocentric" model of mass-production industries may be summarized as follows:[6]

1. There is an ever more refined division of labor. Tasks are broken down into elements that can be learned easily and thoroughly and performed repetitively; these are controlled and coordinated by several layers of management.

2. There is a bureaucratic hierarchy. Clear-cut boundaries separate different work functions and responsibilities; large staffs of functional specialists participate in work design; status differences within management and between supervisory and production workers are sharply defined.

3. There is an implicit belief in one best way to organize and perform factory work. Factory workers are in large measure interchangeable, and, with stable technology, work can be designed according to well-established scientific principles and sustained by close supervision supported by quantitative measures of worker performance.

4. Both workers and managers believe that the interests of workers are best protected from arbitrary and subjective management decisions by carefully drawn-up work rules, well-codified grievance procedures, and detailed, written collective-bargaining agreements negotiated industrywide—a "rule of law" substituting for a "rule of men."

5. It is assumed that productive efficiency requires that management enjoy unchallenged control over the design and introduction of new production technology, investments in plant and equipment, the design of the work process, and plant location. Participation by workers in these decisions is considered neither necessary nor valuable.

6. It is assumed that individual incentives for money and status will be sufficient to motivate the system as a whole.

These beliefs and assumptions are, of course, far from universal, but they tend to dominate in large multiplant firms producing standardized products with electromechanical processes. Although many smaller firms start out with less rigid organizational forms, the large successful firms have established the model for good management, which small firms adopt as they grow.

THE NEW CORPORATE ENVIRONMENT

A whole set of changes in the business environment of the corporation have altered the situation that made these arrangements highly successful in the first half of the twentieth century.

The work force is better educated and expects more autonomy and discretion in the performance of work. Many workers are less willing to accept boring, routine jobs requiring little initiative or brainpower, even when accompanied by rising wages and fringe benefits.

Domestic deregulation and new foreign competitors with new management methods or lower wage levels have increased pressures on corporate managers to cut production and labor costs, improve quality, and, in many cases, customize products and services. The bureaucratic industrial structure with rigid job classifications has become too costly and inefficient.

Because of newly emerging foreign competitors and the saturation of world markets in an increasing number of mature industries and even some of the maturing high-tech industries, the older industrial economies can no longer deliver the constantly rising living standards that production workers have come to expect. As a result, the human costs of traditional scientific management appear less of a bargain to workers.

As production has become more automated, the sharp distinction between production workers and management becomes more and more artificial. This happened first in the continuous-process industries and is now occurring in assembly-type industries. It has become difficult to organize production without according more independent decisionmaking authority to workers on the shop floor.

The changing situation also requires new competencies and higher levels of teamwork and interdependency. Functional boundaries among design, development, and production need to be broken down. Front-line workers need to communicate laterally as well as vertically. Evolving technology requires investments in retraining.

Functional service bureaucracies within manufacturing industries have grown far more quickly than direct production labor. These middle managers fall into neither of the two classical categories of workers—managers as bosses with broad discretionary authority deriving from owners, and production workers as the recipients of orders with essentially no independent decisionmaking power. Instead of a polarization of interests between a monolithic management on one side and a worker proletariat on the other, there is a growing diversity of interests among different parts of the corporate hierarchy. Although they still retain a strong sense of their separate status and interests, middle managers have found themselves to be as expendable as blue-collar workers when companies cut staff functions and decentralize profit centers, especially with the recent popularity of mergers and acquisitions in the United States.

With newer, more automated production technologies, production or services can be maintained for long periods with nonunionized supervisory personnel and middle management. This greatly reduces the effectiveness of the strike threat and, hence, the bargaining power of the union. Union power is further weakened as companies are able to subcontract functions, hire temporary employees, and send some of their operations offshore to cut costs.

As the power of the strike has declined, production quality in a growing number of industries has become more dependent on the positive motivation of workers. Mere passive obedience to detailed, rigid instructions from management does not assure the quality or the productivity necessary to compete in world markets, especially with Japanese industries that have succeeded in developing a much higher degree of employee participation and initiative than their Western competitors.

The rate of change of the product demand mix in world markets and both product and production technology has accelerated. Productivity, once a static concept, has become a dynamic process that involves capital and other input savings, as well as labor efficiency. Changeover times to new products and processes have become at least as important as the static efficiency of the steady-state production process, which is rarely completely achieved. The necessity for rapid organizational adaptation means that rigid definition of jobs and work rules and sharp functional specialization become counterproductive in terms of overall firm performance. The elaborate rules of a collective-bargaining contract, subject to infrequent renegotiation, are simply incompatible with the demands of an ongoing, experimental, and evolutionary process.

The polarity of management and labor has become less relevant to the real world of labor relations. Indeed, the very concept of "labor", which suggests repetitive manual toil, embodies an obsolete notion of the nature of work and of the work force.[7] The relationship between managers and employees is becoming more multilateral: Diverse groupings of employees and managers now have interests that cannot be accommodated by adversarial negotiation between management and union. Furthermore, collective bargaining as practiced under the Wagner Act presumes a degree of union solidarity and discipline that has become almost as distasteful to many younger workers as the unilateral decisionmaking power of management.

Whereas in the 1930s the growing industrial union movement was seen by the public as embodying strong community values working toward the common interest, today, unions are considered increasingly to be just one more special interest vying for a larger share of society's resources at the expense of the consumer or the general public. In fact, the polarized negotiation between large unions and giant corporations is viewed frequently as a cozy conspiracy to capture joint gains for organized labor and management. Although their legitimacy continues to be recognized and even managers admit that they protect the wages of workers, unions and their leaders are increasingly marginal to the liberal coalition, and membership has plummeted except in the public sector, where the adversary is not corporate management representing private owners but elected or appointed officials supposedly representing the general public.

In example after example, Japanese companies, using similar product designs and production technologies, have produced better quality products at lower cost than their American counterparts. Usually, less than a third of the cost differential between Japanese and American firms is attributable to compensation levels. It is increasingly evident that the competitive advantage of the Japanese lies, not in a greater adoption of automation or in inherent cultural differences, but simply in the way the work force is managed, particularly in the involvement of the entire work force, from top to bottom, in a holistic company strategy.[8]

The conclusion that the organization of work, not a superior technology or work ethic, accounts for Japanese success has been supported by the excellent quality and productivity of Japanese-owned firms with American workers in the United States.[9]

To be sure, these changes move more rapidly in some industries than in others. Furthermore, even within large companies, there are major differences in the degree of automation. However, in one way or another, these forces affect all American industry, particularly those competing in the international market.

THE RESPONSE OF U.S. CORPORATIONS AND UNIONS

In response to these general developments, managements and unions in the United States have embarked on a great variety of experiments to change organizations and work relationships.

Changes in the Structure of Work

Walton's high-commitment workplaces based on teamwork and delegated responsibility and Piore and Sabel's "flexible specialization"—horizontal networks with self-coordinating nodes connected to a common data base rather than hierarchical bureaucracies—are two new alternatives to traditional work structures.[10] In another example, Maccoby's "technoservice" model of work, through training and delegating to workers authority to satisfy customer needs and expectations and measurements supporting customer satisfaction, brings the entire work force into better juxtaposition with clients or customers both inside and outside the firm.[11]

All of these new models require much more from the work force—not only individual technical skills and enhanced interpersonal skills of managers and workers, but also better knowledge and competence on the part of unions and union leadership in the stategic aspects of business. The reconciliation of the need for coordination at the organizational level with the need for autonomy and respect at the individual level presents a tremendous challenge.

The "Quality of Working Life" Movement

QWL, Employee Involvement (EI), quality circles, participatory management, industrial democracy, and other such terms, although closely related, are not synonymous; each actually stands for a slightly different flavor in the employment relationship. It is particularly important to distinguish between experiments that are initiated unilaterally by management and those initiated under the joint auspices of unions and management. Joint QWL or EI programs include, among others, many programs in the auto industry, and between the components of the former Bell System and the Communication Workers of America (CWA).[12] In these programs, the goals include both improved competitiveness and enhanced quality of working life.

Management-initiated programs are numerous in nonunionized plants. Early projects of this type were carried out at General Foods, Procter & Gamble, Donnelly Mirrors, and Motorola.[13] While many have been quite successful, organized labor regards them with some suspicion as efforts to avoid unionization—at times, with good justification. Yet, in some successful employee-participation experiments, improved cooperation and joint problem solving at the shop-floor level have spilled over into the collective-bargaining relationship as a result of greater trust built up between unions and management.[14] At Ford, the EI program sparked a development of participative management at all levels of the company, culminating in a new design process that brought together designers, production engineers, suppliers, and workers to participate in designing the highly successful Taurus and Sable cars.[15]

In general, studies of plants in which employee-participation programs have been introduced show improvements in product quality and productivity when compared with conventional workplaces.[16] Such programs, however, are vulnerable to economic downturns or changes in management because management retains the power to change them unilaterally.[17]

Common Interest Forums, Mutual Growth Forums, and Technology Committees

These bodies are established to discuss business strategy and reasons for changes in investments, technology, and employment requirements well in advance of final decisions.[18] At AT&T, the Network Common Interest Forum, addressing the issue of surplus service technicians, worked out ways to offer appropriate training and new jobs to displaced technicians.[19] In 1986, the parties bargained the establishment of a joint training center ("The Alliance") for employees in need of retraining due to changes in market and technology. Similarly, GM and UAW have built a Human Resource Center to provide training and support for QWL, retrain surplus workers, and administer the Paid Education Leave (PEL) program, which puts all GM-UAW local leaders through a four-week course on contemporary economic changes and potential new models for labor-management cooperation.[20]

In cases such as these, the unions gain some say in the strategic decisionmaking of the corporation but no place on the actual decisionmaking bodies. Employee or union representation on boards of directors has been much more common in Europe than in the United States,[21] where it has generally been confined to cases where the company was in serious financial trouble, as at Chrysler and several of the airlines. Such arrangements have often been tied to partial employee ownership of the company.

Employee Ownership to Protect Employment Security

Employee ownership has many degrees and forms, ranging from full cooperatives such as the Mondragon cooperatives in the Basque region of Spain, to employee buy-outs of failing companies as in the cases of Weirton Steel in West Virginia and the Hyatt-Clark ball-bearing plant of General Motors in New Jersey, to partial employee ownership in exchange for wage concessions as at Eastern Airlines.[22] Some of this ownership stems from ESOPs (Employee Stock Ownership Plans), which confer tax benefits to corporations that assist stock purchases by employees.

Employee ownership does not necessarily give rise to genuine employee participation in the strategic governance of the corporation. Employee representatives may be looked upon as management by the rank and file, even though they represent employees as owners.[23] Conflict tends to continue between the short-term interest of employees in job security (as opposed to employment security) and high wages and the policies required for long-term survival and growth. In addition, many cooperatives hire employees who are not members of the cooperative, which further complicates relationships.

In many cooperatives, employee-owners take out too much of the profits and fail to invest sufficiently in new product development, marketing, and other forms of strategic business development for the longer term. Mondragon is a notable exception to this because of the particular nature of the legal arrangements. The cooperative includes over 150 companies, a bank to finance new ventures, and an R-and-D center that serves the entire group.[24]

One of the advantages of cooperatives for employees and the local community is that ownership has an interest in staying put, which provides a good counter-influence to the increasing "footlooseness" of capital in this era of facile communications.[25] Furthermore, cooperatively owned businesses often show higher rates of productivity growth than their separately owned counterparts.[26] Interestingly, ownership without participation can be less effective in improving motivation than participation without ownership.[27]

Pension-Fund Equity

There has been an increase in the use of rapidly growing pension-fund equity participation in corporation ownership to influence corporate social policies and disposition to bargain with unions.[28]

Employee-Rights Legislation

Attempts at legislative and judicial restraints on the right of management to dismiss employees arbitrarily without reasons ("employment-at-will")[29]; legislative mandating of equal opportunity, equal pay for equal responsibility ("comparable worth"), and other policies to guarantee equal treatment; the possible emergence of an employee bill of rights with legislative sanctions and judicial enforceability—all of these developments create some basic employee rights, thereby removing them from the collective-bargaining table.

Occupational Health and Safety Regulations

These regulations, including "right-to-know" legislation in connection with potentially hazardous chemicals in the workplace, constitute another form of government guarantee of individual rights in the workplace. The guarantees of pension rights under ERISA are another example. In addition, unions increasingly influence health and safety in the workplace by bringing suit against employers and conducting or sponsoring with direct employee or union involvement independent research on occupational health and safety issues.[30]

Broadening the Collective-Bargaining Process

Efforts are growing to bring strategic management decisions concerning technology, plant location, employee training, employment security, and investment policies into collective bargaining. A good example is the introduction of corporate outsourcing and subcontracting decisions into collective bargaining in the auto industry. This has generally been most successful in companies where unions have built a cooperative relationship through the QWL/EI process.

International Bargaining

One traditional aim of national unions has been to remove wages, fringe benefits, work rules, and working conditions within an industry as factors in interfirm competition, thereby reducing competitive pressures to erode worker gains in these areas. The internationalization of competition has somewhat undermined this aim. A possible union response would be for unions to go international in order to extend the umbrella of "pattern bargaining" beyond national boundaries. The possibilities of transnational collective-bargaining negotiations are much greater within regions such as northern Europe, where standards of living and legal frameworks are more comparable, than, say, between North America and most of the Pacific Rim, where both labor-management politics and standards of living differ radically.

Multilateral Bargaining

Beyond the inclusion of international constituents, other stakeholders and constituencies affected by labor-management relations demand to be heard—communities in which plants are located, environmental or public interest groups, and organized consumer groups.[31]

Charles Heckscher and other observers suggest that we may be at the threshold of a new model of multilateral or "associational" bargaining inside the firm, as professional groups and lower level management employees begin to feel that their interests have more in common with those of blue-collar workers. Heckscher cites as a possible model the increased recourse to and success of multiparty negotiations regarding environmental and development issues.[32]

Public Policy

There is likely to be an increase in public policies or union-management bargains that facilitate adaptation of the work force to rapid technological and market changes: portable pensions, continuing-education funds, national labor market policies, accelerated private and public investment in retraining programs.[33] Whether these developments will strengthen or weaken unions is not yet clear. If they give union leadership greater flexibility in adapting to change, they will probably strengthen unions.

THE CHALLENGE TO CORPORATIONS AND UNIONS

These developments are still very experimental—manifestations of an urgent search for new paradigms to adapt to a new and rapidly changing environment. Increased employee involvement and the erosion of functional barriers have required considerable effort by dedicated leaders, often pushing against entrenched interests. For this period of experimentation to lead to new, stable labor-management relations, both corporate management and union leadership will have to evolve a new conception of their relationship and develop new competencies and skills, particularly in their interpersonal styles. In Chapter 8 of this book, Bower describes the increased complexity of demands on management in an era of rapid change. Aside from dealing with market strategy, financial markets, and government policy, managers must learn how to build or restructure organizational relationships to establish a motivating corporate culture that will replace detailed rules and procedures with internalized organizational values and norms, even while operating under the continuing tension between the values of a national culture emphasizing individual rights and those of a corporation emphasizing the creation of wealth and the growth of the organization.

A corporation is a subculture that seeks to attract some of the most gifted, motivated, and highly trained members of society and organize them to create wealth. To do this, it must respect the values these people bring with them, but the organization must also compensate for skills and values that are not developed so strongly outside a corporation. Creating a common corporate culture is difficult enough with individualistic employees who are homogeneous in terms of gender and social background; the task for American management with its culturally diverse work force is even more formidable.

The corporation's aim is not to guarantee the individual liberty of its employees but to satisfy customers in a way that generates a competitive return on investment compared to other uses of capital within the boundaries of law and national custom. The corporation requires that people support its strategy. It demands more discipline, more precision, and a greater concern for the quality and consistency of individual and group performance than does the general society. Highly ambitious individuals must see their own futures as being sufficiently bound up with the company's success to justify the submergence of some of their individual goals. Even in a cooperative, members must willingly sacrifice some of their individual freedom for common benefits of employment security and a share of profits. The difference is that a cooperative has the right to expel ineffective or oppressive management.

On the whole, managers in cooperative industries do not appear to behave significantly differently from those in well-run private or publicly held corporations. At Mondragon, for example, despite cooperative ownership and the presence of social committees representing worker interests, a large percentage of workers complain about insufficient participation in shop-floor decisions, and many believe that their interests would be better represented by a union.[34] This echoes the sentiments in many noncooperative companies, where employees see unions or associations as the only sure means to protect their right of self-expression and to secure equitable treatment from managment. Still, in some U.S. companies like IBM, Procter & Gamble, Hewlett-Packard, and Digital Equipment Corporation, managers have created a motivating culture in which there is sufficient respect for the individual and opportunity for learning and self-development that employees have not felt the need to organize.

Managers of many American companies seem to realize that they must increase worker participation, both to improve motivation and efficiency and to take advantage of workers' knowledge and practical shop-floor experience. However, many still see unions as just another external impediment to the growth of more participative and cooperative approaches to corporate problems, claiming that, without unions, they could use the techniques of behavioral science to manage participation and meet worker needs and aspirations more effectively. But can such managerial approaches alone develop the mutual trust needed to sustain participatory management through the changing fortunes of the enterprise?

Evidence from studies in the United States and Japan indicates that the support of a cooperative union enhances the teamwork required by the new workplace.[35] Unions protect workers who have legitimate grievances and offer a process for resolving conflict in a manner that is perceived as fair. Furthermore, they help to create a culture in which workers feel able to speak out and criticize inefficient (or antisocial) practices without fear of punishment or unfair discrimination. Indeed, so far, unions themselves have initiated many of the most successful experiments in participation (e.g., UAW with GM and CWA with AT&T). QWL teams supported by unions have been able to improve organizational effectiveness and deal with special employee needs (e.g., flextime) in a decentralized fashion.

The problem for management is that not all unions are always cooperative; a change in union leadership can quickly undermine a cooperative relationship built up painstakingly over a long time. Some programs have floundered because they became too bureaucratic or politicized or because of strikes. If companies create participative programs, they do not want them to be held hostage by ambitious union leaders with their own private agendas.

For participation to succeed, management must take on more of the initiative, promoting the process, not as a fringe benefit, but as a more effective way of organizing work. When workers see the immediate impact of their work on company success, it is easier to hold down costs, especially if profit-sharing plans replace automatic wage increases. Unions will then have to decide whether they want to oppose these initiatives, thereby risking the disaffection of some of their members, to take a neutral or nonparticipatory stance, or to cooperate fully.

The challenge to union leadership is severe. Unions combine the activities of a movement for justice and a service business. As part of broader societal movements for economic and social justice, unions represent workers in the struggle for democratic rights; as service businesses, they must satisfy the more immediate needs of members who pay the dues. Now, both of these missions require new strategies. As long as large companies gained productivity and profit, unions could demand wage increases; yet when wage increases outpace productivity gains, this can weaken companies' competitive positions. Furthermore, as work becomes more automated, rigid job classifications impede organizational effectiveness and realization of the potential gains from new production technology. It becomes difficult to maintain seniority rules when younger workers are more adept with computer technology than are older workers. Furthermore, younger workers want to participate with management in running the business, and many see unions as obstacles to this. Clearly, unions must modify their approaches if they are to continue to move forward in both of their roles.

Unions will better serve their members by gaining influence over investment decisions that affect employment, work processes, and life on the job. This has happened in Norway and Sweden through laws requiring that unions have a chance to present their views, but leaving the final decisions to management. Union representatives play an active role in the sociotechnical design of work in factories and offices. This works best in companies like Volvo where management helps to educate the union on strategic issues. (To some degree, this has been done by GM with the UAW, particularly in regard to the Saturn Project.)

In these companies, both union and management share essential values. Both want workers to find their work stimulating, challenging, and rewarding, to feel happy to work for the company, and to see a future there. Both want a workplace where everyone is free to express views about improving work. Union and management priorities may differ—the union puts workers' needs first, while management gives precedence to economic concerns—but, where each side respects the other, this divergence can stimulate creative problem solving and negotiations.

However, for management to accept this role for unions, the unions must, like Scandinavian unions and the UAW with GM, succeed in the essential task of organization. To be sure, a significant factor in the unions' recent lack of success in the United States has been an antiunion federal administration's tacit support of business's opposition to organized labor, but demand by workers for union representation has also been falling.[36] Most unions are run by white males who do not pay sufficient attention to the women and minorities entering the workplace. Furthermore, union polling of members and nonmembers shows that younger workers, especially the more educated, want more say, not only in corporate decisionmaking, but also in union affairs.[37] In addition to their wages and benefits, they want unions to further the quality of working life and opportunities for personal development.

One of the oldest craft unions, the Bricklayers and Allied Craftsmen (BAC), has experimented with a new model for union development. BAC's Project 2000 brought together about thirty business agents from all over the country to meet over two years with contractors, architects, other union leaders, marketing experts, and social scientists to plan a strategy for the union's future. They concluded that union strength required improved organizing based on market research and that, to organize, they had to cooperate with contractors and architects to promote masonry and make it competitive with other building materials. Only in this way could they assure jobs. This strategy requires leadership training for local officers and a structure that facilitates both top-down and bottom-up communication and decisionmaking. To educate its membership, BAC instituted study circles led by local officers where members discussed the Project 2000 recommendations.[38]

Of course, the main responsibility for strengthening unions falls on union leadership. But, in the long run, as former Undersecretary of Labor Stephen Schlossberg argues, corporate management must consider the more subtle possible consequences of continued union decline.[39] Companies may face disgruntled individuals and lawyers who lack the union's stake in a long-term relationship with the company and its economic success. Even a small minority of aggrieved workers may appeal successfully to state, local, and national governmental authorities or political candidates, which may result in companies finding themselves enmeshed in new regulations and having to deal with overlapping (or, worse, competing) regulatory bureaucracies.

Many corporate managements feel that, if they treat their workers well, there should be no need for unions. Thus, they regard efforts to organize unions within their plants as rebukes to their managerial competence or as power-seeking moves by labor politicians with no stake in the success of the enterprise and no legitimate grievance. But even the most successful firms may at times be unable to afford the premium treatment of workers that is considered to be essential to keep unions out. At such times, the cooperation of an enlightened and responsible union can help to bring about required adjustments in a way that is more likely to be perceived by the work force as both necessary and fair.

A move toward more cooperative union-management relations requires, not only the development of union leadership and the support of management, but also a more favorable labor law that provides for tougher sanctions against union busting and intimidation of organizers and workers who listen to them, calls for more rapid elections once 30 percent of workers have signed cards of intent, allows lower and perhaps middle management to organize (as is done in Scandinavia), and supports union-management cooperation.

If management expects unions to cooperate in improving company competitiveness, it must accept them as legitimate representatives of the employees' interests with the right to maintain their own political strength and solidarity. The economy, worker aspirations, new technology and increased organizational complexity all combine to require new relationships within the corporation. Both managers and employees could gain by the development of unions and professional associations to protect rights, guarantee fair processes, and promote shared goals through cooperation. To achieve this without causing destructive conflict will entail new attitudes, new visions, and new interpersonal and leadership competencies in both unions and management.

NOTES

1. The rate of participation in the work force for women (married or not) with children under eighteen years of age has grown from 45.9 percent in 1975 to 54.7 percent in 1986. For women with children under three years of age, it has increased from 34.1 to 50.8 percent over this same period.

    The labor-force growth rates for blacks and Hispanics have also been increasing, accounting for 40 percent of the absolute growth in the labor force between 1980 and 1985. The numbers of Asian immigrants in the work force are also growing. See Vernon M. Briggs, Jr., "The Growth and Composition of the U.S. Labor Force," *Science* 238 (October 9, 1987): 176–80.

2. Alexis de Tocqueville, *Democracy in America* (New York: Vintage Books, 1954), vol. 2, p. 168.

3. For an excellent, brief historical sketch of the evolution of manufacturing in the United States, see Wickham Skinner, "The Taming of Lions: How Manufacturing Leadership Evolved, 1780–1984," ch. 2 in Kim B. Clark, Robert H. Hayes, and Christopher Lorenz, eds., *The Uneasy Alliance: Managing the Productivity-Technology Dilemna* (Boston: Harvard Business School Press, 1985), pp. 63–110.

4. N.L.R.B. v. Bell Aerospace Co. Div. of Textron, Inc., 416 U.S. 267, No. 72–1598, decided April 23, 1974, cited as 94 S. Ct. 1747 (1974).

5. See, for example, Edwin T. Layton, Jr., "Measuring the Unmeasurable: Scientific Management and Reform," ch. 6 in *The Revolt of the Engineers: Social Responsibility and the American Engineering Profession* (Cleveland, Ohio: The Press of Case Western Reserve University, 1971), pp. 134–35.

6. Skinner, "The Taming of Lions"; also idem, "Wanted: Managers for the Factory of the Future," *Annals of the American Academy of Political and Social Sciences* 470 (November 1983): 102–14.

7. Hannah Arendt, *The Human Condition* (Chicago: University of Chicago Press, 1958).

8. Harvey Brooks, "Social and Technological Innovation," ch. 1 in E. W. Colglazier, Jr., and Sven B. Lundstedt, eds., *Managing Innovation: The Social Dimensions of Creativity, Invention and Technology* (New York: Pergamon Press, 1981), pp. 1–30; David Garvin, "Quality on the Line," *Harvard Business Review*, September-October 1983, no. 5: 65–74; Ramchandran Jaikumar, "Postindustrial Manufacturing," *Harvard Business Review*, November-December 1986, no. 6:69–76 (reprint no. 86606). John Paul MacDuffie and Michael Maccoby, "The Organizational Implications of New Technologies: An Analytic Framework," Discussion Paper Series, no. 154D. (Boston: John F. Kennedy School of Government, Harvard University, September 1986); Richard Walton, "From Control to Commitment in the Workplace," *Harvard Business Review*, March-April 1985, no. 2, 76–84.

9. Haruo Shimada and J. P. MacDuffie, "Industrial Relations and Humanware," working paper no. 1855–88, (Cambridge, Mass.: Alfred P. Sloan School of Management, MIT, December 1986).

10. Walton, "From Control to Commitment"; Charles F. Sabel, *Work and Politics: The Division of Labor in Industry* (Cambridge, England: Cambridge University Press, 1982), especially chapter 5, "The End of Fordism," pp. 194–231; Michael J. Piore and Charles F. Sabel, *The Second Industrial Divide: Possibilities for Prosperity* (New York: Basic Books, 1984), especially chapter 11, "The United States and Flexible Specialization," pp. 281–308.

11. Michael Maccoby, *Why Work: Leading the New Generation* (New York: Simon & Schuster, 1988).

12. For GM QWL programs, see Michael Maccoby, *The Leader* (New York: Simon & Schuster, 1981); for the Ford EI program, see Ernest J. Savoie, "Creating the Workforce of the Future: The Ford Focus" (statement submitted to the President's Advisory Committee on Mediation and Conciliation, September 16, 1986); Michael Maccoby, "Helping labor and management set up a quality-of-worklife program," *Monthly Labor Review* 107 (March 1984): 28–32.

13. See John Simmons and William Mares, *Working Together* (New York: Knopf, 1983), pp. 197–99 (Donnelly Mirrors), pp. 194–97 (General Foods).

14. For example, see Peter Lazes and Tony Constanza, "Cutting Costs without Layoffs through Union-Management Collaboration," *National Productivity Review* 2, no. 4 (Autumn 1983): 362–70. See also Maccoby, *The Leader*, chapter 6, describing how, as a result of the Work Improvement Program, collective bargaining was achieved sufficiently early for the company to gain significant savings on inventory costs.

15. See T. Kochan, H. Katz, and R. McKersie, *The Transformation of American Industrial Relations* (New York: Basic Books, 1986).

16. Barry Macy, "The Bolivar Quality of Work Life Program: Success or Failure?" chapter 9 in Robert Zager and Michael P. Rosow, eds., *The Innovative Organization: Productivity Programs in Action* (New York: Pergamon Press, 1982), pp. 184–221.

17. Richard Walton, "Work Innovation at Topeka: After Six Years" (Harvard School of Business, Boston, Mass., December 12, 1976, Mimeographed).

18. International Association of Machinists and Aerospace Workers (IAM) Scientists and Engineers Conference, "The Technology Bill of Rights" (New York: IAM, 1981).

19. See Bureau of Labor-Management Relations and Cooperative Programs, *Quality of Work Life: AT&T and CWA Examine Process After Three Years* (Washington, D.C.: U. S. Department of Labor, Bureau of Labor-Management Relations and Cooperative Programs, 1985); also based on Michael Maccoby's personal experience as a consultant to AT&T and CWA.

20. Based on information gathered during Michael Maccoby's personal visits to GM in 1986.

21. "Act concerning the position of a trade-union representative at the work place," SAF Document no. 1528 (SFS 1974:358); Everett M. Kasselow, "Industrial Democracy and Collective Bargaining: A Comparative View," *Labour and Society* 7, no. 3 (July-September 1982): 211–25.

22. "The Question for Unions: Who's In Charge Here?" *Business Week*, April 15, 1985, p. 106.

23. Kirsten Wever, "Power, Weakness, and Membership Support in Four U.S. Unions" (Ph.D. diss., Massachusetts Institute of Technology, September 1986).

24. David P. Ellerman, *The Socialization of Entrepreneurship: The Empressarial Division of the Caja Laboral Popular* (Somerville, Mass.: ICA, 1982).

25. Harvey Brooks, "Seeking Equity and Efficiency: Public and Private Realms," ch. 1 in Harvey Brooks, Lance Liebman, and Corinne S. Schelling, eds., *Public-Private Partnership: New Opportunities for Meeting Social Needs* (Cambridge, Mass.: Ballinger, 1984), pp. 3–30, especially p. 18.

26. Chris Mackin, "Employee Ownership and Job Creation: The Perspective of the Industrial Cooperative Association," in Howard Rosen and S. M. Miller, eds. *Job Generation* (Salt Lake City, Utah: Olympus Publications, forthcoming).

27. Corey Rosen, Katherine Klein, Karen M. Young, eds., *Employee Ownership in America: The Equity Solution* (Lexington, Mass.: Lexington Books, 1986).

28. Jeremy Rifkin and Randy Barber, *The North Will Rise Again: Pensions, Politics and Power in the 1980s* (Boston: Beacon Press, 1978); Peter F. Drucker, *The Unseen Revolution: How Pension Fund Socialism Came to America* (New York: Harper & Row, 1976).

29. See David Ewing, *"Do It My Way or You're Fired": Employee Rights and the Changing Role of Management Prerogatives* (New York: Wiley, 1983).

30. Richard R. Munson and Kenneth K. Nakano, "Mortality Among Rubber Workers," *American Journal of Epidemiology* 103 (March 1976):284–96 (part 1); 297–303 (part 2); Richard R. Munson and Lawrence J. Fine, "Cancer, Mortality and

Morbidity among Rubber Workers," *Journal of the National Cancer Institute* 61 (October 1978):1047–53. The Communication Workers of America are currently sponsoring a study conducted by the National Institute of Occupation Safety and Health (NIOSH) on the relationship of VDTs and reproductive hazards.

31. Maccoby, *The Leader*, ch. 9, pp. 196–218.

32. Charles Heckscher, *The New Unionism: Employee Involvement in the Changing Corporation* (New York, Basic Books, 1988), chapter 10; idem, "Multilateral Negotiation and the Future of American Labor," *Negotiation Journal* 2, no. 2 (April 1986):141–54.

33. Richard M. Cyert and David C. Mowery, eds., National Academy of Sciences Committee on Science, Engineering and Public Policy, *Technology and Employment: Innovation and Growth in the U.S. Economy* (Washington, D.C.: National Academy Press, 1987). For a review of the current situation, see ch. 7, "Current Policies for Worker Adjustment," pp. 137–59. For recommendations for new policies, see ch. 10, "Policy Options and Recommendations," pp. 177–93.

34. Based on Michael Maccoby's conversations in Mondragon, November 1986.

35. Larry Hirschhorn, *Beyond Mechanization: Work and Technology in a Postindustrial Age* (Cambridge, Mass.: MIT Press, 1984); Shimada and MacDuffie, "Industrial Relations and Humanware."

36. Henry S. Farber, "The Recent Decline of Unionization in the United States," *Science* 238 (November 19, 1987):915–20, especially p. 919.

37. Ibid., p. 918.

38. International Union of Bricklayers and Allied Craftsmen, *Project 2000: Committee Report and Recommendations* (Alexandria, Va.: Delancy Press, July 11, 1985).

39. Stephen Schlossberg, former undersecretary of labor (speech to Harman Program, Harvard University, Cambridge, Mass., March 5, 1987).

7 AFTER SOCIAL RESPONSIBILITY

Paul H. Weaver

For about a century now, most U.S. corporations have acknowledged a responsibility to society that goes beyond what is required of them in the marketplace. This ethos, at first glance, looks like an expression of altruism; in fact, it is anything but. As part of its approach to doing business and conducting relations with competitors, customers, and the government, the corporation in the United States used the notion of social responsibility to justify corporate and governmental intrusions into the marketplace in the hope of managing it to its advantage and escaping the disciplines of competition. Thus, what seems like an expression of the corporation's benevolence is actually a reflection of its aggressiveness. The idea that business has social responsibilities has been a weapon wielded by the corporation in its war to wrest advantage from customers and the political system.

Today, the cozy, oligopolistic world described by John Kenneth Galbraith is crumbling under the intense pressures of an increasingly competitive market.[1] The political system that protected, subsidized, and otherwise aided business has become less solicitous of business interests, more influenced by antibusiness and promarket ideologies, and less stable and predictable. As a result, business gets less and less help from the political system—and the little it does get is of less and less benefit.

American business is entering a new era in which it must compete rather than try to rig markets and manipulate public policy to its advantage. Accordingly, corporations must abandon an old self-legitimation that subordinated economics to politics and concealed an appetite for privilege behind a facade of benevolence. They must now embrace a new concept of the corporation based on the original liberal tradition of individual right, limited government, rule of law, free markets, and peaceful, nonimperial international relations. They must accept the disciplines of competition and adopt public postures and policies that reinforce the marketplace and strengthen market institutions.

U.S. companies today are scrambling furiously to develop new strategies that will enable them to survive and prosper in a demanding new global economic environment. In doing so, they must learn new ways of thinking, talking, and acting in the social and political arenas.

THE MODERN CORPORATION

In the second half of the nineteenth century, railroads, life insurance companies, chemical and steel manufacturers, and other businesses began to grow. To manage increasingly far-flung operations, companies set up central offices, run by a widening array of new professionals—marketing experts, financial specialists, corporate communicators. Companies also began growing in new directions— backward toward the production of goods and services for use in their business, forward toward end-user markets, and horizontally to buy up or control competitors.

This was the beginning of the modern corporation, which was both generator and product of a little-understood revolution that transformed American politics and culture in the nineteenth century. It defines the watershed between the popular perception of the American political tradition—the world of Madison and Jefferson—and our own age, dominated by a corporatist ethos that has blurred distinctions between public and private, led government to grow, and established the quest for economic advantage and privilege at the heart of the political process.

The men who created the corporation had a negative attitude toward the marketplace. They thought it inefficient, a drag on progress, a source of difficulty. They intended the corporation to transcend these limitations—to grow faster, become bigger, be more efficient, and advance technologies more than traditional business structures were able to. They meant to realize these ambitions by building on an ethic of social harmony and hierarchy influenced by the philosophy of Auguste Comte, instead of the social bedrock of individual rights and free markets. "The spirit of cooperation is upon us," exulted George Perkins, a leading figure in corporate management and investment banking at the turn of the century. "It must . . . be the next great form of business development and progress." Agreed Frederick W. Taylor, the first great theorist of the corporation: "In the past the man has been first. In the future the system must be first." [2]

For the individualism, competition, and serendipity of traditional capitalism, the corporation substituted, in the phrase of business historian Alfred Chandler, the visible hand of management. [3] Management, in part, meant hierarchy and bureaucracy; as business organizations grew, elaborate chains of control emerged. The corporation curtailed market relationships and caused bureaucratic and political relationships to proliferate.

The corporation sought to extend the reach of the visible hand beyond the organization. Hardly a group, institution, or process relevant to a corporation's line of business was not subject to efforts to influence or control it. Advertising, product differentiation and product cycles to manage consumer demand, economic forecasting with production planning to increase manufacturing efficiency, financial communications and public accountancy to improve the market for corporate debt and equity instruments all signaled attempts to shape the world outside the firm. Most important and characteristic were the corporation's closely related efforts to limit competition among producers and to influence to its own advantage the policy process defining the economic rules of the game.

CONTROL OVER THE MARKETPLACE

In the 1850s the first modern corporations, the big railroads, began lobbying for federal land and cash subsidies. Though, at first, they encountered fierce resistance, eventually they were highly successful, and by the 1870s the industry was a crazy quilt of cutthroat competition and strangulating monopoly. States created regulatory commissions to keep prices down in the uncompetitive markets, and railroads formed cartels to keep prices up in the competitive ones. But the cartels, which generally didn't last for long, did little to curb price competition. The railroads also tried merging; after the severe business downturns of the nineteenth century, waves of mergers swept the industry. But new railroads continued to start up, old ones continued to expand, and competition reappeared. Railroad executives searching for a better solution settled on the concept of a federal commission to set rates. With backing from the railroad lobby and agrarian and labor forces, the first federal regulatory agency, the Interstate Commerce Commission, was created in 1887.

A similar process transformed many manufacturing industries toward the end of the century. New technology and investment increased competition, precipitating efforts to fix prices, including the creation of cartels. When these came to naught, between 1895 and 1904 mergers folded more than 3,000 independent companies into vast new combines called trusts, which often doubled or tripled the market value of the companies involved. However, in many industries, these mergers were followed by an influx of new entrants, new efficiencies, an outburst of competition, falling prices, and dwindling profits. Borrowing a leaf from the railroads, many industries from meat packing to banking turned to regulation in the hope that it would curb competition or confer some other business advantage. The most dramatic examples were the telephone, electric, and gas companies, which begain to lobby state governments for the status of official regulated monopolies around the turn of the century.

Despite variations from industry to industry, the overall pattern—of seeking to control the marketplace wherever possible—was remarkably consistent, as may be judged from the near universality of business support for tariffs in the period in question. The high, wide barriers to foreign competition erected by U.S. tariff laws constituted the fundamental anticompetitive industrial policy running across the entire panorama of American business life.

From the dawn of the modern corporation to its high noon—from just after the Civil War until just after World War II—the business lobby continued its campaign for public policies to keep prices high, provide subsidies and incentives, and control new entrants. This effort reached a climax in the 1920s and 1930s, when more businesses and trades than ever before or since joined the crusade for industrial policy and cartelization and their lobbying met with more success than ever before or since.

In the 1920s, amid an explosion of trade associations, business leaders spoke often of a "business commonwealth," in which industry groups, backed up by government power where required, would set standards and control the behavior of firms and the nation's economic life as a whole. The idea took root most firmly in state and local government, which became extremely active in regulating entry and pricing in a slew of professions and services from taxi cabs and barber shops to funeral homes and dentistry. At the national level, such quasi-cartelist programs sprang up around emerging industries such as broadcasting and air transportation and older ones like shipbuilding.

With the onset of the Depression, business efforts to get government to regulate economic activity grew more feverish. The business lobby's program to end the Depression emphasized a sharp increase in tariffs, a halt to immigration, regulations prohibiting wages and prices from falling further, a governmental authority with power to require producers to manufacture fewer goods, and low-cost federal loans to industry. This strategy was embodied in the National Recovery Act, the Roosevelt Administration's main initial effort to end the depression. Business leaders were exultant. The president of the U.S. Chamber of Commerce hailed the NRA and pledged business's cooperation. Laissez-faire, he said, "must be replaced by a philosophy of planned national economy."[4]

THE BIRTH OF SOCIAL RESPONSIBILITY

One who scans the historical record for examples of executives acting like Daddy Warbucks without Annie searches largely in vain. Even in the nineteenth century, businessmen sought to downplay the self-interest embodied in corporate behavior and acknowledged what they called their social responsibilities to the community, the poor, and other groups and institutions. Not even railroad tycoon William K. Vanderbilt, the man who said, "The public be damned," turns out to be a good example.

Vanderbilt made the statement in 1882, in an interview with two reporters from the *New York Times*. Queried about his New York–New Haven line, Vanderbilt lamented that, though it wasn't profitable, he had to keep it running because competition from another railroad on the same route gave him no choice. "But don't you run it for public benefit?" one of the reporters asked. Vanderbilt took the bait:

> The public be damned. What does the public care for the railroads except to get as much out of them for as small a consideration as possible! I don't take any stock

in this silly nonsense about working for anybody's good but our own because we are not. When we make a move we do it because it is in our interest to do so, not because we expect to do someone else some good. Of course we like to do everything possible for the benefit of humanity in general, but when we do we first see that we are benefiting ourselves. Railroads are not run on sentiment, but on business principles and to pay.[5]

Vanderbilt was merely saying that self-interest and profit are the main motives in business and that altruistic objectives are secondary. Had an economist or journalist made such a statement, the reporters wouldn't have bothered to write it down. But, coming from a big railroad executive, the statement was a bombshell. The dominant theory of corporate behavior and corporate legitimacy was being revealed as a fraud by someone in a position to know.

The next day, when the *Times* printed the story, Vanderbilt, who was as interested in his public image as the next tycoon, was aware that he had blundered. He complained to the editors of the *Times* that he had been misquoted, that he had never said or meant any such thing, that the reporters had made it up. The man who is the source of the quote most widely accepted as typifying the businessman's point of view didn't mean what we imagine he meant and refused to admit that he said it.

The corporation was a tough sell in the nation of Jefferson, Madison, and Jackson, especially in the beginning. What the large majority of Americans believed in—individualism, limited government, free markets—the corporation scorned and worked against. What corporations wanted—subsidies, industrial policy, protection from competition, monopoly—most Americans hated. Unsurprisingly, the turbulent politics of the late nineteenth and early twentieth centuries revolved around the corporation, and, for a time, the corporation's ability to extract what it wanted from the political system and, indeed, its very survival were open questions. The founders' answer was to create a strategy of political self-definition of such subtlety and power that it not only enabled them to achieve their policy objectives but also reshaped the entire landscape of modern politics. They called it publicity—what we know as public relations. But, by any name, the idea of corporate social responsibility was at its heart.

There were three ways to organize relations between the corporation and society, the founders argued. At one extreme was a system of private ownership, private management, and free markets. This, of course, they considered undesirable and unrealistic. To them, competition was the problem, not the solution, and, anyway, they doubted that the public would trust markets to control corporations. At the other extreme was public ownership, public management, and public direction of the economy. The founders dismissed this possibility out of hand. They had shareholders to think of, they had no intention of becoming civil servants, and they were sure that public ownership would quickly self-destruct. "Imagine the Erie and Tammany rings rolled into one and turned

loose on the field of politics," scoffed Charles Francis Adams, "and the result of State ownership would be realized."[6]

The founders preferred a middle course: private ownership, as in the first scenario, with broad governmental direction of the economy, as in the second. The corporation's conduct would be subject to public review and control through extensive disclosure of corporate information, supervision by government regulators, and potential legislative intervention on any outstanding problems. The corporation, in short, would be private property infused with public purpose, sanctified by public approval, disciplined by public authority, answerable to public scrutiny. Corporations were "taking the public into partnership," said Edward L. Bernays, the early-twentieth century inventor of public relations. In Bernays' illuminating oxymoron, the corporation would "make a majority movement of itself."[7]

From the beginning, then, executives defined the corporation as an institution dedicated mainly to the service of society and the welfare of others. "The great semi-public business corporations of the country . . . have in our day become not only vast business enterprises but great trusteeships," said George Perkins. "The larger the corporation becomes, the greater become its responsibilities to the entire community."[8]

To be sure, Perkins and his contemporaries were quick to admit, the corporation wasn't always and everywhere in perfect alignment with the public interest. Unbridled competition could break out; executives could make mistakes. When this happened, Perkins argued, it was usually the result of attitudes left over from the precorporate era. Executives who had once been "in business for themselves" found it hard "to cease looking at questions from the sole standpoint of personal gain and personal advantage, and to take the broader view of looking at them from the standpoint of the community of interest principle."[9]

But, for the most part, the corporation did embody social values—an almost endless list of them, according to the founders. Richard McCurdy, president of Mutual of New York at the turn of the century, said his industry "combined business with pleasure, business with sentiment, business with philanthropy, business with great and ennobling ideas of humanity." In the 1920s U.S. Steel, proud of its worker benefits and anxious to keep the union out, billed itself as "the corporation with a soul." To George Perkins, the corporation "develop[ed] men of a higher order of business ability . . . 'influence,' so called, as an element in selecting men for responsible posts, has been rapidly on the wane. Everything is giving way . . . to the one supreme test of fitness."[10]

As corporations zeroed in on benefits or exemptions they sought from the political system, their identification with social purposes and their enthusiasm for social policy grew. In the early 1850s, when the Illinois Central was lobbying for federal land grants, the company met with stern opposition to its attempts to persuade the national government to break with the tradition of nonintervention. The *American Railroad Journal* said the Illinois Central's executives were offering a plan for "the public to furnish the means necessary to build the road,

while they pocket the profits.'' Asked another opponent: ''Where is the power in this Government to make a donation to A in a manner that pressed [sic] B into paying double price?''[11]

The Illinois Central's lobbying and public-relations team hit upon a brilliant response. At the time, slavery had risen to the top of the national agenda, and fear was growing that the debate would end by destroying the Union. Cleverly, the Illinois Central turned the issue to its advantage. By giving it a subsidy, ran the argument, Congress would be creating the nation's first major north-south railroad. These trains would set up a pattern of intercommunication and interdependency binding North and South ''together so effectually that the idea even of separation'' would become unthinkable.[12] In other words, by giving the Illinois Central what it wanted, the federal government would be funding a social policy to save the Union. Surely, the nation's survival justified a one-time deviation from the traditional relationship between government and business.

This argument, together with some aggressive, expensive lobbying, carried the day. The Illinois Central became the first major railroad to receive federal subsidies. The corporation's new concept of business-government relations took a giant step forward.

Half a century later, when AT&T's share of the telephone market had dwindled alarmingly from 100 to 40 percent and continued to fall, AT&T president Theodore Vail launched his campaign for regulated monopoly status. Arguing that the American people deserved cheaper, better integrated, higher quality phone service than the market was providing, he committed his company to a bold new social policy: AT&T was prepared to meet the emerging social need, but this would require state governments to give AT&T the status of a regulated monopoly.[13]

In the campaign for regulated-monopoly status for electric power companies that was led by Chicago utility tycoon Samuel Insull the pitch was that competition in this industry was unworkable and would lead either to bankruptcy or to inadequate service. This would leave city governments no choice but to step in and take over the electric business—and that would be socialism. But why would Americans embrace that alien ideology when a superior alternative was available?

Today, though competitive electricity is both profitable for companies selling it and cheaper for people buying it, most U.S. markets are served by private monopolies, thanks, in no small part, to Insull's success in manipulating Americans into thinking that monopoly was the realistic alternative to socialism and that utility companies were suffused with the social mission of deflecting the nation from a noncapitalist future.

THE INVISIBLE GOVERNMENT

Government regulation of business was integral to the concept of publicity, and it enjoyed wide acceptance among the founders. George Perkins explained it this way:

If the managers of the giant corporations feel themselves to be semi-public servants, and desire to be so considered, they must of course welcome supervision by the public. . . . The responsibility for the management of a giant corporation is so great that the men in control should be glad to have it shared by proper public officials.[14]

Regulatory commissions were established to free the corporation from the bondage of competition and free markets. Mere private interests would no longer control an industry's destiny; now, the public interest could be the decisive consideration. Someone would be in control; policy rather than personal preferences would prevail. Regulation represented the extension of the visible hand, and the idea of social responsibility, to the marketplace as a whole.

The founders of the corporation meant that hand to be their own. Charles Francis Adams, often cited as the father of regulation, stressed the fact-finding, issue-defining, opinion-leading, initiative-taking functions of the railroad commission he helped create in Massachusetts. It would not set rates but usher in

a new phase of representative government. Work hitherto badly done, spasmodically done, superficially done, ignorantly done, and too often corruptly done by temporary and irresponsible legislative committees, is in future to be reduced to order and science by the labors of permanent bureaus, and placed by them before legislatures for intelligent action.[15]

The regulatory commission was to be, not a source of neutral expertise, but a lever to pry public opinion and public policy away from a legislature that believed in competition and refused to acknowledge Adams's "irresistible law" of economic concentration. Of course, control of the regulatory process could fall into wrong (antibusiness) hands. But the founders believed that risk could be minimized by publicity.

From the beginning, the corporation was a lavishly communicative institution, spending large sums and much energy to put out a flood of information. In the nineteenth century, some corporations owned newspapers, and many distributed canned features and editorials, often without disclosing their source. Bribes and freebies to journalists were commonplace. By 1905 a business group was organizing a program to persuade the current generation of college students of the evils of socialism and the merits of capitalism.

The goal was to create what Edward Bernays called an "invisible government" that would manage all aspects of the corporate environment.

The conscious and intelligent manipulation of the organized habits and opinions of the masses is an important element in democratic society. Those who manipulate this unseen mechanism of society constitute an invisible government which is the true ruling power of our country. . . . It is they who pull the wires which control the public mind, who harness old social forces and contrive new ways to bind and guide the world.[16]

The idea that there were public and private interests that were largely opposed to each other; that private, profit-seeking business untempered by concern for the public interest would subvert democratic society; that society demanded of business a social responsibility going beyond the requirements of law and the disciplines of the marketplace; that if corporations wouldn't voluntarily satisfy such concerns, society would rightly force them to do so through the regulatory process—this was the theme of the "propaganda," as Bernays called it, with which business would control the use of public power over economic life and make regulation safe for business. The myth of social responsibility was an invention of breathtaking brilliance and power, and it has advanced business public policy interests for over a century now. It mobilizes Americans' natural hatred of privilege in support of policies whose very purpose is to create privilege.

THE RETURN OF FREE ENTERPRISE

From the end of the nineteenth century through the first third of the twentieth, business was an ambitious, high-profile, politically active, initiative-taking sector of society, its agenda often dominating the nation's. Since then, it has retreated from leadership and played an increasingly reactive and self-concealing role.

This retreat began in the aftermath of one of business's greatest public policy triumphs, the NRA. The program gave business much of what it had asked for in the way of powers to cartelize industry, but it also gave unions new powers to organize the labor force. The unions grew quickly. Businessmen were aghast, and, within months, a new theme began to stir the hearts of American businessmen: free enterprise.

By the mid-1930s the new mood seemed to have permeated the business community. The American economy was the most productive in the world, argued a new series of economic advertising campaigns. The credit for this achievement was business's. Now, however, false leaders, preaching redistribution, social policy, and interventionist government, were throwing the tradition of free markets and limited government to the winds and coming between the country and its natural leaders. If the planners gained control, the businessmen said, the nation's freedom would be in danger.

The promarket, antigovernment posture was disingenuous, of course. Businessmen remained as certain as ever of the need for cartels and more government spending. They lobbied for programs to regulate trucking, airlines, and broadcasting and to fund the Reconstruction Finance Administration. They said nothing about repealing the Smoot-Hawley tariff. Free enterprise was a weapon with which to fight New Deal policies whose vice was that they interfered with the marketplace to serve labor's interest, rather than business's.

Some historians write of this oppositional posture as if it reduced business to impotence and irrelevance in the 1930s. This is a misreading of history. Business's passionate crusading against the New Deal had a powerful impact. It helped direct many of the twists and turns of New Deal economic policy, which was notably erratic and contradictory, and was an important reason why domestic reform came to an end in 1938, when the prospect of war persuaded FDR that he had to establish more cordial relations with business. In the 1930s, business stood for something.

But the new antigovernment position did weaken business's ability to advance its interests. More and more, it said no to others' initiatives or it said nothing at all. More and more, when it said no, it did so by misrepresenting what businessmen really thought about fundamental political issues. Slowly, business lost influence over the political agenda.

A seeming exception was a loose group of about fifty executives of the biggest U.S. corporations, organized as a kind of business cabinet by Commerce Secretary Daniel C. Roper soon after FDR's inauguration. The Business Advisory and Planning Council (later, the Business Advisory Council and, later still, the Business Council) included the most dazzling luminaries of corporate America; most of them Republicans, as well as some executives from smaller companies who were liberals.

The members of the council were sophisticated exponents of the visible hand, and at times and on issues where the National Association of Manufacturers and U.S. Chamber of Commerce had begun opposing the New Deal, these executives supported it. In exchange for modest changes, the council backed the Social Security Act and the Wagner Act and supported the creation of the Securities and Exchange Commission.

In 1938, as a severe recession underscored the New Deal's failure to revive the economy and a desperate administration turned to spending and antitrust action, the group around the BAC, casting around for new solutions, commissioned a young economist named John Kenneth Galbraith to write a report on the new theories of British economist John Maynard Keynes. So delighted were these executives to discover an antidepression policy strategy that would boost sales right away without entailing punitive steps against big companies that the BAC printed Galbraith's report and began touting it.[17]

Naturally, free enterprisers held members of the BAC in contempt, and BAC people returned the favor. Yet, beneath the surface, the two groups had much in common, for the sophisticates of the BAC were being just as disingenuous and reactive as the free enterprisers. Where the free enterprisers gave up their ability to reform public policy in order to oppose the New Deal, the BAC gave up its ability to resist bad proposals in order to gain whatever concessions they could from the inside. Where free enterprisers misled the public with antigovernment, promarket rhetoric that was inconsistent with the entitlements they still wanted, accommodationists did so by backing policies that, fundamentally, they considered dangerous. Free enterprisers locked themselves out of the policy-reform process that governed their business prospects; accommodationists locked themselves into policies that were not reviving the economy or improving their bottom lines.

Organizational Reform

World War II reshaped the world largely to business's liking. It revived the economy, increased big companies' market shares, changed the government from an adversary into a partner, and expanded the government's role in managing the economy. In a real sense, business's basic agenda had been achieved; Further policy leadership was unnecessary. This drift toward passivity was accelerated by a quiet shift in strategy and structure that swept the corporate world in the 1950s and 1960s and transformed the psychology of corporate managers.

In the beginning, the corporation was a unitary organization—it had what analysts today call a U-form structure. A U-form organization engages in a single line of business and has a single corporate hierarchy. At the top is management; below it are functional divisions contributing the necessary inputs. The top managers coordinate and rule on day-to-day business decisions, and they allocate resources and set broad corporate directions.

After World War II, corporations dropped the U-form in favor of the multidivisional or M-form. In an M-form company, there is a central corporate management, and reporting to it are independent divisions, each with its own functional subdivisions. Divisional managers are responsible for their divisions' bottom lines. The M-form thus diffuses profit-mindedness into the operating levels of corporations, giving middle managers no alternative but to pay attention to the bottom-line implications of their actions. By taking operating decisions out of top executives' hands, the M-form fixes their attention on overall profit and loss, on the relative returns of assets in different lines of business, and the rational allocation of corporate resources among them. It encourages them to think about which new businesses they should be getting into and which old ones they should be phasing out.

When M-form executives foresee trouble, they are likely to try solving the problem and, simultaneously, to ready a strategy of disinvestment. In this sense, an M-form organization is inherently more passive than a U-form company: In the face of damaging public policies, M-form managers have fewer incentives to stand and fight, more incentives to exit.

Thus, in the 1960s and 1970s, when an explosion in social policy and regulatory intervention led to a vast buildup of the business lobby in Washington, business's professions of corporate social responsibility were displaced and somewhat undercut by an increasingly reactive and opportunistic approach to policy. Business still sought entitlements in the name of social responsibility, but it did so in a very different manner. Instead of developing and campaigning for broad, interventionist public policies to advance its interests, business cagily played the angles, working to extract covert entitlements from other people's policy initiatives.

Discarding Social Responsibility

In the 1970s the corporatist, social-responsibility approach to business strategy and public policy began to unravel. The growing political influence of ideology and the news media made government a less generous and less reliable dispenser of corporate entitlements. And the United States' entry into the increasingly competitive world economy has turned what entitlements government does hand out from a boon to a burden. Subsidies, protection from competition, regulation of entry, management of pricing were music to corporate ears in the comfortable world described by John Kenneth Galbraith. But that world is a fading memory. In today's competitive world, corporate welfare is a recipe, not for success, but for disaster.

In the global marketplace, companies either compete or go out of business. There is no third alternative. The dream of an entitlement that will solve an uncompetitive company's problems without weakening its incentive to compete is a delusion. Our politics ensure that no entitlement will be sufficiently massive, long lived, and unconditional to neutralize the effects of the marketplace indefinitely. Sooner or later, even entitled companies have to compete. The landscape is littered today with companies whose sad stories show how entitlements not only don't help, but make a competitive disadvantage worse.

The U.S. corporation needs to unlearn outmoded, dysfunctional political behaviors and to learn new behaviors better suited to its new environment. Since this environment is characterized by markets and competition, the corporation needs public policies that support and assume competition and that help business get and stay competitive. It needs a public that understands the nature of business's environment and companies' need to respond to it. Perhaps above all, it needs to have executives who grasp and accept the logic of the marketplace and the overriding necessity to respond to its imperatives. In short, business must abandon its old, corporatist approach to business strategy and convert to capitalism.

Support Policies that Strengthen Markets and Oppose Policies that Weaken or Flout Markets

Rather than accommodate others in an effort to get subsidies, protection from competition, and other business advantages, capitalist corporations will seek mainly to reduce the competitive risks created by arbitrary, antimarket public policy and to promote policies that improve markets and make companies more efficient. Instead of supinely acquiescing, capitalist corporations will oppose policies that go against their interests and promote policies that help them, letting the political chips fall where they may. Capitalist corporations will accept compromises only in exchange for specific concessions and switch positions only for good reasons—not because they are about to lose or want to create goodwill.

Capitalist corporations will support markets, efficiency, and growth. They will advocate deregulation wherever a regulatory presence is not required. They will support lowering barriers to international trade. They will promote lower business income taxes and strongly urge tax policies that are neutral among industries and types of assets. They will oppose inflation and endorse steady, growth-oriented monetary policy.

Where regulation is needed, capitalist corporations will urge that it create incentives for efficiency, competition, and innovation. In general, broad bureaucratic mandates are the most stultifying, least incentive-creating forms of regulation and should be avoided whenever possible. Taxes, effluent charges, and user fees are better. Regulation should not create competitive advantages, as when it subjects new plants to rules that old ones do not have to meet. Public policy should permit failing companies to fail.

Communicate More and Lobby Less

Business needs a stable, promarket public policy backed by an understanding and supportive public. This is possible only if business has policy positions that will work for the public as well as for business—and only if these positions are communicated far and wide, honestly and tirelessly.

Capitalist corporations will scale back the lobbying, wire-pulling aspects of their public-affairs operations. They will cut back or eliminate Washington lobbying offices and work through business groups and think tanks to converge, not on fleeting entitlements for individual companies, but on long-term interests common to many companies. They will also be less subject to the salami tactics used to turn around individual companies by shaving away their resolve slice by slice.

Capitalist corporations will participate in policy discussion. They will give the same message to all audiences. The language should be clear and sharp, conveying passion, conviction, and earnestness, rather than caution or sophistication.

Capitalist corporations will own up to self-interest and bad news and use them in their advocacy. They will candidly and undefensively discuss the effects of different policy alternatives on the various interests at stake—those of shareholders, workers, customers, and the society as a whole—explaining what trade-offs they would make and why.

When there is bad news for shareholders, customers, workers, or the society as a whole—and particularly when the bad news is caused by public policy—capitalist corporations should clearly and vigorously explain it and what they propose to do in response. Even when the bad news is the result of a market process, executives should explain. What market-driven, profit-seeking institutions do in response to decline and failure is what really sets them apart from public-sector institutions and is a key element of their legitimacy, and capitalism's. Studies show that acknowledging error usually doesn't have any negative impact whatsoever on share prices and may even boost them.

Adopt a Private-Property Justification of Business

The time has come for the corporation to stop masquerading as public property and admit that it is the private property of its owners, an institution engaging in capitalist transactions with consenting adults. It is time, too, for the corporation to adopt the philosophy that justifies private property—the doctrine of classical liberalism: individual right, rule of law, limited government, representative democracy, progressive science, markets, and so forth. The corporation has a vital stake in the repute of these ideas and institutions; it prospers insofar as they do; if they languish, it will, too.

The first principle of corporations should be the primacy of the shareholder interest in its full breadth and complexity—not merely the interest in profit, nor yet that in the share price, but in the well-being of the institution of private ownership and all that goes with it.

This principle needs to be institutionalized. Executive perks should be sharply limited, and the grandiose style to which senior management has become accustomed in most big corporations should be phased out. Executives should pledge formally to put the shareholder interest first. They should also endorse formally the private-property concept of the corporation and the principles behind it. To increase identification with shareholders, profit- and stock-based forms of compensation should be used where possible, and straight salary should be reduced.

Conscientiousness should be the moral style of capitalist corporations. Things should be done for good reasons that can be explained and justified to others. A scrupulously honorable, truthful, customer-oriented, product-honoring approach should prevail.

Conscientiousness flourishes where there is self-knowledge and self-respect, and capitalist corporations should be at pains to encourage both. They should provide executives with extensive continuing-education programs on the industry, company, product, and on the market economy in general. They should also support original research on these topics. Business is a vast, important, and ill-understood subject, among businessmen themselves as well as in the lay public. As they seek to put themselves on a principled footing, capitalist corporations will want to dispel misunderstanding, shed light, and boost their members' morale.

Drop Apologetic PR Programs

Business should not give money to groups or causes that are hostile to market capitalism. Such groups have a right to exist and make an important contribution, but corporations should not support them.

Moreover, corporations should not fund the arts in most cases. Corporations should seek public support on the basis of what they are and, at their best, can be—not on the basis of what they aren't and can't and shouldn't be. Arts that bear some direct relation to a company, its people, or its products are appropriate objects of corporate support. Companies that are themselves involved in the arts can support the arts in all their forms. But corporations that make a point of associating themselves with the arts when these arts have nothing to do with their businesses and are cultivated to blur awareness of those businesses are cynical, manipulative, and dishonest. Such programs have no place in a capitalist corporation.

CONCLUSION

Social responsibility, as it was preached and practiced, was not an authentic business ethic, but propaganda. It misrepresented the actual relations between business and society for the purpose of manipulating citizens and the political system into giving business entitlements.

Most discussions of corporate social responsibility present the idea as new and unconventional, an alternative to older, discredited, market-oriented conceptions of corporate governance. In fact, social responsibility has been in currency for a century. Far from being an avant-garde business idea, it is the orthodox rationale for the corporation's legitimacy.

Most discussions of corporate social responsibility present the idea as an effort to moralize an economically driven institution. In fact, it represents an effort to protect politically bestowed privileges for business.

Most discussions present corporate social responsibility as a liberal idea that, in practice, benefits the poor and powerless. In fact, it is a corporatist and, in that sense, conservative idea that mainly benefits companies and managers. By and large, the practices it legitimates operate at the expense of the poor and powerless.

Most discussions present corporate social responsibility as an idea that justifies corporate responsiveness to external social conditions and public attitudes. In fact, it helps corporations avoid the tests of the marketplace and deflect social and political pressure.

By rejecting the dishonest, manipulative corporatist concept of the corporation and embracing a market-oriented idea of the business-society relationship, companies would free themselves, not merely to become competitive again, but also to be honest. Capitalist executives will be more alert to customers and workers on their own terms, more willing to find areas of mutual interest, more respectful of individual wishes and rights, more willing to acknowledge other views on public policy issues. The new capitalist corporation's sharpened sense of self-interest will make it a better, more thoughtful producer, employer, neighbor, and citizen.

NOTES

1. See John Kenneth Galbraith, *The New Industrial State* (Boston: Houghton Mifflin, 1967).
2. George W. Perkins, "The Modern Corporation" (pamphlet of an address given at Columbia University, New York, N.Y., February 7, 1908), p. 16; Frederick Winslow Taylor, *The Principles of Scientific Management* (New York: Harper and Brothers, 1919), p. 7.
3. See Alfred D. Chandler, *The Visible Hand: The Managerial Revolution in American Business* (Cambridge: Harvard University Press, 1977); see also idem, *Strategy and Structure: Chapters in the History of the American Industrial Enterprise* (Cambridge, Mass.: MIT Press, 1962).
4. In Robert M. Collins, *The Business Response to Keynes, 1929–1964* (New York: Columbia University Press, 1981), pp. 29–30.
5. In Richard S. Tedlow, *Keeping the Corporate Image: Public Relations and Business, 1900–1950* (Greenwich, Conn.: JAI Press, 1979), p. 5.
6. In Thomas K. McCraw, *Prophets of Regulation* (Cambridge: Harvard University Press, 1984), p. 11.
7. Edward L. Bernays, *Propaganda* (New York: Horace Liveright, 1928), pp. 41, 62.
8. Perkins, "The Modern Corporation," pp. 10–11.
9. Ibid., p. 9.
10. Richard McCurdy is quoted in Morton Keller, *The Life Insurance Enterprise, 1885–1910: A Study in the Limits of Corporate Power* (Cambridge: Harvard University Press, 1963), p. 27; Perkins, "The Modern Corporation," pp. 5–6.
11. In Carter Goodrich, *Government Promotion of American Canals and Railroads, 1800–1890* (New York: Columbia University Press, 1960), p. 172.
12. Ibid., p. 171.
13. See John Brooks, *Telephone: The First Hundred Years* (New York: Harper & Row, 1976), pp. 142–45.
14. Perkins, "The Modern Corporation," pp. 12–13.
15. In McCraw, *Prophets of Regulation*, p.15.
16. Bernays, *Propaganda*, pp. 9–10.
17. See Collins, *The Business Response to Keynes*, p. 65.

8 THE MANAGERIAL ESTATE

Joseph L. Bower
Unity in command. Diversity in council.
—Cyrus the Great
Am I a bureaucrat or a manager?
—executive of a French multinational
company

At least from the time the words above were attributed to Cyrus, it has been understood that a leader, working with his or her organization, is accountable for its success. In his autobiography, Alfred Sloan, Jr., quoted from his 1919 organization study, "The responsibility attached to the chief executive of each operation shall in no way be limited. Each organization headed by its chief executive shall be complete in every necessary function and enable[d] to exercise its full initiative and logical development."[1] Fifty years later, Kenneth Andrews expressed the same sentiment in his classic treatise on corporate strategy, "Corporate presidents are responsible for everything that goes on in their organization. . . . Chief executives . . . are first and probably least pleasant persons who are responsible for results attained in the present as designated by plans made previously."[2]

But the French executive quoted above lives in a different world. At the time of his comment, two outstanding company leaders had just been fired by the Mitterand government for pursuing commercial objectives rather than the political aims of the French government. The authority of business leaders seemed substantially undermined by the willingness of ministers to intervene directly in strategic affairs. U.S. managers make the same observation. As one chemical company executive put it, "When we meet in management committees, I sometimes feel that the facts don't mean anything. What we've had to learn is that the public is your peer group, not the other managers in the company."[3]

Contemporary corporations are part of the network of institutional arrangements among politicians, scientists, bureaucrats, and managers through which we make policy and conduct business in industrialized society. Companies cannot be understood as fragmented entrepreneurial units of production guided by the market's invisible hand any more than countries in the Middle Ages can be analyzed independently of their role in Christendom. All companies have interests that other groups in society tend to see as similar—even if the companies do not— and companies band together regularly to achieve common institutional objectives.

Many strategic decisions taken by company managements today have considerable political content.[4] By substantially influencing who gets what and when, managements play an important part in the activity Laswell defined as politics. Those in corporate leadership roles are, in fact, members of a governing establishment representing the managerial estate.[5] With politicians, government administrators, and scientists, they make and implement the policy of our country. The profoundness of this transformation from near-autocratic leader of an economic molecule to influential player in the nation's political economy has not been well recognized in the concepts we use to organize and improve the policymaking process.

Other authors—at least, since Berle and Means—have recognized the emergence of the large, professionally managed corporation: Galbraith's discussion of countervailing power introduced the idea that important prices often are not set in the market in any traditional sense, while Chandler won the Pulitzer prize for his description of the way in which companies often absorbed whole families of transactions from the marketplace into the corporation in order to exploit technological potential.[6] But the changes in the responsibilities and role of top management that came with these economic and organizational trends have not been widely discussed or acknowledged. It makes sense, therefore, to pause briefly to consider the barriers to recognition. There are at least four.

Most important is ideology. Despite enormous changes in the structure of our economy over the last hundred years, we continue to discuss firms and the market as if they had the characteristics hypothesized by economists, perhaps because atomistic economic units correspond closely to the constitutional grounding of our political freedom in property. If property is not fragmented, we are less free. Worse still, from a management perspective, if a business leader's actions are not constrained by the market, then interested parties outside the corporation legitimately may inquire how and by what standards management is held accountable. For managements that think they can do whatever their shareholders will accept, the free market can be a wonderful cloak for irresponsibility.

Economists' continued reliance on the premise of fragmentation is harder to explain, since economics is supposedly an empirical science.[7] Although a number of leading economists have criticized their colleagues' excessive reliance on inadequately grounded theory, most discussions of economic events still assume that the hypotheses of the theory have been confirmed.[8]

A second important obstacle to recognizing management's new role is that our politics have changed rather than the economic structure, which has been relatively static since the evolution of the modern firm a century ago.[9] The railroad builders, Andrew Carnegie, Pierre Du Pont, George F. Baker, and J. P. Morgan were as influential in their day as are their counterparts today. In 1987 people are concerned that Carl Icahn might close mills at U.S. Steel if he succeeds in capturing control of the company, but Andrew Carnegie closed dozens.[10] The corporate restructurings financed by George F. Baker and James P. Morgan must rival those financed by Drexel. The nations of Europe were competing as avidly for market share in the nineteenth century as those of Asia are now. What has changed is the scale of our society and economic undertakings, the power of government, the near-total interdependence of national economies, and, most important of all, the way we think about these phenomena.

The Full Employment Act of 1946 is but one example of the degree to which the performance of the economic system has been deemed to be the proper concern of government. Carter and Reagan attempted to eliminate certain economic regulations, not because they thought regulation was bad per se, but because they considered these particular regulations to be dysfunctional. The reason to "get the government off our backs," was that it was a poor manager, not an illegitimate one. In other words, a new political response developed in reaction to previous economic and institutional changes. Observers tend to focus on the relative stability of the structure of industry during the last half century and to miss the shift in management role occasioned by politics.

A third reason that the shift is not obvious is that corporate managers do not seem to have changed very much. They still look damn powerful. In his foreward to a study of chief executive succession, Alonzo McDonald provides a wonderful portrait of the modern CEO.

> Fundamentally, this is a story of power. Although immersed and rationalized in a maze of worthy motivations, the quest for power—both personal and institutional—is a primary drive for high achievers who press to reach the top rung of the corporate ladder. With power comes most of the rest that one seeks in the quest for career advancement, both the ego-satisfying rewards and the opportunities for more responsible service to society.
>
> Power spawns recognition, latitude for personal action and influence, maximum leverage for one's efforts, high compensation, convenient support infrastructures, and public reputation. In addition, power brings the challenges of leading major commercial enterprises in new directions, imparting new vitality to them, realizing new and greater opportunities for their people, and fulfilling societal needs in a more efficient and satisfying manner.[11]

Questions about whether one is a manager or a bureaucrat or whom one should regard as peers—the public or other managers—do not seem to arise for such an executive.

The final reason for missing the change is paradoxical: In a deep anthropological sense, there has been no change. Capable of resolving problems or not, "corporate presidents are accountable for everything that goes on in his organization [sic]."[12] Even if a leader is weak or inelegant, followers will cloak him or her in the mantle that goes with the role—importance, power, and capability. Power and hierarchy are shifting, but responsibilities and social demands are not.

These four blinders to recognition complicate the task of defining the changes in corporate management because they obscure the evidence. To clarify matters, we will begin by describing the conventional view of corporate management and show how shifts in the competitive environment, government, technology, ownership, and organizational behavior have rendered that view obsolete. The remainder of the chapter argues for a new interpretation of management's role and the changes in public policy that this implies.

THE FUNCTIONS OF THE EXECUTIVE

Chester Barnard conceptualized the firm as an organizational system interacting with an environment.[13] The executive tasks in this system were the provision for and maintenance of communication among the members of the system, the recruitment and motivation of members, and the shaping of corporate purpose. Exchange models governed the relationships between the corporation and its members and between the corporation and the environment. Today, we would say that Barnard introduced the notion of the organization as a system in which individual values and group behavior are recognized as powerful, positive forces integral to the formulation and accomplishment of purpose. Much of the work that followed, such as Simon's or Roethlisberger's, focused on the behavior of the system or its members.[14] Selznick made an important step forward in his examination of the relationship among corporate purpose, the organization's behavior, and the leader's work.[15]

The next major advance was at the Harvard Business School: the development of the concept of strategy. The key contribution was an analysis of what made a "good goal." (Virtually all other discussions of strategy, in economics or in military literature, took a goal as given and developed strategy as a means of achieving the goal.) Accepting Chandler's definition as "the goals and objectives of the firm and the policies and programs adopted to achieve those goals," the concept of strategy was developed as a statement of ends and means, linking such previously disparate fields as industry and competitive analysis with the building and management of organizations and relationships.[16] It also provided a pragmatic calculus for considering noneconomic roles and objectives of the corporation.

The essence of strategic analysis is simple. A good strategy reflects a choice of objectives and programs that matches a company's distinctive competence with opportunity presented by a changing environment. Chandler's work showed that structure (organization, measurement, information, compensation and resource allocation systems) had to change as strategy shifted. Lawrence and Lorsch's work emphasized the value of congruence between structure and environment, with strategy implicitly assumed to be determined by the latter.[17] And, finally, my own work on the process by which resources are actually allocated in a company reveals the effect of structure and systems on the alternatives available to management.[18] In other words, structure shapes the making of strategy.

At the center of this dynamic tension of strategy, structure, and organization members is the general manager—captain of the ship, but also naval architect and cartographer. Donaldson and Lorsch provide an excellent summary of management's view of this work circa 1982. They report that, for managers,

> the first and foremost goal is organizational survival. . . . Closely connected with survival . . . was the desire to succeed . . . and to be seen by others as successful. . . . The personal compulsion to "win," and to continue to win, against specific, respected competitors, by objective and commonly recognized standards, becomes fused in their minds with the goal of survival.[19]

To achieve this goal, Donaldson and Lorsch argue, top managers must balance the competing demands of three constituencies: the market for their products and services, which imposes economic constraints; the market for capital, which imposes yet more; and their organization, which imposes psychological constraints. As these demands change in response to aggregate economic, political, and social forces, top managers adjust the equilibrium to satisfy all three. Interestingly, in this otherwise very modern book, the government—ours or anyone else's—politics, and social change only figure as sources of unpredictable and disruptive turmoil for the three constituencies. Conversation with the authors revealed that they certainly asked about these forces, but the CEOs they interviewed only recognized them as extraneous. After he became CEO of RCA, Thorton Bradshaw declared: "In my concept of the job of chief executive of Atlantic Richfield and RCA, the first and foremost goal is to develop with others where the company is going. Second it is the care and feeding of people who have to get there; and third, it's the financial health of the company."[20] I believe that, in important ways, this view of the job is inconsistent with the role that managers actually play. To the extent that corporate leaders give less than first priority to their part in shaping public policy, they contribute to many of the problems in devising successful economic policies for the nation that we face today. Let us consider briefly how the competitve problem has been affected by changes in the international environment, financial markets, the workplace, and government policies here and abroad.

NATION-STATE STRATEGIES

Nothing has had so powerful an effect on corporate management's formulation of company strategy as the work of government agencies implementing the economic strategies of nation-states. The conventional relationship between governments and competition among companies is shown in Figure 8–1. Companies competed, and governments influenced the domestic macroenvironment of the companies.

In fact, nations typically have strategies—at least, implicitly—by which they pursue their own well-being, usually an increasing standard of living for their

Figure 8–1.   Government and Business: The Old Relationship.

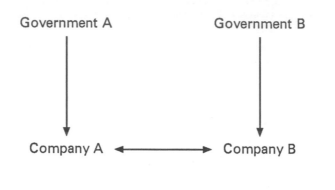

citizens and political independence for the state. The governments of many nations with limited natural resources have seen that the only way to pay for improved economic conditions is to add high value to goods manufactured out of low-value-added raw material and to export those products to high-income markets, principally, Europe and the United States. To develop a competitive base for manufacturing high-value-added products, these countries have usually closed their domestic markets to imports, subsidized investment in plant and equipment, and subsidized early exports.[21] To penetrate markets or maintain volume during recessions, they have also engaged in dumping. One measure of the success of this strategy is the high market share enjoyed by companies in Japan, Taiwan, South Korea, Hong Kong, and Singapore in OECD markets. Right behind the East Asians are Brazil, Thailand, Malaysia, China, and other developing nations.

In the face of such national thrusts, there is no company strategy, other than moving inside the protective wall and accepting a high degree of government tutelage, that can defend a global market position successfully. Even where a company has an historically strong position in a market, a coordinated attack by government and companies can dislodge it from dominance.[22] Consequently, when the management of Company A finally comes to recognize that the attack of Company B is part and parcel of the attack of Government B, it must turn to Government A for assistance. Learning how to get help without being encumbered by the political processes of the government usually takes years. In some countries, it is impossible; typically, immature governments resist leaving independent economic power in the hands of private firms.[23]

Where constitutional arrangements permit a light-handed government, the learning process requires management to develop a detailed understanding of the working of democratic government, a tolerance and indeed a feel for national and legislative political processes—two very different things—and some sort of strategy for dealing with these systems. This inevitably requires the formation of alliances, often with competitive companies or interest groups—rarely can a single company get the help it needs without relatively broad support.[24] Furthermore, the building of a cadre of executives within the organization that can carry out such a strategy takes a good deal of time.

Even then, it will not be obvious what the strategy should be. The combination of slower growth of demand in OECD markets since 1973 and increased capacity for export in the newly industrialized countries (NICs) has created substantial overcapacity in most markets for tradable goods. It is not just shoes and steel that face regular increments of capacity; minicomputers, petrochemicals, and automobiles are all on the industrial-development agendas of new nations.[25]

Raymond Vernon described a process by which technology was developed and exploited for a period of years by the major industrialized countries and then transferred to less advanced nations as the value of the innovation diminished.[26] Now, as the industrializing nations acquire manufacturing capability, they move on to develop design and research skills. They also build up capacity in related services such as banking and accounting. Vernon's cycle no longer represents the transfer of low-value-added activity to young countries but a contest for the location of high-value-added activity. High incomes and the economic and political power that comes from control of the latest technology is the prize.

Perhaps the clearest illustration of this problem is found in the U.S. semiconductor industry. According to a Defense Science Board task force report released in February 1987, this industry will be dominated by the Japanese in the proximate future unless it adopts radical changes in structure and behavior.[27] Restructuring of the Japanese industry, emphasizing vertical integration by computer mainframe manufacturers, a focus on five giant players, subsidies for leasing, government-supported joint-research programs, xenophobic "buy Japanese" programs by the government, and predatory pricing in the U.S. market, had succeeded in achieving dominance for Japanese producers in twelve years.

The United States' leading manufacturer, Intel, must now compete in the U.S. market for chips with vertically integrated Japanese firms and merchant U.S. suppliers such as Motorola, in the market for U.S. engineers with the same firms, and in the market for capital with every other user in the world. As the cost of research has risen, Intel has had to take ever-greater risks, knowing that its customers will abandon it whenever it seems economical to do so. Moreover, any breakthroughs in process-equipment technology will be readily available to Intel's Japanese competition, provided by other U.S. firms eager for sales. IBM's position as a part owner of Intel has helped somewhat to stabilize the situation. But the U.S. government has been reluctant to enforce trade agreements with Japan, so prices in the United States have been depressed, hurting cash flows.[28]

A cooperative agreement such as Sematech—a research and production joint venture of major semiconductor manufacturers, their customers, and their suppliers—looks attractive from a national perspective, but what does it mean for Intel? If the joint venture becomes an advanced producer of chips, will it become yet another competitor? Can the technology developed by the joint venture be restricted to its partners? Or will the Justice Department distribute the benefits to some mythical free market? Can U.S.-Japan partnerships join as American companies? Will the Japanese then have direct access to U.S. technology? How should these decisions be made? In what forum?

THE IMPACT OF THE CHANGED FINANCIAL MARKETS

The 1970s saw a vast increase in the institutional holding of common shares of corporations, as pension funds and mutual funds became preferred forms of investment for individuals.[29] In turn, legislation regulating pension-fund management increased the incentive to use professional managements.[30] Management companies began to compete for the huge fees. Turnover of portfolios began to increase.

At the same time, equity markets responded to the chronically low profits available in markets for tradable manufacturers by depriving these firms of capital. A two-tiered market emerged that ignored basic industry in favor of branded goods and niche products. Providers of debt, too, turned away from the heavy industries toward the more attractive spreads available in the rapidly growing energy field and the newly industrializing nations. This created an opportunity for investment bankers to provide debt to the non-investment-grade companies through the direct issuance of a wide variety of high-yielding securities (the so-called junk bonds).

In time entrepreneurs recognized that the new financing mechanisms made it possible to buy companies mismanaged in the new market circumstances, alter their strategies, and finance the purchase with the resultant change in values. They discovered similar opportunities for leveraged acquisitions where growth-oriented managers had carried conglomeration past reasonable bounds. Again, the undervalued assets of the acquired company financed the transaction. Finally, entrepreneurs discovered that, where investments had been made to modernize companies, support research, and otherwise deal with the international battle, hidden assets were also to be found. Again, an acquisition could be self-financing.

Although statistics now suggest that only 15 percent of high-yield financing was used for takeovers, nonetheless, in combination with debt provided by commercial banks, a market for corporations was suddenly created in which it was possible to transfer a huge company from a set of institutional owners into the hands of entrepreneurs and new management in a way that was not thought possible in the sixties or seventies. Even alert, internationally minded corporate managements now found themselves boxed in by the strategic demands of their markets for a long-term approach to preserving or increasing market share and the financial markets' focus on current performance. Investing for the long term might be good competitive strategy, but if it hurt current earnings in ways that investment analysts could not understand, the stock price would suffer and the company might be put into play. (The caveat is important, for the market ought to support changes that are understood to increase future value.)

The consequence is easily observable in the behavior of managements. Hicks Waldron, CEO of Avon allowed himself to be quoted in a *New York Times Magazine* profile, saying, "You make some pretty stupid judgments, . . . it's highly possible to manage earnings [such as by cutting] out a research-and-development item. These are not necessarily things that are good for the long-term health of the company, but you need the short-term profits."[31] He went on to say that some of the things he has felt pressured to do have hurt the corporation.

The impact on the corporate office is the economic equivalent of headlines' effects on political managers. Neustadt has described vividly the extent to which the power of the president is dependent upon opinions shaped daily or even hourly by the media.[32] Even though the substance of issues will play out over months or years, the political process feeds on rapidly shifting perceptions of whether or not problems are solved.

Although the SEC has contributed to the myth that quarterly earnings are accurate measures of performance, they are in fact inadequate indicators whose management is critical to presidential power in corporations.[33] Serious analysts and managers would argue that only multiyear trends in annual financial statements can begin to provide a meaningful picture. Since publicly held companies are required to report quarterly data, however, managers revert to a form of damage control by "managing" their earnings—building reserves and taking charges in a way that reveals to the public a steady pattern of progress. The investments demanded by the international competitive battle impose short-term impacts on current earnings that can look unaffordable to a corporate management sensitized to reported earnings that feels vulnerable to a takeover. A *New York Times* story grimly summarized the managerial dilemma: "With survival at stake, only market leadership, strong profits, and a high stock price can be allowed to matter."[34]

On the other hand, managements, too, can benefit from the changed market. They can now consider acquisitions unimaginable since the turn of the century. GE can buy RCA, Texaco can buy Getty, and Hoechst can buy Celanese. In swift, dramatic moves, corporations can alter their strategic positions and radically restructure an industry. As forward-looking managers examine the international competitive arena, it is precisely such large-scale moves that look attractive. Too many competitors clutter most industries; using comtemporary capital markets to finance concentration makes sense. In socialist France, coalition-led Italy,

MITI-led Japan, and free-market America, the pattern has been the same: a consolidation of assets by industry. The difference for corporate management in the United States (and also in the United Kingdom) has been the extent to which free-capital markets permit sudden, unanticipated shifts in management control and ownership and very skewed distributions of the costs and benefits of the changes.

CHANGES IN THE WORKPLACE COMPLICATE THE RESPONSE

Both management cadres and workers increasingly expect to be consulted during the formulation of policy that affects them, and research reveals that organizational performance has been enhanced significantly when involvement is well managed and extensive.[35] New information-processing technology has improved the ability of shop-floor levels to contribute to results, which calls into question conventional notions about hierarchy and the role of middle management.[36] These new expectations and capabilities are reflected in changing laws and customs throughout the world.[37] For top management, this means that successful strategic change requires extensive work with the organization in order to tap employees' creativity and maintain their commitment—even if the consequence for part of the organization may be layoffs. In some countries, this also entails extensive work with national and local governments.

It is the conjunction of external circumstances of crisis with the necessity to draw on those within the organization to develop and execute options that makes contemporary management so difficult. "When top managements turn to their organization for help in developing plans to deal with crisis circumstances, they usually find that lower levels of managers are not persuaded that the problem exists. Usually a division's response to a request for an exit plan is a request to spend new money."[38] The work force is even further removed from the problem; if they do recognize it, they blame management.

In these circumstances, it is common to call on outsiders, usually consultants, to help devise plans for traumatic moves. Megadollar consulting catastrophes can develop. A successful arrangement requires the marriage of technical knowledge and experience embedded in the organization with the analytic skills and perspective of the outsider. The relationship is seldom easy to manage, especially when the outsider counsels retrenchment.

Establishing the legitimacy of the solution may be even more difficult. Restructuring industry is a form of economic surgery. Pieces of a living organization are sold off or shut down. Relative prices, new technology, and international competition are often very abstract concepts to operating managers and workers. Inevitably, they think in terms of personal and local stakes.

Here, the new model of human-resource management has been particularly useful. The executives cited in the *Times* article emphasize vehemently the necessity for organizational involvement. "All we can offer them is blood, sweat, and tears" is at least an honest commitment to competitiveness, often made even more palatable by the promise of extensive profit sharing for the survivors.[39] Where, as at Ford Motor company, a long-term comprehensive program of change, involving product redesign, new manufacturing processes, and reconceived marketing, has been coupled with worker and union involvement, the results can be dramatic. In 1986, Ford boasted waiting lists for its cars comparable to those at Toyota and Honda, and its profits surpassed GM's for the first time in sixty-two years.

In human-resource terms, worker involvement makes sense as a form of motivation and a way of encouraging organizational learning. But, as workers acquire computerized tools, they actually need less management. While presenting a wonderful opportunity to improve the productivity of firms, this exacerbates the vulnerability of middle managers caught between corporate leaders seeking strategic change and a work force seeking involvement. New questions arise about how an organization should work, how careers should be organized, and how people should be measured and rewarded. Where top management may see the answer to their competitive problems, middle managers may see only the end of their careers.

When law or custom operate to constrain managerial discretion in responding to strategic threat, the management task is even harder. In Europe, managements face a wide variety of legislation defining workers' rights to employment, or even to their particular jobs, or codetermination in management.[40] Japan has faced similar difficulties as the tradition of lifetime employment in large firms, long-term relationships with suppliers, and membership obligations to a keiretsu have slowed and sometimes blocked companies' responses to shifting markets and new competition.[41] Managers in Europe and Japan often comment enviously on the freedom to alter arrangements that they see in the United States. U.S. managers would argue that there is less to their freedom than one might think. ERISA has turned unfunded pension and health benefits into a major obstacle to change for some firms.[42]

Indeed, sources of conflict abound in any effort to change work-force arrangements. At Continental Airlines, Frank Lorenzo's attempts to reduce work-force costs by lowering the wages of dishwashers and cleaning crews from $13 an hour to the market's $6 or $7 led to a strike, bankruptcy, and attacks in Congress.[43] If Continental succeeds in the end, Lorenzo and his associates will have negotiated new working relationships with groups as varied as pilots, maintenance crews, commercial bankers, the bankruptcy court judge, investment bankers, the managements of Eastern Airlines and People's Express, the Department of Transportation, and congressional committees.

In such negotiations, it is always necessary to relate the demands of a specific situation to the strategic needs of the company. To do this, management must have a firm grasp of the fundamental changes under way industrywide. At the same time, management must often explain why the success of the company is in the broader public interest. To help frame the arguments relating Continental's success to the national interest, Lorenzo called upon his president, Phil Bakse, ex-senatorial aide to the committee that drafted the airline deregulation legislation, and a board of directors that included Alfred Kahn, former chairman of the Civil Aeronautics Board and high priest of deregulation in the United States, and John Robson, another former chairman of the CAB. This was a management team constructed to deal with a much more complex environment than one consisting solely of airline passengers and bankers.

The manufacturers of computers and semiconductors are making the same argument about national purpose and need when they join together to request government support for a research and production consortium, as are the steel manufacturers seeking government funding for industry restructuring. When Don Peterson, chairman of Ford Motor company, told the press that "we [Ford] have one imperative. We simply must continue making improvement to the point that we are fully competitive on an international scale," he was asserting that the United States' need for a competitive domestic automobile manufacturer justifies whatever constitutes "making improvement" at Ford.[44]

THE MANAGERIAL ESTATE

When the president of GE speaks, does he think first of his shareholders or of the interest of the United States? I believe that, if he understands his role as a member of the U.S. managerial estate, he must, at a minimum, be able to speak credibly in the national interest or *he cannot help his company*. But if he is to serve in that role, politicians who disagree with his positions must be careful not to challenge his patriotism. It is a delicate balance.

As participants in the process of defining the community need by shaping industry-specific objectives, policy, and law, company managers take part in the making of public policy.[45] As spokespeople for their industries' interests, they also contribute to the shaping of macroeconomic policy. In both activities, they fulfill what Don Price would call the functions of the managerial estate.[46] Drawing on an analogy to the three estates of medieval Europe, Price suggests that, on a spectrum ranging from truth to power, four estates work together in the development and implementation of policy in the United States: scientists, members of professions (e.g., law, medicine, and the clergy), administrators, and politicians. Price's analysis addresses the way in which public policy is shaped when the multiple truths needed to inform policy reside in science and the professions, but legitimacy and the power to act reside with politicians. Decisions relating to the deployment and use of nuclear arms exemplify his concern.

Price offers three lessons that, I believe, provide insight into the work of today's corporate managers:

> First, the scientists and professionals, in order to do their own jobs, must be involved in the formulation of policy, and must be granted wide discretion in their own work. Second, politicians and administrators must control the key aspects of technological plans if they are to protect their own ability to make responsible decisions. Third, the ability of a free society to make effective use of science and technology depends on some workable (though probably informal) system of checks and balances among the four estates.[47]

To relate this to business, company managers are responsible by and large for the application of new science and technology in the economy, a demanding process during periods, such as the present, when dramatic innovation is a constant and the economy is in turmoil. Both politicians and businessmen are aware of the precedent-setting quality of decisions concerning product and process. The battle among manufacturers, regulators, and politicians over pollution and toxic substances is exemplary.[48] The changes in the environmental protection laws that required the EPA to consider economic cost are a recognition of the complex relationships among what is technically possible, what is politically desirable, and what makes sense economically.[49] Clearly, some cooperative arrangement (probably informal) that involves all four estates is necessary to make intelligent economic policy. In this process, it is vital that, while politicians receive respect as sources of public legitimacy, they also give to business managers the respect that they merit as mediators of technical expertise.

In complex questions such as trade and regional economic development, it is uncertain what knowledge can be regarded as scientific and entirely unclear which forum is best for interchange among representatives of the estates. Unless the role of corporate managers is better defined, it will be very hard to understand their position in the debate. Common usage has it that ''where you stand is a function of where you sit.'' But where does a multinational conglomerate headquartered in the Midwest sit?

Even more confusing is the role that economists should be regarded as playing: Are they scientists bringing knowledge to the debate or clergy explicating deeply held beliefs? If Galbraith is right, they are closer to the clergy. He suggests that ''everyday discourse, except economic textbooks, recognizes [the] change'' in the corporation from entrepreneurial unit to organizational manager of ''modern technology and planning.''[50] In 1987, as the value of the dollar drops and U.S. factories continue to lose market share, it is only economists who argue that industrial competitiveness is not a fundamental problem. Even if the economists are scientists and their evaluation is correct, what we have is a breakdown in the relationships among the estates. Politicians are dealing directly with scientists in a way that makes no sense.

But the earlier point is more relevant here: How should business leaders regard themselves? If they are economic animals interpreting self-interest in particular market niches, they have no obvious role in the making of policy. But if they seek a role—and I believe that they have achieved it as a consequence of economic history—then they must understand the kinds of behavior that are appropriate for the members of an estate that contributes to the definition and satisfaction of the community need.

Managing the Corporation

In the end, the strength of the economy depends on the strength of individual companies. No mix of facilitating policies by a government is sufficient to make a company competitive over a significant period of time. The company's products and services must be able to compete in changing markets; capital must be focused on a limited number of important opportunities promising sustainable growth; organizational arrangements and systems must be devised to make the best use of the talents and aspirations of members; and the people of the organization must be helped to grow as workers and managers. In the existing context of radical change, this is no easy task. The high turnover in top management suggests that many cannot meet the challenge.[51]

It is the argument of this chapter, however, that, in carrying out the traditional management role, leaders are inevitably caught in a web of interdependence with other companies and other institutions. In dealing with issues such as environmental legislation, nuclear power, tort law, or trade policy, managers must work with scientists, the professions, and politicians—the other estates.

In working with these groups, managers must be careful to recognize when they are functioning in their traditional roles and when they are functioning as representatives or stewards for a group of economic and human assets that are part of the nation's economic and social potential. Often, the same decisions represent moves in both the company's competitive battle and its position in political negotiations.

For example, when in 1984 General Motors paid large bonuses to its management shortly after negotiating give-backs from its union, the company was widely thought to have lost a great deal of its legitimacy, both in its dealings in Washington and in its decade-long efforts to improve union-management relationships. Yet, some company spokespersons clearly felt that no inconsistency should have been inferred. Similarly, the management of U.S. Steel did not seem to consider it inappropriate to seek wage reductions from steelworkers and tariff protection from the government at the same time that it was transferring resources to the oil industry and seeking to import slab from British Steel.

In the public's perception and in the perception of other groups on whom these companies were dependent, these actions were only technically legal. In a broader sense, they were illegitimate. They indicated that, in their relations with other interest groups, the companies would only take. When they argued in the public policy arena, they could be counted on to be speaking solely for their self-interest, regardless of how they cloaked their intent.

It may not be pleasant, but the world has changed. The U.S. chemical company executive quoted at the opening of this chapter was well aware that his company's overseas activities were affected by the tax laws, by tariffs here and abroad, by subsidies that affected his feedstock costs, and by an endless list of other laws and policies. He thought it perfectly natural that the company organize itself to lobby the processes by which those policies were made and recognized—as U.S. Steel did not—that his company's positions ought consistently to take into account the national interest. But he did not seem to see that, once he entered the national debate over what was best for the country, *the members of the other estates were his peer group*. The evolution of the technology and scale of economic enterprise had brought his activities out of the mythical world of the invisible hand and into the smoky backrooms of negotiated politics and the hectic bedlam of the six o'clock news.

Defining the Community Need

In public policy debates, one critical ingredient that business managers often lack is a clear, easily articulated view of the effects of their companies or industries on the national interest. Usually, well-informed executives understand how national policy ought to be slanted so that it will help their companies. Quite frequently, their views on broader issues are framed ideologically—and often inconsistently with the particular positions they have taken for their companies.

This dichotomy cannot continue. As members of the managerial estate contributing to the shaping of public policy, executives must develop a broad view of the national interest and then be sure that their companies' positions are consistent. An international view and an educated perspective on major national issues are important to their effectiveness in their new role. For many U.S. executives, this is a problem. Our economy is open to entrepreneurial efforts of all kinds by all comers. Top managements have very varied educational backgrounds. Higher degrees tend to be in business, science, and engineering. A weakness of our educational system is that it teaches relatively little about history and the workings of government.

Managing in a Politicized Environment

The times may demand hands-on management, limited hierarchy, and opportunism, but they also require corporate leaders to operate in a politicized environment in which they ought to play an important part. Essential strategic decisions taken by major firms are politically salient. Only a fool would ignore the likely public reverberations.

The managers of restructuring that I have studied all spoke of the need to deal with the politics of their decisions. For some, speed was important—a decision might make sense for the nation, but the injured might mobilize political sentiment, so it was deemed best to present the government with a fait accompli. For others, such action was unimaginable until public sentiment was prepared by the government. For all, the great necessity has been to learn how to persuade those outside the company—the scientists, professionals, and politicians—that the decisions being taken made sense, not only for the company, but for the country as well. In this delicate negotiation and positioning, it is often the scientists in their role as objective experts or the politicians as representatives of the people who can provide the legitimacy needed for a controversial course of action. The Sematech joint venture was sufficiently controversial that it required the blessing of professors who could testify to competitive problems with Japan and that of government technocrats who could assert the community's need.

MAKING THE MANAGERIAL ESTATE WORK

Most of the imaginative strategic responses being devised to meet the market challenges of the next decade have similar features. For companies to apply their planning and operating skills best, their institutional and/or microeconomic context must be adjusted in significant ways. For a program to succeed, it must be understood and supported by the other estates. This is true for battered industries like steel that wish to reconfigure and refinance their companies in order to rebuild and for nascent industries like biotechnology that have provoked severe criticism from some religious and other quarters.

Many countries have routine procedures for bringing together the relevant estates to consider important questions. Japan's ''Industry Structure Committee'' and Germany's Federation of German Industry are just two examples. The procedures are helpful in their own right as elements of national managerial apparatus. But they are also important signals to managers and the members of other estates of their shared roles in leading the nation.

In the United States, we may never wish to have so institutionalized a recognition of the estates. Don Price is careful to use the adjective ''informal'' to characterize the negotiations among them. But we should be much more aware of and ready to support the efforts of estate members to get together in various forums in order to shape policy. We cannot make orderly progress with our complex economic problems until we recognize that the marriage of science, the professions, politics, and business management is unholy to contemplate but truly made in heaven.

NOTES

1. Alfred Sloan, Jr., *My Years with General Motors*, ed. John McDonald with Catharine Stevens (New York: Doubleday, 1963), p. 53.

2. Kenneth R. Andrews, Jr., *The Concept of Corporate Strategy*, 3rd ed. (Homewood, Ill.: Irwin, 1980), p. 3.

3. An industry manager, interview with the author, September 1982.

4. My recent study, *When Markets Quake* (Boston: Harvard Business School Press, 1986), describes the extensive political content of the decisions taken by managements responding to the fundamental economic and technological forces that are restructuring industry. Other industry studies, such as those in John Zysman and Laura Tyson *American Industry in International Competition* (Ithaca, N.Y.: Cornell University Press, 1983), and Bruce Scott and George Lodge, *U.S. Competitiveness* (Boston: Harvard Business School Press, 1984), reveal the extent to which decisions taken on a company basis to determine the location of plants and employment, the level of investment in new technology, and sources for components and materials have dramatic implications for countries concerned with employment, balance of payments, and national security. Other works such as Robert Reich, *New Deals* (New York: Times Books, 1985), and Lester Thurow, *The Zero-Sum Solution: Building a World-Class American Economy* (New York: Simon and Schuster, 1985), discuss the same issues of public policy from a perspective that questions the wisdom of leaving these strategic decisions in the hands of private company managements. George Lodge, *The American Disease* (New York: Knopf, 1984), argues that the unwillingness to recognize the political content of company decisions has serious dysfunctional consequences flowing from obsolete ideological foundations.

5. This is not a normative proposition. Berle and Means, Mason, Kaysen, and others have noted the phenomenon but have tended to treat it as pathology requiring rationalization, because the motive behind corporate action was presumed to be economic self-interest. Weaver's chapter in this volume, "After Social Responsibility," reflects the same approach. See, for example, Carl Kaysen, "The Corporation: How Much Power? What Scope?" in Edward S. Mason, ed., *The Corporation in Modern Society* (Cambridge: Harvard University Press, 1960), pp. 85–105; and Edward S. Mason, "The Apologetics of Managerialism," *Journal of Business* 31, no. 1 (January 1958): 1–4.

6. Adolf A. Berle, Jr., and Gardiner C. Means, *The Modern Corporation and Private Property* (New York: Macmillan, 1933); John Kenneth Galbraith, *American Capitalism: The Concept of Countervailing Power* (Boston: Houghton Mifflin, 1952); Alfred D. Chandler, Jr., *The Visible Hand* (Boston: Harvard Business School Press, 1978).

7. Although, in his 1969 presidential address to the American Economic Association, John Kenneth Galbraith described "economics as a system of belief" (address to the American Economic Association, New York, N.Y., December 25, 1969).

8. A particularly egregious example of the unwillingness to accept changed circumstances can be found in Walter Adams and James Brock, *The Bigness Complex* (New York: Pantheon, 1987). They argue valiantly for political values that Justice

Brandeis would admire (see Thomas K. McCraw, *Prophets of Regulation* [Cambridge: Harvard University Press, 1984]), apparently oblivious to fundamental changes in market mechanisms.

9.   For definitive descriptions of the development of modern corporate management, see Alfred D. Chandler, Jr., *Strategy and Structure: Chapters in the History of the Industrial Enterprise* (Cambridge, Mass.: MIT Press, 1962); and idem, *The Visible Hand*.

10. Harold C. Livesay, *Andrew Carnegie and the Rise of Big Business* (Boston: Little, Brown, 1975), pp. 93–128.

11. Alonzo McDonald, foreward to Richard F. Vancil, *Passing the Baton: Managing the Process of CEO Succession* (Boston: Harvard Business School Press, 1987).

12. Andrews, *The Concept of Corporate Strategy*, pp. 2–3.

13. Chester I. Barnard, *The Functions of the Executive* (Cambridge: Harvard University Press, 1953).

14. Herbert A Simon, *Administrative Behavior*, 2nd ed. (New York: Macmillan, 1960); Fritz J. Roethlisberger and William J. Dickson, *Management and the Worker* (New York: John Wiley & Sons, Science Editions, 1964).

15. Philip Selznick, *Leadership in Administration: A Sociological Interpretation* (New York: Harper & Row, 1954).

16. Chandler, *Strategy and Structure*; idem, *The Visible Hand*.

17. Paul Lawrence and Jay W. Lorsch, *Organization and Environment* (Boston: Harvard Business School, Division of Research, 1969).

18. Joseph L. Bower, *Managing the Resource Allocation Process*, (Boston: Harvard Business School, Division of Research, 1970).

19. Gordon Donaldson and Jay W. Lorsch, *Decision Making at the Top* (New York: Basic Books, 1983), p. 160.

20. Quoted in ibid., p. 14.

21. See Roy Hofheinz, Jr., and Kent E. Calder, *The Eastasia Edge* (New York: Basis Books, 1982).

22. For an example, see the description of MITI's successful attack on IBM Japan in Defense Science Board, "Report of Defense Science Board Task Force on Defense Semiconductor Dependency" (Washington, D.C.: Office of the Undersecretary of Defense for Acquisition, February 1987)

23. Taieb Hafsi, "*The Strategic Decision-Making Process in State-Owned Enterprises*" (DBA thesis, Harvard Business School, 1981).

24. See, for example, Joseph Badaracco's chapter "Changing Forms of the Corporation," in this volume.

25. See, for example, Scott and Lodge, *U.S. Competitiveness*, chapter 2.

26. William H. Gruber, Dileep Mehta, and Raymond Vernon, "The R&D Factor in International Trade and International Investment," *The Journal of Political Economy* 75, no. 1 (February 1967): 20–37.

27. Defense Science Board, "Report."

28. *The Wall Street Journal*, February 17, 1988, p. 1, col. 1.

29. See, for example, F.M. Scherer's chapter, "Corporate Ownership and Control," in this volume.

30. Employee Retirement Income Security Act of 1974, *U.S. Code, Congressional and Administrative News*, 93rd Congress, 2nd Session, 1974.

31. N.R. Kleinfield, "What It Takes: The Life of a *CEO*, " *New York Times Magazine*, December 1, 1985, p. 48.

32. Richard E. Neustadt, *Presidential Power: The Politics of Leadership from F.D.R. to Carter* (New York: Wiley, 1980).

33. H. Thomas Johnson and Robert S. Kaplan, *Relevance Lost* (Boston: Harvard Business School Press, 1987), provides an excellent discussion of the decline of the meaning of financial accounting.

34. Steven Prokesch, "Remaking the American CEO," *New York Times*, January 25, 1987, sec. 3, p. 1.

35. Writing for a colloquium on trends and challenges in human-resource management, Beer and Spector provide a useful summary of the changed assumptions underlying the "new HRM model." They note, "We have come to believe that the transformation we are observing amounts to more than a subtle shift in the traditional practices of personnel. . . . Instead, the transformation amounts to a new model. . ." (pp. 231–32). In the old model, workers were treated as a factor of production to be dealt with from the top as a variable cost through piecemeal adversarial bargaining. Now, organizations are considered to be systems of people sharing a long-term coincidence of interest, which is best encouraged by power equalization, open communication, and a commitment to goals that are accepted as legitimate, in part because all individuals within the system participated in their definition. See Michael Beer and Bert Spector, "Transformation in HR Management," in Richard E. Walton and Paul R. Lawrence, eds., *Human Resource Management, Trends and Challenges* (Boston: Harvard Business School Press, 1985), pp. 219–53.

36. Shoshana Zuboff, "Technologies That Informate: Implications for Human Resource Management in the Computerized Industrial Workplace," in Richard E. Walton and Paul R. Lawrence, eds., *Human Resource Management, Trends and Challenges* (Boston: Harvard Business School Press, 1985), pp. 103–39.

37. Janice McCormick, "Europe in Disarray," review of *A Continent Astray: Europe 1970–1978*, by Walter Laqueur, *Havard International Review* 2, no. 2 (October 1979): 30–31.

38. Bower, *When Markets Quake*, p. 209.

39. Prokesh, "Remaking the American CEO," p. 8.

40. Michael Emerson, "Regulation and Deregulation of the Labour Market: Policy Regimes for Recruitment and Dismissal of Employees in the Industrialised Countries," preliminary draft (Cambridge: Center for International Affairs, Harvard University, June 1986).

41. See, for example, Douglas D. Anderson, "Managing Retreat: Disinvestment Policy," and Thomas K. McCraw and Patricia A. O'Brien, "Production and Distribution: Competitive Policy and Industry Structure," in Thomas K. McCraw, ed., *America Versus Japan* (Boston: Harvard Business School Press, 1986), pp. 77–116, 117–50; or Bower, *When Markets Quake*.

42. See Debra Casale, "Unfunded Pension Liabilities: Should You Be Concerned?" *Journal of Commercial Bank Lending* 66, no. 3 (November 1983): 2, 10; or

Kimberly Blanton, "Unfunded Liabilities Plague Firm," *Pension Investment Age* 10 (September 13, 1982): 1, 62.

43.   Martha W. Weinberg, *Continental Airlines*, (A) 9–385–006, (B) 9–385–007, videotape 9–885–012 (Boston: Harvard Business School, 1984).

44.   Quoted in Prokesh, "Remaking the American CEO," p. 1.

45.   George C. Lodge, *The New American Ideology* (New York: Knopf, 1975).

46.   Don K. Price, *The Scientific Estate* (Cambridge, Mass.: The Belknap Press, 1985), p. 135.

47.   Ibid., pp. 144–45.

48.   Joseph A Badaracco, Jr., *Loading the Dice: A Five-Country Study of Vinyl Chloride Regulation* (Boston: Harvard Business School Press, 1985).

49.   See Robert Reich, *Minding America's Business* (New York: Basic Books, 1983), for several fine descriptions of de facto U.S. industrial policy.

50.   John Kenneth Galbraith, *The New Industrial State* (Boston: Houghton Mifflin, 1967), p. 163.

51.   Prokesh, "Remaking the American CEO," pp. 1, 8.

9 CAN THE BOARD OF DIRECTORS HELP THE AMERICAN CORPORATION EARN THE IMMORTALITY IT HOLDS SO DEAR?

Winthrop Knowlton and Ira M. Millstein

With a handful of notable exceptions, there is little useful material available today on what American corporate directors actually do.[1] Few case writers or investigative reporters have penetrated the mysterious recesses of that holy of holies, the boardroom. Press releases emanating from it report the most turbulent and troublesome events in prose as bland and comforting as a surgeon's postoperative report to a patient's family. Even the minutes of board proceedings, if one can get one's hands on them, prove—thanks to the careful ministrations of corporate counsel—to be as lean and elusive as the most exquisite Zen haiku.

Yet, the U.S. corporation is currently under great stress, faced with a multiplicity of responsibilities, chief among them the need to cope more effectively with global competition. Corporate takeovers, for better or for worse, have assumed a major role, creating still more stress and, on occasion, genuine institutional trauma. A vast and necessary transition is taking place, involving a restructuring of attitudes, practices, and, sometimes, the corporate organism itself. At the core of this change is a heightened awareness of the need to serve the shareholders better. An informed, sensitive, and active board—itself restructured in some important respects—can, we believe, help management through this difficult period so that necessary institutional change is effected, the relevant obligations are met, and destructive trauma is avoided.

During their working lives, the authors of this chapter have either served on or helped represent the boards of directors of more than thirty corporations, ranging from small, struggling start-up enterprises to corporate giants with tens of billions of dollars of assets in the manufacturing, financial-services, entertainment, and high-tech sectors of the economy. We have seen hundreds of directors in action during periods of corporate ascendancy and decline, under conditions of calm and stress, during episodes of excruciating boredom and high drama. Blending this actual experience with our more theoretical interest in corporate governance, we will examine here how directors might better help the managements they have installed carry out their increasingly complex and demanding tasks.

THE CORPORATION

The Nature of the Corporation

The corporation's two principal attributes are perpetual life and limited liability. Corporations today can engage in virtually any type of endeavor, sometimes requiring special permission from state or federal governments, but more frequently subject to enabling legislation and regulations applicable to corporations in general.[2] The corporation need not end after exhausting its original business purpose; it can be perpetual: Under law, it can modify or change totally the products and services it offers; acquire other corporations vertically or horizontally; conglomerate; divest or abandon facilities; and grow, shrink, move, or internationalize.

In perpetuating itself, the corporation attracts capital by offering its equity contributors no liability beyond the equity that they invest. In addition, to contract with lenders, it defines the rights of those lenders to an annual return and establishes their claims on assets. The corporation's borrowing and equity-raising techniques are limited less by law than by the ingenuity of entrepreneurs.[3]

If the corporation encounters serious financial difficulties, it can seek the protection of the courts, renegotiate its obligations to lenders and creditors, dilute the equity interests of its shareholders, and emerge again ready to do business at the old or, possibly, a new stand.[4] Thus, the corporation does not have only one chance at perpetual life; if its first incarnation fails, it has a very serious shot at rebirth. Plain mortals should be so fortunate. Small wonder, then, that it is the premier vehicle for organizing the private sector. Indeed, corporations today *are* the private sector, and the ultimate purpose of, as well as the locus of discretion and power over, their self perpetuation affect us as individuals, as communities, and as a nation.

The Purpose of the Corporation

The fundamental purpose of the corporation—so clear that we tend frequently to lose sight of it—is to mobilize financial, physical, and human resources to produce goods and services of sufficiently high quality to entice consumers to buy them in sufficient quantity and over a long enough period of time to make the organization a going concern (or, stated differently, to earn it immortality). To realize this aim, the corporation must provide first the promise and ultimately the reality of some minimum threshold return to its investors, without whose capital there would be no means to assemble and utilize the other resources, human and material, that every business venture needs. Then, however difficult the exercise, corporate boards and managers eventually will have to decide what rate of return their companies can earn for their shareholders over the long term and then persuade investors that this return is sufficiently sustainable and superior to other plausible alternatives to warrant investment.

Deciding on the best way to meet this primary obligation to shareholders—so that the fundamental purpose of the enterprise can be carried out—is what running a business is all about. Plans are hatched, investments made, people hired, goods produced and marketed. If enough goods are sold and if the price is right and costs are controlled, a return is generated. The board of directors helps oversee this process, making sure, at least in theory, that the right goods and services are produced and the best possible return is made, both in compliance with the law and in an ethical manner.

If this work is carried out over any meaningful length of time—a generation, say—and if the enterprise grows to some substantial size, the rules of the game under which the corporation operates are certain to change. The nature of competition itself changes (today, for example, it is global; and, since certain foreign countries and competitors play by different rules, the rules change for American corporations, too). Technology changes (which means, for example, that workers in biotechnology laboratories are different from paid hands in metal-bending factories at the turn of the century). Social mores change (today, child labor and dirty air are not socially acceptable; safe workplaces and equal employment opportunities are socially demanded). And, gradually, the *formal* rules change, too: Society's new demands are translated into legislative and judicial prescriptions. All of these changes create a new web of secondary obligations—a network of new constituents—which must be recognized and served if the corporation is to honor its primary obligation to its shareholders.

In the past, governance insensitive to the effects of a changing environment on corporate purpose—especially the obligation to the shareholders—doomed the enterprise; today, it is more likely to doom itself first. In the current market for corporate control, if an acquirer, friendly or otherwise, sees that existing governors are not exploiting fully some value in the acquired company's assets, it may replace them. To achieve a "better" use of certain assets, they may be sold, in whole or in part, or "restructured," with costs cut, jobs eliminated, and a variety of efficiencies and synergies sought. Or, in a proxy contest, shareholders dissatisfied with existing governors may seek to replace them, again with the aim of "better" using the corporation's assets. In both cases, by failing to recognize values, old governance gives way to new, whether voluntarily or not. When a company slides into a corporate reorganization in or out of Chapter 11, the more violent the need for reorganization, the more creditors will demand new governance.

Our System of Corporate Governance

Shareholders, managers, and directors are the key actors in our system of corporate governance. Their rights, their behavior, and their interrelations are determined by a combination of state and federal statutes, court-made law and societal pressures.

The Shareholders.   From the beginning, corporate law conceived of the shareholder as an investor in and an owner of an enterprise chartered by the state, and corporate law continues to define the rights of the shareholder and to prescribe the means to protect them.[5]

The nature of the shareholder has changed dramatically over time. At first, shareholders were a smaller, identifiable group of investors who delegated to identified managers power to run a business under the shareholders' watchful eyes and, to a degree, control. In the last half century, a more complex and puzzling set of relationships has evolved. First, shareholding became more diffuse, and the typical small shareholder became more "passive" (to use a term from Berle and Means) and less concerned with controlling the business.[6] In effect, "owners" traded control for liquidity. Today's shareholder is evolving again and is more likely to be an "it" (a pension fund or other type of institution) than a "she" or a "he."[7]

It is fashionable today to characterize the contemporary institutional shareholder as a transient, a rentier interested only in short-term gains. Reality is more complex. A remarkably broad range of responsibilities, perceptions, motivations, and patterns of behavior falls under the rubric of institutional shareholder. While they all have legal obligations to act in the best interests of their beneficiaries, some institutional fiduciaries invest for the very long term, others for the short term. Many now index their investments. The larger ones may not have the ability to buy and sell shares without affecting the market and, hence, the values of their own shares. Some are interested in special causes, like apartheid in South Africa or religious disputes in Northern Ireland, and buy and sell shares accordingly. Some are now interested in a shareholders' "bill of rights." Others are morally neutral and turn their decisions over to computer programs. And then there are arbitrageurs, the "one-event" investors: the true shareholder transient.

Corporate law makes no significant distinction between the various kinds of shareholders (mom, pop, type of fund, arbitrageur, fiduciary, etc.); nor is it interested in whether they are, philosophically, "owners," "investors," or "speculators" or whether their concerns are transient or long term. "Shareholders" remain, despite the evolution in ownership, the principal beneficiaries of the protections provided by corporate law. While governance mechanisms may well have to take the institutional shareholder development into account, corporate law has not yet differentiated.

It is state law that spells out the nature of the contract between this diverse group of owners and the corporation, covering such matters as how the corporation is to be formed, how its purposes are to be defined, how the board of directors is to be elected and what (in general) directors are to do, how officers are to be selected and what they are to do, whether and how the officers and directors can be indemnified, the nature and rights that inhere in stock and other securities that the corporation can issue, and so forth.[8] Federal law imposes other, still more sophisticated obligations on directors and managers toward shareholders.[9]

And shareholders are not without remedies to enforce these obligations. As developed in the courts, the law treats the manager and especially the director as the shareholders' fiduciaries. As fiduciaries, managers and directors have the obligation to manage the corporation with care and loyalty—that is to say, honestly, in good faith, as would a reasonably prudent person in similar circumstances, and in a manner that the manager or director believes to be in the best interests of the corporation, which, for most purposes, means in the best interests of the shareholders.

Loyalty, honesty, and care in the exercise of business judgment are normally enough to satisfy the courts that this fiduciary responsibility has been properly discharged. But the interpretation of what constitutes these qualities can be the subject of litigation by shareholders who believe that management/director action has harmed the corporation. This derivative litigation on behalf of the corporation is a significant means for shareholders to enforce good-faith performance by their surrogates.[10] State and federal statutes also provide shareholders with recourse in court against managers and directors for damages and injunctive relief in situations where the shareholders are caused direct harm by a violation of federal or state law. Securities law violations by managers are a prime example.[11]

In short, by statute, regulation, and common law, alert shareholders have a significant bundle of rights to protect them from a derelict management and/or board of directors. They can elect and remove directors; they can obtain substantial information; they can enforce rights judicially to redress harm to the corporation and to themselves. And, because markets are liquid, they can sell their shares whenever they wish, either individually on the open market or en masse to potential new owners. Most importantly, they can threaten some or all of the foregoing or be perceived by management/directors to be so threatening.

Nevertheless, there is still much that shareholders cannot do. They cannot have much of a role in the day-to-day operations of the firm, nor can they usually influence directly how managers are paid or motivated (the kinds of compensation arrangements that are submitted for shareholder approval are often arcane and virtually always rubber stamped). Many aspects of corporate democracy—the annual meeting, the proxy process—are cumbersome, even a little unreal.

While large institutional investors can sometimes alter some aspects of corporate behavior or induce fundamental reform, the former actions are usually issue specific and marginal in relation to the corporation's central activities, and the latter are usually responses after important aspects of corporate performance have gone wrong. The behavior of institutional investors shows signs of change, but it is too early as yet to determine its direction and extent.

In general, then, stockholder rights provide remedies only after the enterprise has been harmed.[12] Yet, while voting out management, suing boards and management, and selling stock are after-the-fact remedies, they nevertheless, together with the fiduciary responsibilities existing under the law, supply the practical and philosophical reasons why shareholders must be the key concern of management and the directors. Ultimately, shareholders control the destinies of management, directors, and the corporation, and beware the management or director who loses sight of this fundamental.

The fact that shareholders are multifarious in kind and, often, in opinion is a challenge for managers and directors but not an excuse for not attempting to divine what is in their best interests. Setting the wrong course today can be fatal. The remedies, reactive though they are, are becoming more certain. There are fewer places to hide.

The Managers.   Under state law and corporate organic documents, the chair of the board and the chief executive officer are normally elected by the board of directors. They need not be the same person. Ordinarily, the chair or CEO designates the remaining officers of the corporation, and typically the board confirms these choices.[13]

The manager's task is as complex as the industry (or the company) he or she manages. As a group and individually, managers are constrained by law, by custom, and by the need to interact effectively with a variety of constituents, employees, and governments at almost every turn.[14] The marketplace, of course, provides the ultimate constraint, for, in the end, the manager must succeed in each market in which the corporation competes: the market for capital; for managerial talent; for employees; for the company's goods and services; and, as we are discovering, for corporate control itself.

When managers fail, they are replaced, at least in theory, by their superiors; when the CEO fails, he or she, in theory and sometimes in practice, is replaced by the board. Except in emergencies, the board usually tries to remain uninvolved in day-to-day management. Responsibility for setting strategy, on the other hand, is shared by management and the board.

The Board of Directors.   State statutes stipulate that the business of the corporation be managed "by" or "under the direction of" the board of directors.[15] These mandates are not taken literally in practice or by the courts. On the other hand, court opinions and state statutes do not define precisely what the board is to do other than select the officers and perform a few mandated functions. They are largely silent on the specifics of day-to-day board behavior, except for stating that work should be done honestly, prudently, and loyally.

An American Law Institute proposal summarizes the modern distinctions between board and management:

3.01 Management of the Corporation's Business: Powers and Functions of Senior Executives

The management of the business of a publicly held corporation . . . should be conducted by or under the supervision of such senior executives . . . as may be designated by the board of directors in accordance with the standards of the corporation, . . . and by those other officers . . . and employees to whom the management function is delegated by those executives, subject to the powers and functions of the board. . . .

3.02 Powers and Functions of the Board of Directors

(a) Except as otherwise provided by statute, the board of directors of a publicly held corporation . . . should:

(1) Elect, evaluate, and, where appropriate, dismiss the principal senior executives. . . .

(2) Oversee the conduct of the corporation's business with a view to evaluating, on an ongoing basis, whether the corporation's resources are being managed in a manner consistent with the [purposes of the corporation].

(3) Review and approve corporate plans and actions that the board or the principal senior executives consider major, and changes in accounting principles and practices that the board or the principal senior executives consider material.

(4) Perform such other functions as are prescribed by law, or assigned to the board under a standard of the corporation. . . .

(b) Except as otherwise provided by statute or by a standard of the corporation, the board of directors of a publicly held corporation should also have power to:

(1) Make recommendations to shareholders.

(2) Initiate and adopt major corporate plans, commitments, and actions, and material changes in accounting principles and practices; instruct any committee, officer, . . . or other employee; and review the actions of any committee, officer, or other employee.

(3) Manage the business of the corporation.

(4) Act as to all other corporate matters not requiring shareholder approval.

(c) Except as otherwise specifically provided by statute or by a standard of
the corporation, and subject to the board's ultimate responsibility for
oversight, . . . the board may delegate to its committees authority to
perform any of its functions and exercise any of its powers.[16]

There is widespread agreement—among both critics and supporters of
boards—that directors cannot, except in the most dire circumstances, manage the
day-to-day affairs of the corporation and that the board's role in hiring, evaluating,
and, if necessary, firing management is more than a statutory formality—it is a
core responsibility.[17] Between these two extremes, there can be enormous
variations in board activities, attitudes, and styles.

It is in this gray area that the essential character of a corporate board manifests
itself over the long run. Whether boards respond only to crisis or to specific kinds
of issues and the rest of the time restrict their activities to formal, even ritualistic
review or take a more active interest in the day-to-day operations of the business
depends in large measure on the kinds of people the directors are, the personality
and operating style of the CEO, past board practice, and the challenge that the
particular corporation faces.[18]

The Board's Responsiveness to Criticism

In recent decades, the American corporation has been subjected to sporadic but
harsh waves of criticism, much of it directed at specific alleged instances of
inattention at the top that resulted in wrongdoing or outright failure. The collapse
of Penn Central and near-collapse of Chrysler, the use of false and misleading
information in proxy statements by Bar-Chris, the use of inside information in
Texas Gulf Sulphur, the massive frauds of Equity Funding, the overseas payoffs
by a host of respectable enterprises, and the corporate political contributions
involved in Watergate—all inspired demands for tighter corporate self-control as
well as public regulation.[19]

In 1980 the proposal of a Corporate Democracy Act was the culmination of
escalating demands for federal corporate regulation. If enacted, the proposed
statute would have prescribed federal rules as to who could serve on boards,
various new duties for boards (including assuring law compliance), new board
committees and functions, greater shareholder review of the corporation's
activities, greater corporate disclosure, and a long list of other reforms.[20]

The proposal garnered little congressional support; after a while, it evaporated.
The academic debate before and after its introduction, however, aroused the
interest of major business organizations such as the Business Roundtable.[21]
Corporate leaders recognized the legitimate concerns that were being expressed
about lack of diligence and law compliance, and many adjusted governance

mechanisms accordingly. While certain new board duties have been prompted by laws like the Foreign Corrupt Practices Act, the essential changes have been voluntary.[22]

The principal corporate response was to increase the numbers and functions of outside directors, that is, directors who are not managers of or otherwise closely related to the corporation. Today, as a result, more than half the members of the typical board of the large corporation are outsiders.[23] The number of corporations with nominating committees responsible for selecting directors has increased from 9.2 percent in 1976 to 89.9 percent in 1986. Over 99 percent of these companies have audit committees, and, in our experience, these committees spend far more time at their work, paying attention to a larger range of issues in much greater detail than they would have ten or fifteen years ago.[24]

With outside directors came not only more attention and diligence, but an awareness of the need to respond to greater social expectations. During the sixties and seventies, corporations were lectured and written to about the need to consider the effect their actions have on society, in terms of specifics such as product (or service) pricing, quality, and advertising; fair treatment of employees; health and safety in the workplace; plant openings and closings; the environment; community impact; philanthropy; and the welfare of suppliers and customers.[25] Perhaps grudgingly and under pressure, the corporation assimilated the concepts of "accountability" and "responsibility," again without the need for special legislation. As a credo, subsequently endorsed by the American Law Institute, the Business Roundtable in 1981 urged:

> While it would be neither sensible nor possible to direct the full thrust of the corporate community efforts to curing all the nation's social ills, it is important that each corporation give attention to all of the consequences of its activities. Business enterprises are not designed to be either political or cultural institutions, but the business community will be well served by a habit of mind that stays alert to social currents. . . . A corporation's responsibilities include how the whole business is conducted every day. It must be a thoughtful institution which rises above the bottom line to consider the impact of its actions on all, from shareholders to the society at large. Its business activities must make social sense just as its social activities must make business sense.[26]

In a few short years, in response to a host of internal and external changes, the purpose of the self-perpetuating corporation was subtly but importantly modified. Under these new circumstances, the outside director is faced with a great variety of responsibilities—the traditional one of overseeing management and guarding shareholder interests and the newer ones of "social responsibility" and "accountability" to nonshareholder constituents. Moreover, boards rely increasingly on outside directors when they may need to demonstrate that their decisions are independent of management interest. (Examples are nominating, audit, compensation, and special board committees.) And, most prominently, courts give the discretion and business judgment of outside directors significant weight in decisions relating to contests for corporate control.[27]

With this increased responsibility has come the fear of increased liability. But the courts have been remarkably generous in not holding directors liable to the corporation for their normal run-of-the-mill business decisions.[28] Indeed, Delaware and a number of other states have recently made it clear through statutory amendments that a corporate charter may provide that directors will not be liable for monetary damages for decisionmaking relating to the running of the business, as long as their decisions are free of dishonesty or self-aggrandizement and the decisionmaking process is pursued in good faith.[29]

The outside director is, then, an important, relatively new corporate actor, with great freedom to act and even to make mistakes, as long as the actions are undertaken with care, loyalty, and respect for the corporation's obligations to its shareholders.

THE NEW CONTEXT FOR CORPORATE DECISIONS

Today, American corporations and, by implication, their boards of directors, face a new challenge: the task of sustaining or restoring (as the individual case may be) American competitiveness in what we all recognize—at last—as a fiercely competitive global economy. But they also have more freedom and flexibility (and perhaps even credibility) to meet this challenge than they could possibly have imagined a few short years ago. A variety of forces, some intellectual and philosophical, others more political and practical, have left the market system more unfettered by various kinds of public restraint than in a very long time indeed.

An example is the movement toward deregulation, whether manifesting itself in explicit policies—as in the case of the airline industry—or less explicitly in a relaxation of regulatory standards or in funding cuts for regulatory agencies, or in a growing, generalized suspicion of traditional "command and control" types of government interventions.

The government's attitude toward antitrust is another case in point. Today, mergers, joint ventures, and restructurings, even industrywide ventures, are limited only by the imaginations of the parties involved. Since the Reagan administration took office, very few mergers and no joint ventures that we know of have reached the courts because of government protest; instead, they are handled through administrative review by market-oriented federal agency appointees. Delineating interpretations of the law for mergers and joint ventures, the Justice Department's merger guidelines and other official statements of policy reflect a new kind of economic thinking: Big is not necessarily bad; barriers to entry and efficiencies are important factors to consider; worldwide competition, where appropriate, should be used to define markets.[30] In the past, if the antitrust enforcement agencies saw a problem, they would sue; now, the government will tell the parties how to do the merger right. The government's free-market approach and its willingness to become a partner in structuring mergers and joint ventures have made possible many transactions that no one would have dared to consider ten years ago.

There is more at work here than the hands-off policy of a particular (conservative) Washington administration, although this is a factor, of course, as is the new federal fiscal distress, which will call for less of many kinds of public activity for some time to come. But also involved is a more sophisticated appraisal—by government practitioners and academics alike—of the economic consequences of a variety of public policies.[31] We are more humble about the ability of public interventions to bring about the results we wish, more willing to figure out ways in which the market itself—or market-like devices such as auctions—can help solve problems.[32]

Along with these changed attitudes, there are some important changed realities. Whether we like it (or understand it) or not, technology keeps breaking down regulatory barriers, creating entirely new industries—the financial-services industry is a conspicuous example—so that traditional restraints (like the Glass-Steagall Act prohibiting commercial banks from engaging in securities activities) become anachronistic and irrelevant.[33] The global economy, itself born of new technologies in communications and information processing, is almost beyond the power of traditional regulatory authorities to comprehend. Thus, today, we have, instead of Bretton Woods, a system (or nonsystem) of floating exchange rates. We have, instead of manageable (i.e., regulatable) domestic capital markets, a worldwide Eurodollar market of such scope and complexity that we can barely imagine it.[34]

A variety of forces, then, seem to have conspired to tilt the balance of societal power. The extent of the shift toward a freer enterprise system can be measured by what has not happened—that is to say, by the failure of the proponents of an American industrial policy to gather support for a federal program, not to regulate business or somehow make it more responsible, but to help it be competitive in global markets.

This new freedom places an ever-greater responsibility on the governance of the corporation; with less government direction of traffic, there is more room for private discretion.

THE CHALLENGE FOR THE BOARD

The pervading criticism of American corporations and their governance had to do in decades past with specific kinds of inattentiveness and lack of social responsibility; more recent concerns go to the very core of corporate purpose. Are businesses being run well enough to survive in today's competitive world? Are American products and services a match, in quality and price, for those of foreign competitors? Are employees adequately motivated? Are plants modern enough? Managers flexible enough? Boards of directors informed and wise enough to understand how the enterprises under their stewardship might be managed better?

One need not subscribe to popular doomsday scenarios about the deindustrialization of America to regard these as important and relevant concerns. In some industries, there are problems of worldwide overcapacity; others face the challenge of profound technological change; still others, the difficulties of endemic bureaucratic inertia. A look at the steel industry, which suffers from all of these hardships, suggests how knotty the problems are and how difficult it has been for many American managers and boards of directors to face up to them.

Although outside societal pressures and threatened government interventions played a role, the attention of corporate leadership was focused particularly sharply by the current takeover phenomenon. Seeing values in certain corporate assets that their managers often do not, entrepreneurs are willing to take financial risks to acquire those assets from their current owners. We do not here take a normative position on Pickens et al., who make, or attempt, their acquisitions hostilely and then redistribute assets to pay for the purchase, thereby incurring the wrath of the establishment and some commentators for being "bust-up artists" who pile debt on the national economy, wrecking lives and communities in the process, and cause greed and excesses in the marketplace for control of corporations.[35] But we do note that there are serious commentators to the contrary and that some of our very best managed companies have made acquisitions with similar characteristics—transforming their own and the acquired businesses mightily by pruning jobs and business segments and selling assets to reduce acquisition debt—and have attracted the envy and approbation of the establishment.[36]

Good or bad, friendly or unfriendly, takeovers are now a fact of corporate life, providing a mighty goad to corporate self-examination as to whether use of the corporation's assets is being maximized in the best interests of its shareholders. Any corporation that doesn't engage in this self-analysis (i.e., "think like a raider") will undoubtedly receive assistance—wanted or unwanted—in the marketplace for corporate control. Obviously, we are not advocating wholesale adoption of all potential raider actions, from threatening a takeover to greenmail. Rather, we mean that the use of corporate assets should be reevaluated and, if necessary, altered to a more efficient course of action—by selling off underutilized assets, by buying and merging subsets, through closings and layoffs, and, sometimes, through stock buybacks, when no better corporate purpose appears. Where top management is key, the solution may be to increase its equity interest so that it has true entrepreneurial interest in the outcome. In short, the responses are as varied as the corporations that make them.

Spurred by takeover threats and by competitive realities, major restructuring is now taking place in many companies.[37] The challenge facing the American private corporation is to get back to basics—to understand that its purpose is to operate for the benefit of its shareholders, profitably and responsibly, in an intensely competitive world that will not stay put. Perpetuation is not a right; it must be earned every day in the marketplace.

Restored or enhanced competitiveness is an important part of society's agenda as well. Jobs and the health of many communities, and perhaps even our long-term fiscal stability, are at stake. The economic dimension now present in so many public policies is evidence of our better understanding of the contribution that economic strength makes to the achievement of all our other goals. There even seems to be a tacit acknowledgment of the fact that initially we may have to dispense with jobs—by laying workers off or shutting down plants—in order to build an economic base efficient enough to provide growth and vitality over the long run. (Whether this trade-off is truly understood and whether the public sector will accept and ameliorate adequately, as it should, the human costs of economic restructuring remains to be seen.)

It is hard to see how the board of directors can escape playing a central role in helping the American corporation meet this new (and, indeed, very old) challenge. The board, after all, is the surrogate for the corporation's owner, the stockholder, who, while capable of effecting current changes at the margin, can influence basic corporate behavior only with blunt instruments and after the fact—often too late. The board is also the on-line evaluator of management. It is management, of course, that has to get the job done; but how quickly and well it gets it done is a question with which the board, in our judgment, must increasingly concern itself. In a sense, the board—many boards, at any rate—has relied too heavily on its own particular blunt instrument: the ability to fire the CEO if things don't work out. This is analogous to the shareholders' ability to sell their shares if they lose faith in the company's prospects. The trouble is that this power tends to give those who have it a false sense of security. And it is a power exercised only after a good deal of damage—sometimes irreparable—has been done.

IS THE BOARD EQUIPPED TO MEET THE CHALLENGE?

The average board of the Fortune 1000 company consists of fourteen people. Of these, eight are independent or outside directors, and the rest are either members of management or in some way affiliated with it. The typical board now meets eight times a year, and directors spend, on average, approximately sixteen days a year on board matters.[38]

Compensation for outside directors averages a little more than $20,000 annually, or about $1,300 per day of work.[39] This is less than half the rate charged by the senior partners of top metropolitan law firms and about 90 percent of that charged by the partners of major certified public accounting firms. Obviously, this rate is lower for the more diligent directors who spend more time preparing for their board work. Stated somewhat differently, the aggregate cost of outside directors for all of the Fortune 1000 firms, employing 23 million people and with estimated net profits of $130 billion, comes to $160 million a year (excluding the cost of liability insurance, travel, and a variety of fringe benefits)—little more than one-tenth of one percent of the earnings of the companies in question.[40]

Today's board differs from that of the 1960s in at least four respects: (1) it has, as we have already mentioned, a far larger component of independent directors; (2) it has more committees, which meet more often; (3) its members do considerably more work; and (4) the selection of new members is done in a more orderly and comprehensive way. Furthermore, in recent years, corporate counsel have taken special pains to remind directors of their "duty of care"—their responsibility to be prudent and methodical as they engage in their directorial activities.

In our judgment, these various changes have been useful, on balance. The U.S. board of directors today is a more serious, knowledgeable, and hardworking group than before. It is also, in some important respects, more cautious and conservative. A recent survey of Fortune 1000 board chairs seems to confirm this. Nearly 45 percent of them ranked their boards' performance as caretakers—concerned with "protecting assets for the long-term interest of the shareholders"—as "outstanding." Only 15 percent gave their boards the same high marks for their roles as *progenitors*—concerned with "planning for short-term growth in profits and capital gains."[41]

We find, then, paradoxes and frustrations. A relatively small group of men and women has been charged with great responsibility. They are more acutely aware of the seriousness of these obligations than ever before, especially of the risks to them if they are not careful. They spend more hours on the job. They appear, in theory, to have immense power and flexibility. They can help shape their corporations' missions in a great variety of ways, provided only that they offer plausible evidence that they have taken their primary obligation to shareholders adequately into account. They can (and do) stimulate CEOs to formulate long-range plans. They can dismiss CEOs if they do not like their plans or the way they are carried out. They can urge management on to higher standards of performance with an arsenal of sophisticated incentives: salary increases, bonuses, options, and a variety of grants. And yet, their gut feeling is that their role is exceedingly limited. They feel that they do not have time enough to get to know the company's products well, especially how competitive these products truly are. They do not have time enough to tour company plants, talk to middle managers, hear alternative points of view. While they can criticize CEOs, punish them, and even remove them, there is immense unwillingness to do so. This is an individual they themselves have selected, an individual who has far more information at hand than they do, who is (surprising as it may seem to many corporate critics) usually devoting every waking hour to the firm's affairs, and who is in need of every bit of support the board can give.[42] Outside directors who have managed or continue to manage companies of their own may be particularly sensitive to this.

And so, for reasons of both fiduciary caution and operational practicability, directors are forced to spend a great deal of their time—in our view, most of it—going by the numbers and by the book, endlessly reviewing financial results, making sure their tracks are covered, and helping their companies mostly, we feel, by the exercise of negative virtues: reducing risks, preventing egregious mistakes, making sure things are in order.

There are exceptions, of course. In some companies, especially smaller ones where survival is taken less for granted, boards seem to be more bound up, organically, in the life of the enterprise; relationships are so close that the whole question of meddling in day-to-day affairs becomes somewhat academic. During acute, heartrending crises, managements and boards of corporations of virtually any size will come together to pool their formidable personal resources in remarkably creative and exciting ways, sometimes redirecting profoundly the fortunes of the enterprise. It is at times like these when one realizes how much latent possibility has been gathered in the board room all along. One realizes, too, how lamentably the job of anticipating the crisis at hand has been done in all the preceding years.

As we see it, and as history confirms, the board possesses the organizational capability to modify itself and the ability to act forcefully. It should, therefore, be able to meet the new challenge of overseeing the organization of the corporation's endeavors before there is trauma such as a contest for corporate control or a serious management failure, so that the corporation can operate for the benefit of shareholders, profitably and responsibly, in new globally competitive markets where change is the single constant. But most boards do not appear to share our conviction; rather, they stand by, somewhat ready to deal with crisis and trauma after the fact, meanwhile doing things by the book, trying to avoid risk and major error.

HOW SHOULD BOARDS BE CHANGED?

There is profound uneasiness in corporate board rooms. It is becoming much more difficult to be a member of a board, and there are signs now that it is also becoming more difficult to persuade talented outsiders to serve.[43] Nevertheless, we believe that the answer to today's challenge is clear: The board must play a more active role, not only in "overseeing" the operations of the firm and "evaluating" the situation, but in bringing about decisions as to which assets are being managed effectively and which should be managed differently by different people—either in its own corporation or in someone else's.[44]

In its present mode of operation, the typical board is not equipped to fulfill these new responsibilities. Directors have some information but not enough. They give some time to the task but not enough. Most of them have other things on their minds. Inside directors work full-time for particular parts of the company, and most outside directors have other jobs. The outside director has many reasons— practical, philosophical, emotional—for playing a more passive role than the one we espouse. In their permissive and passive stances, most boards are likely: (1) not to appraise the performance of CEOs critically enough; (2) to overestimate the ability of managers to manage different kinds of businesses well; (3) to allow managers to build enterprises that may be too large and diversified for anyone to manage well; and (4) to wait too long to respond to ongoing political, social, and economic change.

We propose a number of changes to give boards resources commensurate with the responsibilities they should assume. These suggestions are intended to help the board render assistance to the management that it has installed. In our view, rendering assistance requires more than passive approval until disaster strikes. The board, harkening back to words from the Business Roundtable itself, must be more than "supportive and positive" regarding the CEO, it "should be challenging. . . . Strong independent directors, well informed on the problems to be discussed, openly debate the pros and cons of questions presented . . . searching questions are welcomed."[45] Other commentators have characterized a good board as a forum for open but structured dissent.[46] Our suggestions are designed to achieve such boards.

Our first suggestion is designed to give the board control over its own agenda, so that it is not constantly put in the position of responding to management's (or, essentially, the CEO's) notions of what issues should be addressed, in what depth, and when. The way to accomplish this is to have as chair an outside director who prepares his or her own agenda for the meeting, in close consultation with the CEO, management, and fellow directors. In larger corporations, this may require extra compensation, since the job will demand more time and attention.[47]

The second suggestion is to give the chair the resources he or she needs to study issues and to hear alternative points of view so that the right agenda can, in fact, be created and acted upon. Information is the key to action. There are today outside directors who serve as chairs but remain dependent upon management because they have no organizational capacity with which to function independently. We propose that, in major corporations, chairs be given professional advisors who will help them and their board colleagues obtain information, organize agendas, and follow up. (We emphasize again the importance of information flow—such advisors should make sure the board receives information in a readily digestible form, rather than reams of paper designed to discourage the most willing director.) Depending on the need, this function would be filled by a financial advisor, a management consultant, a lawyer, a person on staff, or an outsider; by one person or by a series of persons. There should be no hard and fast rule, only the recognition that the chair will need professional assistance. In periods of crisis, this is precisely what directors do to protect themselves in the legal sense. Perhaps some crises could have been averted had there been recourse to such a facility in the first instance.

Third, the board must be a more active advisor to and nurturer of the CEO. There should be open and regular communication, not just formal board-meeting interchanges and casual golf outings. In the great majority of cases with which we are familiar, the CEO and the board spend far more time appraising the performances of the firm's other top executives than that of the CEO. In part, this is because board members find it somewhat awkward to criticize the executive with whom they work most closely and, in part, because the board has ultimate recourse to its blunt instrument—firing. But the board's role must go beyond simply hiring and firing: It must advise and broaden the CEO, bringing to bear its members' presumably wide range of experiences, their different view of the outside world. Board members may not be any wiser, but, at the least, they were chosen for their different perspectives, expertise, and judgment, and this resource should be tapped.

In order to carry out all of this, directors must spend more time on the job (and be compensated for doing so). This means that directors should not serve on too many boards at any one time: two should be the limit (one, if it is a major corporation) if a director is also holding down a full-time job; three to five, depending on the size of the corporations, if the director is retired. We believe that so-called professional directors who sit on many boards are often merely going through the motions—doing routine housework but never really facing up to difficult issues. If directors are to spend more time on the job and receive more compensation for doing so, some portion of their pay should be in the form of equity in the company. No director should fail to feel the impact of poor performance on shareholders.

Structured dissent, challenging, and open debate require a high degree of mutual respect and something less than a town-meeting atmosphere. Smaller boards are preferable to larger ones, if such an atmosphere is to be achieved. As a rule of thumb, we suggest that boards should include a maximum of ten to fifteen members, no more than a third of whom should be insiders.

Finally, we believe that directors exercising these kinds of responsibility in good faith should be exempt from monetary liability to the corporation—that, in essence, the new Delaware statute should be adopted universally.[48]

These suggestions will not be greeted with enthusiasm by either boards or managers. In fact, a recent survey of Fortune 1000 chairmen drew an 87 percent negative response to the suggestion that "boards would be more effective headed by independent chairmen who are not CEOs of the organizations they chair." Not surprisingly, the same group disputed overwhelmingly the notion that "today's hostile takeovers represent a correction for past managerial abuses by elevating more talented executives and putting productive capital to use."[49]

The reasons why these proposals will not be popular with established managers are obvious. They usurp what tradition has assumed were managerial prerogatives; they open the door to asserted "meddling," "delay," and "second-guessing" by the board. Board members, too, will have reservations. Some of these will have to do with an increased sense of exposure (What will I be sued for next?). Others will relate more to a genuine reluctance to interfere, interference being perceived as unseemly and a little unfair to those charged with such considerable day-to-day responsibility. And some directors have very real doubts about their ability to play this role effectively—all the more reason to give them the tools they need.

CEOs can view these proposals as a disguised palace coup, depriving them of a degree of power and prestige. Or they can recognize that a rapidly changing world has imposed enormous new responsibilities on them and that, quite simply, they need support. Today's CEOs need to look outward, not only to other parts of the globe, but to other players on the global scene—politicians, government regulators, statesmen, scientists, the media, and a host of outside specialists.[50] They must at the same time look more penetratingly inside their own organizations, for here, too, much change is (or sought to be) taking place: changes in the way work is organized, employees are motivated, sources of supply deployed.[51] Everywhere, there is likely today to be blurring of formal, traditional boundaries. Nothing is entirely safe—neither hierarchical lines of command, organizational divisions, nor even our former sure sense of what, exactly, is public and what private—and experimentation is rife.[52]

It is unreasonable to expect that the corporate boardroom—and its occupants— can remain untouched by this change. A more subtle, complex, and demanding set of board-CEO relationships and responsibilities is inescapable.

There is no one right way to govern the corporation. The genius of our governance system is that it permits each company to evolve the system that suits it best. The board can adopt most of our suggestions by itself for itself, if it wishes to. That is not to say that every company will or necessarily should. Some are performing beautifully in the traditional manner with chairs who are also CEOs.[53] Other chairs are former CEOs. Some companies are led by entrepreneurial founders who dominate both boards and management (and own substantial blocks of stock). Some are led in the way we suggest. In times of crisis, most systems of corporate governance tend to resemble the one we propose—perhaps not formally but in actual practice. We believe that average American companies— those that are neither brilliantly run nor in total disrepair—will benefit most over the long run from the changes we suggest. It is the performance of these corporations that must be improved if we are to meet the competitive challenges at hand.

We know of no case where an American corporation has been made less competitive over the long run because its board of directors was playing too active a role. We know of many whose competitiveness has deteriorated, at least in part, because boards have been too passive and did not challenge management to see what was coming and to act before the crisis occurred.[54]

EPILOGUE

What if boards do not play this kind of role? Either American corporations will prove that they can meet their competitive challenges anyway, or many will fail to do so, and boards will be perceived as having been part of the problem. Under such circumstances, our system of corporate governance will lose credibility. That great pendulum of forces that swings the balance of power from the public sector to the private and back again is likely to sway once again toward more public solutions, more public controls, more public oversight—this time of governance mechanisms themselves.

At present, our private-sector governors have been given immense responsibility, and immense flexibility to meet it. This will not always necessarily be so. Just as boards are charged with seeing that the corporations under their stewardship "earn" their immortality, so, at the same time, are they preserving their own independence and the right to meet these challenges in the way they see fit. The board's immortality is at stake, too.

NOTES

1. The works of Professors Myles L. Mace and Kenneth Andrews of the Harvard Business School are among the exceptions.
2. See, for example, Del. Gen. Corp. Law §§ 121, 122.
3. High-yield securities ("junk bonds") are but one of a number of innovative financing devices being developed that lubricate rapid restructurings. Congressional Research Service, *The Role of High Yield Bonds (Junk Bonds) in Capital Markets and Corporate Takeovers: Public Policy Implications: Report for the Subcommittee on Telecommunications, Consumer Protection and Finance of the Committee on Energy and Commerce*, 99th Cong., 1st sess., 1985, Committee print; Congressional Research Service, "Corporate Takeover: Alternatives for Merger Finance," report no. 87-254E (Washington, D.C.: Congressional Research Service, March 26, 1987).
4. See 11 U.S.C. §§ 1101 *et seq.*, detailing provisions for reorganization under Chapter 11 of the U.S. Bankruptcy Code. For a comprehensive review of the workings of Chapter 11, see M. Bienenstock, *Bankruptcy Reorganization* (New York: Practising Law Institute, 1987).
5. See, for example, Del. Gen. Corp. Law §§ 151, 220, 262, and 326; I. M. Millstein, "Takeover Reform: Common Sense From The Common Law," *Harvard Business Review*, July–August 1986, no. 4:16.

6. A. A. Berle, Jr., and G. C. Means, *The Modern Corporation and Private Property* (New York: Macmillan, 1932).
7. See F. M. Scherer's chapter, "Corporate Ownership and Control," in this volume; and Professor Robert Clark's astute analysis of the changing role of shareholder fiduciaries, "The Four Stages of Capitalism: Reflections on Investment Management Treatises," *Harvard Law Review* 94 (January 1981): 561–82. See also G. Jarrell, "Institutional Ownership, Tender Offers, and Long-Term Investments" (study by the Office of the Chief Economist, Securities and Exchange Commission, Washington, D.C., April 19, 1985); M. Blumstein, "How the Institutions Rule the Market," *The New York Times*, November 25, 1984, sec. 3, p. 1, col. 2; "Will Money Managers Wreck the Economy?" *Business Week*, August 13, 1984, p. 86.
8. See, for example, Del. Gen. Corp. Law § 101(a) (formation of corporation); Del. Gen. Corp. Law § 102(a)(3) (definition of corporate purpose); Del. Gen. Corp. Law § 141 (election and function of Board of Directors); Del. Gen. Corp. Law § 142 (selection and function of officers); Del. Gen. Corp. Law § 145 (indemnification of officers and directors); Del. Gen. Corp. Law § 151 (nature and rights that inhere in stock).
9. Securities laws, legislative and court made, for example, are designed to cause disclosure of information and to prevent manipulation and fraud in securities transactions by managers and directors, as well as shareholders. See Section 10(b) of the Securities Exchange Act of 1934 (manipulative and deceptive devices) (codified at 15 U.S.C. § 78j) and Section 13 of the Securities Exchange Act of 1934 (periodical and other reports) (codified at 15 U.S.C. § 78m).
10. See generally D. Block, N. Barton, and S. Radin, *The Business Judgment Rule* (Clifton, N. J.: Prentice Hall Law & Business, 1987) pp. 26–30 (for standard of care owed by directors), 213–99 (for discussion of shareholder derivative litigation).
11. Section 16(b) of the Securities Exchange Act of 1934 (codified at 15 U.S.C. § 78p[b]).
12. See L. Lowenstein, *What's Wrong with Wall Street: Short-term Gain and the Absentee Shareholder* (Reading, Mass.: Addison-Wesley, 1988), urging that shareholders, especially institutional shareholders, have a responsibility to be interested in the ongoing affairs of the corporation, not just the performance of its stock in an overheated stock market. The author suggests means to motivate that interest, including greater participation in nominating and electing directors.
13. Del. Gen. Corp. Law § 142; N.Y. Bus. Corp. Law § 715.
14. See J. Bower's chapter, "The Managerial Estate," in this volume, for an excellent discussion of the increasingly complex role of the chief executive officer, who needs now to interact with politicians, government administrators, scientists, and professionals. The CEO's role has shifted from "near-autocratic leader" to "influential player."
15. Del. Gen. Corp. Law § 141(a); N.Y. Bus. Corp. Law § 701.
16. American Law Institute, "Principles of Corporate Governance: Analysis and Recommendations," tentative draft no. 2 (Philadelphia: American Law Institute, April 13, 1984), pp. 61, 66–67.
17. For example, ibid., pp. 67–69; The Business Roundtable, "The Role and Composition of the Board of Directors of the Large Publicly Owned Corporation: Statement of The Business Roundtable," *The Business Lawyer* 33 (July 1978):2094, 2097–98.

18. See C. P. Alderfer, "The Invisible Director on Corporate Boards," *Harvard Business Review*, November–December 1986, no. 6: 38; idem, "An Intergroup Perspective on Group Dynamics," in J. W. Lorsch, ed., *Handbook of Organizational Behavior* (New York: Prentice-Hall, 1986), pp. 190–222.

19. See "A Chrysler Crisis for IOU's," *Business Week*, August 20, 1979, p. 112; R. Reich and J. Donahue, *New Deals: The Chrysler Revival and The American System* (New York: Times Books, 1984); Escott v. BarChris Construction Corp., 283 F. Supp. 643 (S.D.N.Y. 1968); Securities and Exchange Commission v. Texas Gulf Sulphur Co., 401 F. 2d 833 (2d Cir. 1968); "Equity's Sentencing," *Business Week*, March 31, 1975, p. 30; "Overseas Payoffs," *Business Week*, January 10, 1977, p. 34; "The Attacks Mount on Political Gifts," *Business Week*, March 24, 1975, p. 32.

20. Corporate Democracy Act, H.R. 7010, 96th Cong., 2d sess., 1980.

21. As early as 1978, the Business Roundtable acknowledged the following criticisms in a tract that suggested substantive and procedural means to reduce the bases of those criticisms: (1) directors do not spend enough time on corporate affairs to be effective; (2) they are "hand-picked . . . rubber stamps"; (3) shareholders have no voice in director nominations; (4) directors are poorly informed; (5) they are too homogeneous. See The Business Roundtable, "The Role and Composition of the Board," pp. 2083, 2092.

22. Pub. L. No. 95–213, 91 Stat. 1494 (1977) (amending the Securities Exchange Act of 1934) (codified at 15 U.S.C. § 78m [b][2]–[3], 78dd-1, 78dd-2, and 78ff [1978]).

23. Heidrick and Struggles, Inc. *The Changing Board* (Chicago: Heidrick and Struggles, Inc., 1986).

24. Ibid.

25. See, for example, M. Mintz and J. Cohen, *America, Inc.* (New York: Dial, 1971); R. Nader, M. Green, and J. Seligman, *Taming the Giant Corporation* (New York: Norton, 1976).

26. The Business Roundtable, *Statement on Corporate Responsibility* (New York: The Business Roundtable, October 1981), p. 14.

27. The presence of outside independent directors on the board enhances the good-faith presumption of the business judgment rule, since these outside directors do not depend on the corporation for their livelihood and are therefore more likely to be objective and less likely to entrench themselves. See Unocal Corp. v. Mesa Petroleum Co., 493 A.2d 946 (Del. 1985); Moran v. Household International, Inc., 500 A.2d 1346 (Del. 1985); Panter v. Marshall Field & Co., 646 F.2d 271 (7th Cir.), *cert. denied*, 454 U.S. 1092 (1981); Enterra Corp. v. SGS Associates, 600 F. Supp. 678 (E.D. Pa. 1985). There are exceptions where the presence of outside directors is not accepted as evidence of good faith. See, for example, Norlin Corp. v. Rooney, Pace, Inc., 744 F.2d 255 (2d Cir. 1984); Hanson Trust PLC v. ML SCM Acquisition Inc., 781 F.2d 264 (2d Cir. 1986). See generally Block, Barton, and Radin, *The Business Judgment Rule*, pp. 86–90.

28. See Joy v. North, 692 F.2d 880 (2d Cir. 1982), *cert. denied*, 460 U.S. 1051 (1983). See generally Block, Barton, and Radin, *The Business Judgment Rule*, pp. 30–34; S. R. Cohn, "Demise of the Director's Duty of Care: Judicial Avoidance of Standards and Sanctions Through the Business Judgment Rule," *Texas Law Review* no. 4 (1983): 591.

29. See Del. Gen. Corp. Law § 102(b)(7); Ind. Bus. Corp. Law § 23-1-35(i)(e); Va. Stock Corp. Act § 13.1-690(A), (C). The Corporate Director's Guidebook characterizes the duty of loyalty as an "allegiance to the enterprise and acknowledges that the best interests of the corporation and its shareholders must prevail over any individual interest of [the director's] own." It further states that the "basic principle to be observed is that the director should not use his corporate position to make a personal profit or gain other personal advantage." The Corporate Director's Guidebook, *Business Lawyer* 33 (1978): 1591, 1599. See also Guth v. Loft, Inc., 5 A.2d 503, 510 (Del. 1939).

30. United States Department of Justice Merger Guidelines, 2 Trade Reg. Rep. (CCH) ¶¶ 4490 *et seq.* (1984); FTC Statement Regarding Horizontal Mergers, 2 Trade Reg. Rep. (CCH) ¶ 4516 (1982); U.S. Department of Justice Vertical Restraints Guidelines, 48 Antitrust & Trade Reg. Rep. (BNA) 1199 (1985).

31. C. Schultze, *The Public Use of Private Interest* (Washington, D.C.: The Brookings Institution, 1977).

32. See R. Reich, "Of Markets and Myths," *Commentary* 83, no. 2 (February 1987):38–42.

33. Banking Act of 1933, Pub. L. No. 66, 48 Stat. 162 (codified as amended in scattered sections of 12 U.S.C.).

34. For a discussion of the implications of international competition for domestic regulation, see W. Knowlton, "The Pain of Regulation," *Harvard Business Review*, November–December 1985, no. 6:180–2, 184, 188, 190.

35. See, for example, U.S. Congress, Senate Banking Committee, "Hearing on Corporate Takeovers before the Senate Banking Committee," 100th Congress, 1st sess., March 4, 1987; W. Law, "A Corporation Is More than Its Stock," *Harvard Business Review*, May–June 1986, no. 3:80; P. Drucker, "Taming the Corporate Takeover," *Wall Street Journal*, October 30, 1984, p. 30; M. Kalin, "Takeover Abuses Demand Congressional Reform," *Legal Times* 7 (June 25, 1984): 12; P. Elicker, "Corporate Takeover Should Not Be Made Easier," *Industry Week* 223, no. 3 (October 29, 1984): 14; Lowenstein, *What's Wrong with Wall Street.*

36. See, for example, J. K. Glassman, "Après Ivan," *The New Republic* 195 (December 15, 1986): 11; M. Magnet, "Restructuring Really Works," *Fortune*, March 2, 1987, p. 38; M. Jensen, "Takeovers: Folklore and Science," *Harvard Business Review*, November–December 1984, no. 6: 329. See also J. R. Norman, "General Electric Stalking Big Game Again," *Business Week*, March 1987, p. 112.

37. See "Restructuring Really Works," p. 38.

38. Heidrick and Struggles, Inc., *The Changing Board.*

39. Ibid.

40. "The Fortune Review 500," *Fortune*, June 9, 1986, p. 122; "The Fortune 500," *Fortune*, April 28, 1986, p. 210; Heidrick and Struggles, Inc., *The Changing Board.*

41. Heidrick and Struggles, Inc., *The Changing Board.*

42. The increasing extent to which top managers rely on outside experts—consultants and investment bankers among them—to authenticate their judgment makes the distribution of information even more asymmetrical than before.

43. "The Job No One Wants," *Business Week*, September 8, 1986.

44. See American Law Institute, "Principles of Corporate Governance," § 3.02, p. 66.

45. The Business Roundtable, "The Role and Composition of the Board," pp. 2110–11.

46. We are grateful to James S. Coleman of the University of Chicago for providing the term "structured dissent" to describe a desirable boardroom atmosphere.

47. This idea is hardly new, having been debated in and out of business circles for years. See, for example, The Business Roundtable, "The Role and Composition of the Board," pp. 2111–12. Hopefully, its time has now come.

48. Del. Gen. Corp. Law § 102(b)(7).

49. Heidrick and Struggles, Inc., *The Changing Board*.

50. See J. Bower, "The Managerial Estate," in this volume.

51. See H. Brooks and M. Maccoby, "Corporations and the Work Force," in this volume.

52. See J. Badaracco, "Changing Forms of the Corporation," in this volume; R. Zeckhauser, "The Muddled Responsibilities of Public and Private America," in W. Knowlton and R. Zeckhauser, eds., *American Society: Public and Private Responsibilities* (Cambridge, Mass.: Ballinger, 1986), pp. 45–77.

53. Our own observation is that these are also the companies with highly active, interested, and informed boards.

54. We leave for another forum the issue of nominating and electing outside directors. Early on, the Business Roundtable noted the need for outside board members to be credible and independent, as free as possible from the charge of being "handpicked" by and hence "submissive" to the CEO—that is, "rubber stamps." In 1977 it suggested that the SEC revise, if necessary, Rule 14a-8, to ". . . permit share owners to propose amendments of corporate by-laws which would provide for share owner nominations of candidates for election to the board of directors." The Business Roundtable, "The Role and Composition of the Board," pp. 2092, 2095. With the advent of the large institutional shareholder adverted to earlier, further evolution of this concept must be anticipated. J. Heard and H. Sherman, *Conflicts of Interest in the Proxy Voting System* (Washington, D.C.: Investor Responsibility Research Center, 1987).

10 EFFICIENCY, MORALITY, AND MANAGERIAL EFFECTIVENESS

James M. Gustafson and Elmer W. Johnson

During the 1960s and 1970s, critics of the corporation focused almost exclusively on the responsibilities of business to its employees and publics.[1] Their hero was the socially responsible manager. With the advent of the fiercely competitive global markets of the 1980s, however, a new set of critics assumed center stage and riveted our attention on the competitiveness of U.S. industry. And they honored a different pantheon of business heroes: the brutally efficient manager and the takeover artist.[2] Yet recent revelations of Wall Street skullduggery and managerial insensitivity to human and social values require us to consider anew the ethical aspects of corporate governance, not in the abstract, but in the context of the modern marketplace.

TENSIONS AND CONFLICTS

Corporate activities impinge upon a variety of constituencies in society: customers, employees, stockholders, and wider publics such as the communities in which operations are located, groups interested in the protection of the environment, and so on. Each has interests and values that are threatened or sustained and enhanced by the decisions and actions of management. There is no automatic harmony among these interests and values; tensions often erupt into open conflicts. To bring our inquiry into sharper focus, we have isolated three tensions.

The first is tension within the large corporation, between its structures of authority and accountability on the one hand and the necessary conditions for personal initiative and corporate adaptability on the other. Both accountability and adaptability are necessary to corporate well-being, which itself is the sine qua non to all of the corporation's purposes and responsibilities.

The second tension is between the broad, long-term responsibilities of boards of directors and managers and the narrow, more immediate self-interests often pursued by certain constituencies. Directors and managers are stewards of organizations that are built up as partnerships between generations (as Burke once said of the British government). The long-term orientation of managerial decisionmaking determines the well-being of both the corporation and its constituencies. The short-term self-interest of management, employees, or stockholders, exacerbated by deficiencies in our corporate governance mechanisms, can jeopardize that well-being.

The third tension is more complex. The interests of the corporation's stockholders are sometimes at odds with the well-being of its employees, its customers, and the outside community. This conflict ceases to be an issue if the social responsibility of the corporation is defined as the maximization of stockholder wealth within legal (and perhaps ethical) limits. In this view, any unfortunate or deleterious outcomes of lawful, profit-making activities are beyond the responsibility of the corporation, and the corporate manager is therefore absolved from having to act as a moral agent. Another aspect of this tension derives from the competing claims on the corporation of employees and various interest groups, which cannot all be accommodated in light of limited resources.

A MORAL PERSPECTIVE

Some or all of these tensions have been well addressed from the perspectives of economics, law, history, and sociology.[3] This chapter proceeds primarily from a moral perspective. We do not mean to deny or even limit other points of view, nor do we claim that defensible moral considerations are sufficient or overriding in the development of policies and courses of action. Rather, our conviction is that ethical analysis and argument draw particular features of policies and actions to the attention of management and that they ought to inform decisions, giving direction to policies without necessarily determining them.

"Social responsibility" is an ethical term in this chapter, and, as such, it is not reducible to legal responsibility. For legal responsibility, there are clearer and more definite criteria of compliance and structures of enforcement. Prima facie moral claims can be in tension with legally binding responsibilities—this is implied in the statement "not every moral claim is a legal entitlement." From the moral perspective of this chapter, management makes choices informed by ethical principles and human values in the context of legal rules and other conditions. As theologians are wont to say, the right and the good are sought within the conditions of finitude, that is, within the existing constraints and enabling conditions or within the realm of the possible as defined by prevailing economic, legal, and social factors.[4]

A moral point of view is based on the assumption that actors or agents (in this case, primarily managers) making choices in pursuit of their purposes are accountable for both the goodness of the purposes that they pursue and the foreseeable outcomes of their choices.[5] Outcomes can be stated in economic, political, social, or other kinds of terms. We assume that a generally moral dimension is also present in outcomes primarily described in other terms, that is, that outcomes affect the well-being and the presumptive moral rights of persons and communities. For example, outsourcing of production is justified on the grounds of economic efficiency, but the decision to outsource affects the well-being of persons and communities—both those from which and those to which production facilities are moved. From a moral point of view, those effects on well-being must be considered in making decisions.[6]

Thus, the ethical conception of social responsibility used in this chapter is not reducible to eleemosynary activity. Rather, it is based upon a descriptive and analytical account of corporate purposes in the social and economic world, and even the natural world, in which human agents participate. Managerial decisions and actions affect the well-being of other institutions and persons, just as decisions and actions by others have outcomes for corporations and managers. These patterns and processes of interdependence and interaction, necessary and inevitable, are the basis for ascribing social responsibility in a moral sense.

The Western moral tradition that attends to the "common good" also enters into our moral perspective. While it is difficult to formulate a precise concept of the common good, what it refers to is acknowledged intuitively in various moral theories. Some "whole" is perceived specifically or alluded to casually, the parts of which are interdependent. Thus, to serve the interests or values of one part of the whole—for example, maximization of employee benefits—necessarily affects other parts of the whole—prices. Our procedure is to consider a notion of common good, that is, the relevant whole to which our moral perspective must relate. But whose interests should be taken into account in the interdependence of outcomes when one is thinking about corporate activities? An expansion of those interests clearly complicates corporate policy choices and the role of government. For example, environmental protection expands the whole to include the impact of activities on the natural world. Since the justifiable interests and values of all entities deemed relevant to the whole are difficult (perhaps impossible) to fullfil simultaneously, it is imperative to consider as fairly as possible the principles of allocation that attend to them.

A descriptive premise of patterns and processes of interdependence both makes possible and requires an assessment of the extent of an agent's responsibility for outcomes. Are there degrees of social responsibility based, in a moral sense, on priorities among corporate purpose and, in a causal sense, on the proximity and efficacy of the outcomes of activity?[7] Some order of precedence is determined by legal obligations, but, where law does not determine an order, moral arguments and judgments most often can be made in favor of one constituency at some expense to the others.

For management to develop and use a moral perspective to analyze corporate activity, it must have a proper understanding of corporate purposes. It is our belief that management should look upon the corporation under its stewardship as an implicit compact among its principal constituencies, comprehending a hierarchical community of generally long-term employees, a highly mobile, atomistic conglomeration of common stockholders, existing and potential consumers of its products and services, and the various publics that are likely to be affected by its operations.[8]

Under the compact, management is entrusted, subject to a host of laws and governance requirements, with the stewardship and mobilization of the employee community and the stockholders' capital, on the following set of understandings: (1) Management and the employees will strive to produce goods and services that meet or exceed customer expectations as to quality and value, in a manner that will yield the best possible long-term return to the common stockholders consistent with the other terms of the compact; (2) management will strive to provide a work environment that respects the equal and inestimable dignity of all employees, offers strong encouragement and equal opportunity to develop employees' individual talents and their capacity for team cooperation, and promotes and rewards them based on individual and team performance; and (3) management and the employees will strive to protect and advance, to the full extent feasible under a competitive market system, those legitimate social interests on which the corporation's operations have a significant impact.

Each constituency has certain rights designed to enforce the compact. Stockholders can sell their stock, pursue rights of action against the directors, and vote their shares against management. Employees can organize and exercise their collective rights to bargain and to strike, quit and seek other employment, and utilize open-door procedures within the corporation. Customers can take their business elsewhere and pursue various rights of action, individually or collectively. The various publics can act through the regulatory agencies or pursue private rights of action.

Most of these rights and ultimate checks on corporate conduct are costly to all of society; much damage can occur before they bring about corrective action. If the purposes of the compact are to be realized efficiently and well, management must learn to deal with the difficult issues involving tensions among the constituencies in an ethically effective manner. It must weigh the relative importance of competing claims and make painful, often gut-wrenching trade-offs that can be defended on moral, economic, and other grounds.[9]

What are the general principles that should guide the ethically effective manager in considering and determining such trade-offs? First, as we have said, the ethical manager must be guided by an adequate view of the corporate purposes, a view that takes into account the common good and humanity's shared goals and values. Management should work out and reconsider periodically broad statements of purpose, such as that outlined above, with heavy input from employees in various disciplines and at different levels in the organization. This overall sense of direction will help the manager to sort out the relevant facts and frame the key issues and alternative responses.

Some alternatives will be screened out immediately because they would violate what can be viewed as boundary conditions on choices. Some acts would be unlawful. Some would constitute dishonesty or a betrayal of trust or aid and abet breaches of trust by officials of other organizations (e.g., bribery). Some would transgress the basic dignity of persons. While there are necessarily different levels of authority and responsibility in the enterprise, all employees are equal as human beings, and their personal and social interests far transcend the commercial goals of the corporation.[10] Employees cannot be considered as merely another resource in addition to plant, tools, and equipment; they should never be referred to as human capital.

Management must place a high priority on the fitness and health of the corporation (its well-being), so that it can attend to its basic purposes on a stable, long-term basis. Yet, while management can exercise a considerable degree of discretion in attending to its responsibilities in areas involving important social interests, this autonomy is not without limits. For example, the competitive market system very promptly penalizes and ultimately bankrupts the firm that promotes social goals at the extreme expense of private profit. When there are important social interests that the market fails to protect, even with the application of long-term, enlightened corporate self-interest, management's overriding obligation may be to protect the financial health of the entity and then to solicit appropriate government intervention for the protection of those social interests.[11] In such cases, management should utilize its experience and judgment to suggest the best means for removing and overcoming competitive impediments to corporate social responsibility.

In all cases, management should consider whether the moral issue at hand would be addressed more appropriately or effectively through changes in the legislative or corporate governance framework than by the corporation acting alone or with others within the existing framework. If so, management may well have a duty, in alliance with others, to propose and pursue legal or regulatory reform.

Instead of presuming an irreconcilable conflict of interests among constituencies, the ethically effective manager will consider the extent to which constituencies have shared goals. For example, management's responsibilities to employees and to shareholders have a great deal in common. The well-being of both constituencies depends on the long-term competitiveness of the corporation. The manager should strive to design compensation and other kinds of mechanisms that will dramatize this alignment of interests and reduce the potential for conflict.

After real, irreducible conflicts have been identified, the manager must consider whether there are hierarchies of values that will help determine the course of action. For example, compromises in basic product safety to achieve improved product styling or reduced manufacturing costs are morally unacceptable.

Given the enormity of legitimate claims on the corporation's limited resources, management must allocate its energies and resources to those claims where it can have the greatest efficacy by reason of the corporation's relative proximity to the problem, its unique knowledge or expertise, its strategic ability to form alliances of shared responsibility, or otherwise.

These are the principal guidelines, often overlapping and not necessarily congruent, that will inform the ethically effective manager's decisions. They will be of little use in the case of the manager who has no heart—who has little or no empathy for the people and communities whom his or her decisions affect. The process of moral discernment we have proposed presupposes a manager who can feel the hurt and pain of others. It also presupposes a manager who has a sense of the possibilities and limitations of time and place—the conditions of finitude.

HIERARCHY VERSUS INITIATIVE

Our first tension, stated above, is between the need for structures of authority and accountability and the need for incentives to initiative and adaptability.[12] Put more abstractly, this is a tension between order and freedom. Clearly defined formal structures of authority and accountability are necessary for order, and order is necessary to serve the ends of efficiency, itself a precondition to the survival and prosperity of a corporation. Yet, excessive segmentation of roles can constrict freedom and initiative, creativity and adaptability, and thus impede the larger ends that efficiency is meant to serve.[13] Creativity and adaptability, however, do require some stable and ordered conditions; a degree of order is necessary for freedom. The benefits of maintaining this delicate balance accrue, not only to the corporation as a whole, but also to individual participants in terms of enhancing their sense of self-respect or self-esteem.

Harvey Brooks and Michael Maccoby describe the institutionalization of this tension in U.S. labor-management relations within large bureaucratic manufacturing enterprises: ". . . productive efficiency requires that management enjoy unchallenged control over the design and introduction of new production technology, . . . the design of the work process, and plant location."[14] The assumption here is that workers are not competent to participate in such matters. Management must do all the thinking and decisionmaking; workers carry out orders.

Brooks and Maccoby go on to describe how changes in the work environment have made this ethos obsolete. From the moral perspective, however, we would argue that it was fundamentally flawed from the beginning. Human beings have always deserved to be treated with equal respect and dignity. Authoritarian structures, justified in the name of efficiency, tend over time to produce oppressive managers.[15] It is true that the American ethos "worked" for forty years or more, but mainly because the effects of alienating working conditions were masked or offset by ever-increasing levels of wages, benefits, and job security.[16] As long as American manufacturers dominated American and free world markets, the costs of these offsets could be passed on to consumers, and the system could continue to function. When this dominance waned, the system began to crumble.

While we do not hold out the Japanese manufacturing systems as a moral ideal, there is no doubt that the best of them have exposed serious flaws in both our institutional mechanisms and our managerial practices pertaining to the mobilization of human resources.[17] The advantages of authority and hierarchy, in terms of personal discipline and accountability, are not likely to be realized except in an environment conducive to worker initiative, pride of product, and a rewarding association with one's fellow workers. For example, at NUMMI, the Toyota-operated joint venture with General Motors in Fremont, California, workers may be terminated once they exceed a certain level of absenteeism. But these and other tough disciplinary provisions in the labor pact are combined with numerous forms of employee participation. Personal initiative and resourcefulness, hitherto grossly underutilized sources of efficiency, are now being tapped through this combination of personal accountability and team cooperation.

Yet, there is a paradox. These sources are not likely to be tapped by the manager who fails to recognize that accountability and participation are valuable in their own right, that they help to instill a commonality of purpose and build ties of affection and loyalty.[18] If employees sense that the manager is merely using the incentives of participation to achieve the solitary goal of efficiency and that their human and social goals are intermediate and instrumental at best, the incentives will be ineffective.[19]

If one were to sample the attitudes of factory floor workers in the automobile industry today, one would hear vehement expressions from workers who yearn for a better way but have become distrustful of both union and management leadership. Here is an example given to one of the coauthors in the course of such an inquiry:

> They ignore the input of their most valuable resource—the common workers, and now that they are in deep trouble they send out SOS signals. . . . But I have a real credibility problem. I don't trust management and I don't feel that they have ever trusted me. . . . So when I hear these signals and am asked to get involved, I am torn between a spirit of cooperation and a spirit of rebellion against a company that has caused my guts to burn and my hair to thin and turn gray through years of mistrustful dealings.

> Knowing that I never had a chance to be anything within the Company, . . . the next obvious move was for me to become active in the Local Union, and I did. I

now had a cause and that cause was not to contribute anything worthwhile to the corporation but rather to screw the sons of bitches in management that had been too good to recognize me as another human being.

I now became the Champion of the Faith and the Defender of the Truth as I inflicted pain and doled out agony to management people that chose not to agree with me. I picked on bad management people and good management people. It made no difference. I learned to justify my hatred every step of the way and through a seventeen-year process became a very bitter, bitter person.

Then one morning, shortly after my last election, I woke up with a different attitude . . . I was tired. I thought there must be a better way. —I'm ready for a change.

There is a whole lot wrong with both sides. We have to truly change if we are to survive. We have to care about the consumer. We have to care about the stockholders. We have to care about the people we represent. But most important, management people and the workers have to care about each other. . . . The leadership, both management and union, had better show the world that the employees are their most important asset.[20]

To us, our first tension points to very profound issues that sometimes are not addressed in literature about corporate activities—issues of trust and distrust, of confidence or lack of confidence in persons within corporations. In our view, one of management's tasks in relation to this first tension is to sustain an ethos in which various persons and echelons gain the confidence of others through their own trustworthiness and in which common interests among potentially conflicting parties can be accented and relationships of mutual trust sustained and enhanced. During the 1987 negotiations between the UAW and both Ford and General Motors, the union's central demand was that of unconditional job security. But, behind all the rhetoric, both union and management leaders were keenly aware of the harsh competitive realities of the current global marketplace and knew that the companies' competitive strength, to which the long-term interests of both stockholders and employees are tied, depended on continuous improvements in product quality and employee productivity. Further, both sides realized that a prerequisite to such gains is the establishment of an atmosphere of mutual trust and confidence.

In this area, management must take the initiative. It must demonstrate by conduct and behavior and by the values observed in daily decisionmaking that employees can trust their dedication to product excellence, their fair play, their competence, and their judgment. In a large corporation, senior management has the additional challenge of spreading this ethos throughout widely dispersed operations and enhancing the skill and judgment of hundreds or thousands of individuals throughout the ranks of management. Statements of corporate purpose such as those described earlier (and the participative process of articulating such a mission statement) may be useful in disseminating management's philosophy throughout the company.

Ethically effective managers must be committed in their minds and their hearts to this vision of corporate purpose and to the human values that it upholds. Character, integrity, patience, courage, and practical wisdom (i.e., prudence) are key, for, without these, none of the other virtues can be translated into effective action.

We have tried, from a moral perspective, to explain how and why very large, necessarily hierarchic, bureaucratic corporations might pursue simultaneously goals of efficiency and of employee initiative and well-being. Yet a good many of the corporate reorganizations of the last few years have reflected the downsizing of corporate America, carried out almost entirely for the purpose of maximizing stock values. These reorganizations have often taken a considerable toll in terms of worker displacement and community impact. What if the brutally efficient manager also had deeply humane values? Would the pursuit of the employee-oriented purposes of the large corporation also require such a manager to consider further subdividing or downsizing kinds of actions? We strongly suspect so.[21]

LONG-TERM STEWARDSHIP VERSUS SHORT-TERM SELF-INTEREST

Our earlier discussion of the development of labor-management relations provides a good illustration of this tension. With the advantage of ethical hindsight, it now appears that both management and labor have struck bargains over the years that have enabled management to retain its authority and prerogatives and labor to gain important economic benefits at the expense of long-term competitiveness. Domestic industry was thus exposed to considerable danger when global competition emerged. Now, under the pressure of external forces, labor and management are beginning to sense how much they have in common and to think in much longer terms.

This second tension is also well demonstrated by the phenomenon of the corporate takeover, which is often followed by plant closings and other business "rationalizations." A moral analysis of this phenomenon rests on twin principles: Public corporations are institutions that must be built over decades and even generations if their management and employees are to approximate the full possibilities of the corporate compact outlined above; and the managers of such institutions must be subject to removal when knowledgeable shareholders deem them to be incompetent or disloyal.

Free-market economists focus on the second principle and argue forcefully that takeovers create a market for corporate control that promotes competitiveness and efficiency. In this view, tender offers and leveraged buyouts are simply mechanisms by which ownership and control are transferred to persons who believe they can manage the corporation's assets more efficiently. Accordingly, the wake of a takeover often brings the elimination of excess or obsolete productive capacity and the sale of individual assets or businesses, which may also provide funds to service acquisition debt. These consequences are justified in the name of efficiency, without regard to the compact between management and employees.[22]

Critics of current takeover practice argue that it is too easy to put an established enterprise into play and virtually force it into a "bust up" takeover or the adoption of a recapitalization or other defensive maneuver.[23] Takeovers often have little to do with incompetent or disloyal management. Instead, they are frequently driven by the perceived benefits of leverage: the tax deductibility of interest payments encourages bidders and target companies to issue debt in order to finance the purchase of equity.[24] The takeover game all too often involves the acquisition of companies with strong balance sheets, structured for long-term stability, with the result that their equity is replaced with debt and their assets are sold off or retired.

A takeover bid confronts ethical managers with the worst of dilemmas. In many cases, they must decide whether to give in and permit the bidder to take control or to attempt to ward off the takeover by leveraged recapitalizations or other voguish strategies. If they make the former choice, it is often because they conclude that a long battle for control, even if successful, might inflict greater harm on the corporation and its constituencies than would a successful takeover and the adverse consequences to the long-term stability of the enterprise.

Many of the proposals for legislative or regulatory reform in this area seek to preserve legitimate takeover activity while avoiding the abuses described above. For example, the Supreme Court recently upheld the constitutionality of one such approach, in which Indiana restricted the voting rights of acquirers of controlling stock positions unless the other shareholders voted to restore such rights.[25] We do not propose a moral assessment of specific proposals, but we do believe that the legal rules in this area need to be changed in order to enable and encourage managers and shareholders to conduct themselves in a manner consistent with the corporate compact as envisioned in this chapter. From this perspective, the soundest proposals are likely to be those that focus on the responsibilities of stock ownership rather than solely on stockholder rights. We believe that corporate, securities, and tax laws should promote a longer term and more complete view by requiring a reasonable duration of stock ownership as a condition of full access to voting rights, capital-gains treatment, and other benefits of investment in public corporations.

EFFICIENCY VERSUS EQUITY

We have stated our third tension in different ways, the most basic being the tension between the prima facie claims on the corporation of its stockholders, on the one hand, and of employees, consumers, and publics, on the other. Our descriptive principle underlies this tension: The actions of the corporation affect the interests, values, and well-being of large numbers of persons and institutions. To some extent, laws and regulations impose ordering principles on these interests, while other outcomes evoke at least prima facie moral claims on corporations. As noted above, where the causal accountability of the corporation is most singular—for example, in product safety—a stronger claim can be made on its moral responsibility. And, since most events that give rise to conflicting claims have complex multiple causes, there are areas in which corporations will share moral responsibility with other persons and institutions.

The principal moral issue here is one of fairness or distributive justice.[26] Our moral perspective assumes that considerations of justice are proper in the determination of corporate policy. But they, too, must be worked out in the context of economic, legal, and social conditions. Legal obligations to stockholders have to be met; managers must sustain and develop the well-being of the corporation to fulfill those obligations as well as to produce goods and services that meet customers' expectations. These obligations have priority, and other nonlegal responsibilities must be negotiated with reference to them. It is at this point that the tensions between efficiency and fairness or justice can become acute. Attention to these prior obligations often requires the sacrifice of prima facie claims of fairness by employees and other constituencies, especially in highly competitive international markets. This has been evident in the elimination of domestic jobs through the outsourcing of production to countries with lower labor costs.

Manufacturing companies have long been required under their labor agreements to cushion the financial blow of layoffs resulting from outsourcing, but in 1987, in the UAW negotiations with Ford and GM, unions obtained for the first time almost absolute job guarantees (except in the event of market-related downturns in business volume) on a massive scale. Unless the newly established joint processes for improving productivity are utilized effectively, the competitiveness of these companies in international markets could be seriously jeopardized.

In 1987 General Motors wrestled with this issue. How could hourly workers make their maximum contribution to the goal of competitiveness if this required them to work toward the elimination of their jobs or the jobs of their fellow employees? How could management and labor work out terms relating to job security, productivity, profit sharing, plant closings, outsourcing, and other matters that would enable GM both to tap the full potential of its work force and to compete flexibly and cost-effectively in global markets? If management liquidated or sold unprofitable and marginal components operations and relied on outsourcing as the primary solutions to the problem of competitiveness, this would eliminate any possibility of unleashing the skills and energies of the work force.[27]

In the negotiations, the union argued that top management ought to be more accountable for such things as strategic blunders that have long-term adverse effects on the entire work force; management practices that are not respectful of human and social values; the retention of rigid, authoritarian plant managers who destroy the possibilities of worker cooperation; and the failure to scale down the cost and size of the salaried work force. Likewise, management pointed out problems involving the hourly work force. For example, 5 percent of the hourly work force accounted for 50 percent of unexcused absenteeism. Unexcused absences at GM averaged 8.5 percent of required work time in 1986, compared to 2.5 percent at NUMMI. A reduction of only two percentage points at GM would amount to a savings of hundreds of millions of dollars, which could be used to benefit all the employees rather than the 5 percent who accounted for the waste. Other problem areas included relief-time abuses, health-care abuses, obsolete work rules, the inability to fire high-problem employees without recourse to complex grievance procedures, and the union's insistence that wages and benefits be negotiated at the national level but that productivity issues be addressed only at the local level.

On the positive and creative side, both parties knew that they had to work together to keep improving quality and productivity, install more effective programs for the retraining of employees, and develop new roles for unions. It may turn out that the most significant innovation of the 1987 agreement was the establishment of continuous joint processes for addressing specific issues at the local or plant level and designing solutions to fit the peculiar needs of particular units to improve efficiency and product quality.

We have focused much of our attention on the employees, but the corporation also has responsibilities to the customer. Its most important responsibility to consumers is to make safe products, and this is an area that is covered increasingly by law and regulation. The question is whether corporations have responsibilities that exceed legal standards. That some corporations have thought so can be illustrated by the actions of Johnson & Johnson after criminal tampering with Tylenol capsules resulted in the poisoning of innocent consumers. While it might have been economically more efficient for the firm to increase advertising to focus on Tylenol's medicinal value and assure consumers that the tampering cases were isolated, Johnson & Johnson promptly removed all Tylenol capsules from the market until it was satisfied with a sealing technology believed to be impossible to penetrate. It is interesting to note that Johnson & Johnson employees have been guided since 1947 by a credo written by the company's founder and elaborated on by successive generations of senior management. The credo makes clear that the company's first responsibility is to the doctors, patients, parents, and other consumers who use its products. "In meeting their needs, everything we do must be of high quality."[28]

While corporate managers have no special qualifications to make decisions about broad social policy, their causal accountability for wide social effects requires them to consider social policy issues. The well-being of local communities, for example, is deeply affected by managerial decisions: A host of persons, businesses, and institutions, such as schools and churches, is affected if facilities are closed in the name of economic efficiency; communities and wider publics are affected by the disposal of pollutants from production. There is a prima facie claim upon management at least to cooperate with government and other agencies to reduce adverse outcomes. The question of justice, or fairness, must be asked: What is due to communities and other publics that are bearers, however remote, of both the benefits and harms of corporate policies?

CONCLUSION

From the moral perspective developed in this chapter, there are ethical dimensions to choices and activities that are described and analyzed primarily in social, economic, and legal terms. Moral considerations cannot always be determinative; management has to seek "the good" within the possibilities and constraints that exist legally and economically. It is our view, however, that moral considerations should be consciously addressed, that the tensions between morally justifiable interests and values should be articulated explicitly, and that resolutions within the realm of the possible should take them into account. We do not adhere to the quasi-theological belief of those who assume that the greatest good to all will result automatically when corporations pursue the single aim of economic efficiency.

NOTES

The authors wish to acknowledge the substantial assistance of Robert S. Osborne, a partner of the Chicago law firm of Kirkland & Ellis, in the preparation of this chapter.

1. For example, see Christopher Stone, *Where The Law Ends* (New York: Harper & Row, 1975); and C. Walton, ed., *The Ethics of Corporate Conduct* (New York: Prentice-Hall, 1977). For an early and important statement of this concern, see Howard R. Bowen, *Social Responsibility of the Businessman* (New York: Harper and Brothers, 1953). This book was one of a series on ethics and economic life produced by a study committee of the Federal Council of Churches, chaired by Charles P. Taft.

2. The new order of business heroes "eschews loyalty to workers, products, corporate structure, businesses, factories, communities, even the nation." Steven Prokesch, "The Remaking of the American C.E.O.," *New York Times*, January 25, 1987, sect. 3, p. 1. Ivan Boesky, a Wall Street arbitrageur subsequently indicted for securities law violations, summed it up: "Greed is all right, by the way. . . . You can be greedy and still feel good about yourself." "True Greed," *Newsweek*, December 1, 1986, p. 48.

3. Each discipline highlights certain features of the modern corporation and accents causal factors that are relevant from that perspective. Proposed resolutions follow from the data and concepts that dominate the analysis. Two recent books are particularly instructive because of their multidimensional analyses: Klaus J. Hopt and Gunther Teubner, eds., *Corporate Governance and Directors' Liability: Legal, Economic and Sociological Analyses of Corporate Social Responsibility* (Berlin and New York: Walter de Gruyter, 1985); and Oliver E. Williamson, *The Economic Institutions of Capitalism: Firms, Markets, Relational Contracting* (New York: The Free Press, 1985). Neither of these injects a moral point of view into its discussion (note the absence of "Ethical" in the subtitle of the first); arguments from both, however, could be redescribed and reanalyzed from a moral point of view.

4. From this perspective, the more explicitly ethical question, "What ought we to do?" must be pursued in tandem with a more empirical analytical question, "What is going on?" An interpretation and assessment of circumstances, supplied by social, economic, and legal analysis, is required to understand both the constraints upon and the positive possibilities for alternative courses of action that will recognize moral claims raised by the first question. The morally desirable must be worked out within the conditions of possibility and within the patterns and processes of interdependence. This perspective is not that of an ideal moral observer, totally external to the dense circumstances of corporate life, which would develop a more purely ethical theoretical approach, nor does it resemble that of the single-purpose interest group, which would develop a rigid primacy of one ethical goal and measure all conduct against that one standard.

5. Alan Gewirth makes this general point by describing two generic features of action, "voluntariness or freedom and purposiveness or intentionality. By an action's being voluntary or free I mean that its performance is under the agent's control in that he unforcedly chooses to act as he does, knowing the relevant proximate circumstances of his action. By an action's being purposive or intentional I mean that the agent acts for some end or purpose that constitutes his reason for acting; this purpose may consist in the action itself or in something to be achieved by the action." Alan Gewirth, *Reason and Morality* (Chicago: University of Chicago Press, 1978), p. 27.

6. We have introduced the term "well-being," which suggests the primacy of the outcomes of activity and raises serious philosophical issues about the criteria to be used to judge what constitutes beneficial or harmful outcomes. In our usage, well-being is not reducible to economic well-being, although some level of economic well-being is necessary for other qualities of life and thus is a very appropriate consideration when thinking about the social responsibilities of the corporation. To define satisfactorily what is included in well-being, or a desirable quality of life for persons and communities, requires more attention than we can give; it is a multidimensional concept, some aspects of which receive attention subsequently, for example, a sense of satisfaction and fulfillment in one's work.

The vocabulary of rights is also evident in current discussions. In a moral perspective using that term dominantly, one would describe the tensions as existing between conflicting rights. One would argue for or against a moral right to employment, for example, just as one would argue for or against a moral right not to be harmed by poorly designed and manufactured products.

There are mixed moral arguments that use concepts drawn from different moral theories, and there are different theories and vocabularies of ethics. The choice of one over others involves much more extensive justification than is appropriate for this chapter. Our purpose here is modest: We will use ethical terms that are appropriate to the descriptions and analyses of the three tensions; we choose not to argue for one ethical theory over another or to formulate at an abstract level a coherent theory of our own. Rather, we use terms for their heuristic value in relation to tensions defined primarily in policy terms derived from corporate organization and activity.

7. Technical and precise arguments about the concept of responsibility are found in legal, philosophical, and theological literature. See, for example, H. L. A. Hart, *Punishment and Responsibility: Essays in the Philosophy of Law* (New York: Oxford University Press, 1968); Kurt Baier, "Responsibility and Freedom," in Richard T. DeGeorge, ed., *Ethics and Society: Original Essays on Contemporary Moral Problems* (New York: Doubleday Anchor Books, 1966), pp. 49–84; and H. Richard Niebuhr, *The Responsible Self: An Essay in Christian Moral Philosophy* (New York: Harper & Row, 1963). Its most common usage refers to the ascription of accountability for actions, usually ex post facto, but theological literature often adds a more forward-looking usage, that is, that responsibility involves the capacity to be responsive to needs and claims and to assume voluntarily activity for the sake of others' well-being.

8. See Thomas Donaldson, "Constructing a Social Contract for Business," ch. 3 in *Corporations and Morality* (New York: Prentice Hall, 1982).

9. See the discussion of "transaction costs" in Williamson, *The Economic Institutions of Capitalism*, pp. 18–22. To the calculative mind, the ethical caliber of management and those corporate governance mechanisms designed to encourage ethical conduct are part of the "private ordering" for reducing transaction costs. But see page 199 of this chapter.

10. See Frank H. Knight, *The Ethics of Competition and Other Essays* (New York: Harper and Brothers, 1935; Chicago: University of Chicago Press, Midway Reprints, 1976), pp. 59–61.

11. See W. J. Baumol, "Matching Private Incentives to Public Goals," in Harvey Brooks, Lance Liebman, and Corinne S. Schelling, eds., *Public-Private Partnership: New Opportunities for Meeting Social Needs* (Cambridge, Mass.: Ballinger, 1984), pp. 184–86.

12. Literature on large-scale social organizations has long pointed out the social and functional problems that stem from the coexistence of these needs. One earlier study is Robert K. Merton, "Bureaucratic Structure and Personality" and "Role of the Intellectual in Public Bureaucracy," chs. 5 and 6 in *Social Theory and Social Structure* (Glencoe, Ill.: The Free Press, 1949), pp. 151–78. For a highly amusing and perceptive account of this tension within government, see Jonathan Lynn and Antony Jay, eds., *The Complete Yes Minister* (Topfield, Mass.: Salem House, 1987).

13. Moral responsibilities, especially in large, highly structured organizations, are defined to a considerable extent by role responsibilities, for example, the moral responsibilities of the General Counsel or the Vice President of Environmental Activities are defined by their distinctive roles in the corporation. Officers are morally accountable to boards of directors, as other executives are to internal boards for safety or environmental affairs, and so on. The obligations come with the voluntary acceptance of positions.

Theological literature has long recognized and addressed the moral quandaries that emerge from a distinction between one's "office," or social role, and one's "person," or one's capacities to be self-determining according to one's own conscience; different resolutions have been proposed on a very broad spectrum of possibilities. See, for example, Martin Luther, "Temporal Authority: To What Extent It Should Be Obeyed," in *The Christian in Society II*, vol. 45 of *Luther's Works* (Philadelphia: Muhlenberg Press, 1962), pp. 81–129.

14. See "Corporations and the Work Force," in this volume, p. 118.
15. The American Protestant theologian, Reinhold Niebuhr, made this point rather dramatically: "The man of power, though humane impulses may awaken in him, always remains something of a beast of prey." Reinhold Niebuhr, *Moral Man and Immoral Society* (New York: Scribners, 1932), p. 13.
16. Lucia Dunn, "The Effect of Firm Size on Wages, Fringe Benefits, and Work Disability," in Betty Bock, Harvey J. Goldschmid, Ira M. Millstein, and F. M. Scherer, eds., *The Impact of the Modern Corporation* (Columbia University Press, 1984), pp. 5–58.
17. Although one of the coauthors, who recently visited a number of Japanese manufacturing operations, found a certain grimness and intensity among Japanese workers and a degree of subordination of the individual to the group that derogates from the dignity and worth of persons.
18. Charles E. Lindblom, *Politics and Markets: The World's Political Economic Systems* (New York: Basic Books, 1977), p. 333.
19. Williamson, *The Economic Institutions of Capitalism*, p. 405.
20. Excerpted form a letter by Terry Busch, an hourly employee of General Motors and member of the UAW, dated July 18, 1987, to one of his high school classmates, a member of GM management. Both are now in their early forties. Mr. Busch shared the letter with Elmer Johnson during an interview in October 1987. At that time, he authorized the use of the excerpt that appears in the text.
21. For an excellent discussion, see Williamson, "The Limits of Firms: Incentive and Bureaucratic Features," ch. 6 in *The Economic Institutions of Capitalism*, particularly pp. 148–53, in which the author laments the "underdeveloped state of bureaucratic failure literature" but speculates as to the outcome of further studies: "I will be surprised, however, if the principal limits to vertical integration turn out to have non-bureaucratic origins" (p. 153). The authors of this chapter will also be surprised if such limits don't have much to do with the propensity to "micromanage" and with the emotional distance of top management from the human and social impacts of their decisions.
22. A leading exposition of this view, which turns on the "efficient capital market hypothesis," is Frank H. Easterbrook and David R. Fischel, "The Proper Role of a Target's Management in Responding to a Tender Offer," *Harvard Law Review* 94 (1981): 1161.
23. Critics of unbridled takeovers also point to front-end loaded offers and other *in terrorem* tactics used by takeover artists to create the conditions for panic selling by shareholders. These abuses are compounded by the fraudulent and illegal use of inside information that often seems to accompany current takeover practice.
24. "[V]irtually the entire current value of a company's assets is realized as a maximum amount of debt is imposed on the company, while the remaining equity retains significant investment value as an option on future increases in the value of the

company. In addition, given a company with limited opportunities for internal investment, value is enhanced by removing cash from the company on a pre-tax basis as interest payments, as opposed to a post-tax basis as dividends." Lawrence Lederman and Michael Goroff, "Recapitalization Transactions," *Review of Securities and Commodities Regulation* 19 (1986): 241, 245. The development of liquid markets for junk bonds has provided a ready source for the financing.

25. CTS Corp. v. Dynamics Corp. of America, 55 U.S.L.W. 4478 (April 21, 1987).

26. The concept of justice is not developed here in its technical complexity; there are many important treatises on the concept, and a vast literature applies it to many human and institutional relationships and problems, including writings on business ethics. The most discussed modern treatise is John Rawls, *A Theory of Justice* (Cambridge: Harvard University Press, 1971). For our purposes, it is sufficient to remind readers of two formulations of the formal aspects of the concept in Western thought: "to each his or her due" and "equals (or similar cases) should be treated equally (or similarly)." Judgments about the material (as opposed to formal) aspects of the concept answer the questions, "*What* is due to *whom* and *why*?" and "*Who* are the equals to be treated equally and *how*?"

27. It is clear that, by reason of external forces, including the twin onslaughts of rapid technological change and global competition, GM has no choice but to manage a shrinking work force over the longterm. To the extent that these forces are truly external to GM and threaten its long-term competitive health despite its best efforts to expand sales, its employees should accept the need for shrinkage on terms that strike a fair balance between their immediate interests and those of long-term corporate survival and prosperity. It would also be appropriate for management and labor to work in partnership with government to ease the impact of structural competitive change. For example, government involvement could help ease the adjustment of displaced workers and their communities by bearing a substantial portion of the costs of job training and other programs to facilitate change.

28. Other aspects of the credo are relevant to our discussion. The company is also "responsible to our employees. . . . Everyone must be considered as an individual. We must respect their dignity and recognize their merit." Further, "we are responsible to the communities in which we live and work and to the world community as well." And, "our final responsibility is to our stockholders. . . . When we operate according to these principles, the stockholders should realize a fair return."

11 EPILOGUE: FOR WHOM DOES THE CORPORATION TOIL?

John R. Meyer and James M. Gustafson

Originally, the corporation, as inherited by the colonies from British antecedents, was a political instrument, given a special charter (often an exclusive franchise or monopoly) to pursue some royal or governmental purpose. As McCraw notes in his historical essay, "The Evolution of the Corporation in the United States," royal exclusivity quickly was eliminated after the North American colonies achieved independence. By the middle of the nineteenth century, if not before, business incorporation could be done easily and freely in the United States, becoming more of a right than a privilege.

The corporation thus became a convenient means to accumulate the large commitments of capital needed to develop the new country. Individual investors could commit their capital in widely varying amounts, more or less anonymously, with liability limited to whatever amount they advanced. In the nineteenth and early twentieth centuries, accumulations of sufficient size were created to carry out such large tasks as linking the two North American coasts by rail, establishing a modern steel industry, and initiating large utility and communications networks.

Subsequently, an interacting or reinforcing advantage of the corporation was sometimes discerned. Very large enterprises could only be undertaken if they were big enough to control their environments, say, by creating a stable pricing framework or political context. Accordingly, even if a particular activity did not require a large scale for technological reasons, such scale was often sought, perhaps even needed, to control or overcome other, nontechnological environmental constraints.[1]

The corporate form was also extremely flexible. Capital could be raised more or less in close conformance with financial need, in easily transferable and divisible units. Increasing numbers and scale made it relatively easy to create a broadly based financial market for corporate-ownership certificates, adding the attribute of liquidity.

Certain convenient governance characteristics also came with the corporation. Corporations are self-perpetuating bodies; replacements or additions to the governing board usually are voted by the existing or established governing group. With this characteristic, corporations possessed what amounted to perpetual life. In particular, a convenient process was created for transferring power from one generation of leadership to another, as the occasion necessitated.

All of these attributes might have been achieved by other institutional forms, but there was little incentive to search for alternatives as long as the corporation succeeded. The corporation may not have been a perfect fit in every application, but it certainly covered a wide variety of business situations quite adequately. The corporate format also became easily implementable. Even the youngest lawyer knew the standard legal forms and requisite registrations.

Quite understandably, then, the corporation came to dominate the American business scene. As Scherer points out in his chapter on "Corporate Ownership and Control," corporations accounted for 87 percent of U.S. industrial activity in 1978, up from 74 percent as recently as 1958. Increased use of the corporate form has been accompanied by widespread diffusion of corporate ownership and a corresponding decline in the prominence of corporations owned preponderantly by managers (at least until leveraged buyouts became fashionable in the 1980's).

As is frequently the case with economic institutions, the corporation's weaknesses often have stemmed from its strengths. The first major criticism of corporations, appearing in the early years of the twentieth century in the United States, was that they had simply become too big. The public policy reaction was to enact antitrust laws to circumscribe the growth of major corporations and the extent to which any single corporation could dominate its particular market. These initial adverse reactions to corporate bigness were based on both economic and political considerations. Economically, a market monopoly could eliminate most of the gains that a competitive market environment might otherwise bestow. Politically, there was the Jeffersonian notion that bigness might be antithetical to democratic processes.

Some observers also felt that certain enterprises might become too big to be managed efficiently by the usual hierarchical structures. Indeed, in textbooks and much of their literature, economists memorialized this concern in the "U-shaped" cost curve—an average total cost curve for the enterprise that declined with scale to a certain point, bottomed out, and then began to rise inexorably thereafter. When pressed to defend the U-shaped cost curve, especially under the onslaughts of expanding technology and economies of scale, economists generally pointed to limitations on the scope or reach of control and management processes.[2] Managers and students of business administration explored much the same phenomena as they became concerned about means of maintaining authority while delegating responsibilities down through ever-larger organizations (as McCraw details in his chapter).

Questions also arose at a very early stage as to whether large corporations were compatible with innovation and entrepreneurship. The early wisdom, perhaps best exemplified by Schumpeter's eloquent statement in 1911 of the case for the individual entrepreneur, suggested that large organizations might stifle both.[3] It was therefore somewhat surprising when Schumpeter himself argued in 1942 that bigness was not only compatible with innovation but perhaps a necessary condition for it.[4] Specifically, he maintained that only big firms could afford the large expenditures necessary to develop the new technologies required for increasingly advanced and scientifically complex manufacturing processes. So striking was the contrast between Schumpeter's emphasis on bigness in the mid-1940s and his earlier work attributing heroic, almost romantic qualities to the individual entrepreneur that some scholars came to identify two different Schumpeters and to wonder which described more accurately the development process.[5] Interestingly, when these conflicting Schumpeterian hypotheses have been put to the empirical test, the tentative consensus seems to be that neither extreme of large monopoly or microscopic competition best serves innovation and development; rather, something in between, say, an oligopolistic market of five to ten participants, may be best.[6] Much also seems to depend on the capital intensity, market concentration, unionization, labor-skill requirements, product differentiation, and other characteristics of a particular industry.[7] Nevertheless, a strong belief persists that scale does facilitate innovation, as in Galbraith's *The New Industrial State* and Reich's *Tales of a New America*.[8] Reich, in fact, blends a bit of the old and new Schumpeters, coining the term "collective entrepreneurship" to describe the large-scale collaborative research and development that he considers necessary under modern conditions.

Large corporations also came to be viewed as sometimes being too big to adapt easily even to evolutionary changes in markets or technologies. Perhaps because of their deep pockets and easy access to capital markets, corporations tend to continue doing things the old way long after such old ways have outlived their usefulness. As Gustafson and Johnson point out in their essay on "Efficiency, Morality, and Managerial Effectiveness," an inevitable tension may also have arisen between the accountability requirements of a large corporation and the flexibility required to act expeditiously. The most dramatic recent application of this line of criticism has been to the U.S. automobile industry in the 1970s, as it encountered successively major challenges from overseas competitors, government requirements to meet certain environmental and fuel standards, and basic demographic shifts in markets.[9] The charge that large, successful, and established corporations can all too easily fall victim to the hubris of considering themselves above normal market considerations, thereby becoming incapable of adaptation, has also been leveled at railroads, textiles, steel, and several other industries.[10]

By contrast, Coleman, in his chapter on the "Social Organization of the Corporation," suggests that size may have little to do with a corporation's ability to adapt, at least directly. Coleman's emphasis is on the "constitutional" allocation of rights and responsibilities within the corporation. He therefore believes that the rate of innovation is influenced heavily by how the corporation assigns the ownership rights to innovations. Where these rights are shared by the corporation and the person or group originating the idea, the rate of innovation is increased, often by creating new spin-off companies. Furthermore, he speculates that, while innovational capabilities are commonly associated with certain industries (computer software, microchips, biotech) and not with others (automobiles, steel), the real difference may have little to do with an industry's technology, or a company's size, but instead relate more to the industry's traditions with respect to sharing these ownership rights.

If Coleman is correct, the implications could be far-reaching, since the ability to adapt and innovate could be at the very heart of determining a business's viability. Indeed, McCraw maintains that the basic challenge facing U.S. corporations today is essentially their age-old problem: how to adapt to shifts in the economic environment brought on by technological change. He apparently considers it an open question whether bigness helps or hinders such adaptation.

Bigness might also be identified as the root of still another commonly criticized characteristic of the corporate form: the separation of ownership and control.[11] This separation allegedly could lead to economic inefficiency, since professional managers can become more interested in size for its own sake, its attendant power, or their personal compensation than in efficiency and profit maximization. Scherer discusses theories of the behavioral consequences of ownership structure and concludes that there is lack of agreement on how seriously the goals of owners and managers diverge, how small the ownership share of leading stockholders must be before managers can pursue their own goals, and what incentive mechanisms most effectively reconcile owner and manager goals. Like Berle and Means, Scherer concludes that ''ownership structure can make a difference'' but is uncertain what difference it makes.

In the extreme, expansion or growth for its own sake can lead to the collection of diverse and unrelated businesses into one corporate entity, so-called conglomerate business enterprises.[12] Such unrelated diversification can intensify the perennial problem of hierarchical control, making the corporation even more subject to rapidly diminishing returns on expanded activity. The standard defense of conglomeration, generally preferred in the 1960s when conglomerates were under particularly active development, was that it provided risk diversification. Unfortunately for this defense, the liquidity, divisibility, and other qualities that make the creation of a financial market in corporate-ownership shares so attractive and easy also provide a very simple means for individual investors to diversify the risks attached to corporate stock ownership. Modern financial theory, in fact, suggests that individual investors can achieve risk diversification at least as easily on their own as by participating in conglomerations.[13] Furthermore, the financial markets apparently did not believe that the conglomerate achieved much risk reduction, evaluating them as being approximately 50 percent more risky than the average publicly traded firm.[14]

The ease of creating corporations may also have led to their use in situations where their basic characteristics of perpetuity and continuing access to capital markets were inappropriate, or at least of little value. For example, the perpetual nature of the corporation is not obviously an advantage when exploiting a depletable natural resource; in such cases, there is usually some automatic time limit (exhaustion of the resource) on the particular enterprise or activity, going beyond which creates temptations or problems that are better avoided. The same rules of finite life may be almost as applicable to many other types of business activities. For instance, technologies and production processes can become as passé as a depleted mining resource because of new technologies or shifts in consumer tastes. Accordingly, the ability to perpetuate a business's existence may not always be a blessing. While there are many examples of corporations making successful transitions from one set of technologies or industries to another, there are also many cases where a particular corporation probably had outlived its usefulness so that dissolution and dispersal of the assets to shareholders would have been best.

Certain of these weaknesses in the corporate form have been reinforced by yet another characteristic of the corporation: its convenience as a target for government taxation. Corporations are devices under which individuals or groups come together to participate in different guises—as employees, consumers, management, investors, and so forth. In view of this, corporations, as such, do not pay taxes, but, rather, are intermediaries through which taxes are collected from the different constituencies. Very little is known about exactly which constituents typically pay corporate taxes, as the incidence depends on a number of difficult-to-determine characteristics such as the relative degree of competition in product and supplier markets. [15] Since nobody really knows who pays, corporate taxes have the political advantage of obscurity or anonymity. On the other hand, activities organized within the corporation are to some extent subjected to double taxation; stockholders, employees, and investors usually pay taxes on their individual incomes as well.

Double taxation, in turn, creates potentially unfortunate consequences for economic efficiency. Obviously, no one likes paying taxes twice. One of the simpler ways to avoid such double taxation is for the corporation not to transfer profits to stockholders. Furthermore, earnings retained in the corporation and reinvested are likely to be taxed only after a delay and possibly at an advantageous capital-gains rate. Incentives are thus established for the stockholder to delegate some investment decisions to the managers of profitable corporations. As long as corporate and individual income-tax rates are reasonably high, the corporate manager as investor would have to be rather incompetent not to achieve higher after-tax returns than individual investors could achieve making investment decisions on their own after double taxation. Whenever personal income-tax rates for the stockholder are higher than tax rates on capital gains, these effects are magnified. These tax considerations clearly create a permissive environment for managers to pursue their own goals independent of ownership (though often with the tacit or explicit permission of the owners). Some of this independence apparently has been pursued to the point where managers-cum-investors have sometimes achieved the near impossible, realizing net returns after taxes lower than the individual investor might have made even with full dispersal of corporate proceeds and double taxation![16]

Recognition of these weaknesses in the corporate form has given rise to several adaptations or alternatives. In natural-resource industries, for example, a royalty trust or master limited partnership has sometimes replaced the corporation. While either the trust or the master limited partnership provides a means to transfer profits to owners without double taxation, a potential disadvantage is that virtually all positive cash flow must be passed through relatively promptly. This may create managerial and other problems in times of economic downturn by limiting the accumulation of reserves to weather adversity.

The large corporation's potential inability to adapt to new problems and markets has also led to considerable experimentation with various hybrid organizational forms. Badaracco, in his chapter on "Changing Forms of the Corporation," contends that the traditional corporate relationship based on specific contractual and market relationships and responsibilities is being replaced increasingly by networks of cooperative arrangements in which authority, ownership, operations, and, sometimes, even corporate identity are shared. For example, like Coleman, he sees spin-offs being used to set up independent entities to develop new technologies, with those originating or implementing the new technologies participating substantially in the ownership and, therefore, the potential rewards if the technology succeeds. Similarly, joint ventures can be established between or among different corporations, in order to meet new problems and challenges better. Joint ventures, moreover, are not necessarily limited to cooperation among traditional profit-seeking corporations; the biotechnical area, for instance, provides many examples of joint ventures between corporations and universities or other nonprofit research institutions. Trade associations and industrywide cooperative ventures are other ways of pursuing these goals. Even labor unions have sometimes joined in such partnerships.

The Japanese apparently adopted these cooperative corporate institutional arrangements earlier than the United States, perhaps more for cultural or historic reasons than by deliberate design. As described by Peck in his chapter, "The Large Japanese Corporation," the Japanese have long had zaibatsu (after World War II, keiretsu) to combine or coordinate business activities under one unifying financial oversight, usually provided by a large bank, within which various cooperative joint ventures and arrangements have become quite commonplace. At least part of the Japanese corporation's apparent ability to adapt to change without much benefit of takeovers or other financial restructurings may reside in the presence of the keiretsu, with their history of experimentation with diverse organizational combinations. In essence, within the keiretsu, corporate restructurings can be achieved without necessarily enduring the substantial dislocations of extensive reorganization of a corporation's central office or governance.

Somewhat ironically, some of the new institutional forms or adaptations supplanting the corporation have also become defensive mechanisms by which corporate managements can protect themselves from external threats. For example, an unfriendly takeover is rather difficult to achieve against a master limited partnership, since voting control in such circumstances is normally vested in a very small group of general partners. Similarly, the Japanese may have experienced relatively few takeovers because keiretsu can provide various defenses against them, including, again, vesting control in small groups.

Thus, while the large U.S. corporation may sometimes display weaknesses in adapting to change, it certainly has not displayed any substantial lack of innovation in financial or organizational terms. These innovations, moreover, have provided not only corrections to certain perceived and often real weaknesses but also defensive mechanisms for hindering unsolicited or ostensibly hostile solutions to some of these same problems. A very interesting question is how these various tendencies, both good and bad, will prove out in the longer run. Much, of course, may also depend on future public policy choices and evolving notions of the responsibilities of the corporation.

Indeed, a key question concerning the modern corporation is: Exactly to whom does it owe its ultimate allegiance and responsibilities? In conventional economic and financial theory, the answer is apparently simple: The goal of management is to maximize the value of the firm as the agent of stockholder-owner principals. In common law, at least historically, the relationship has been a bit more complex but, in the end, much the same: The corporation as an entity should be governed by its directors working in the best interests of the corporate entity (rather than just the stockholders), who are elected by the stockholders (but not always on a one-share one-vote basis).

In both law and economics, much of the underlying logic for this position flows from the fact that the ultimate risk in the corporation is borne by stockholders: If the business fails, their equity investment is wiped out. Since stockholders bear this risk, they seem entitled to most of the profits if the business succeeds. As the ultimate risk bearers and owners of the corporation, stockholders also have the ultimate right to select corporate strategy and management; theirs should be the final say.

Others think this view is much too simplistic, arguing that corporations have responsibilities to many constituencies and must balance the conflicting claims made by these different groups. For example, Brooks and Maccoby, in their chapter on "Corporations and the Work Force," assert that a number of developments in society (rising worker aspirations, new technologies, increased organizational complexity) have all coalesced to make the historical bipolar relationship between management and labor less and less relevant; specifically, relations between managers and employees have become more interdependent and multilateral. A related but somewhat different point is made by Gustafson and Johnson in their chapter. They feel that managers should work at perceiving the interests and values that corporations share with their various constituencies and that the welfare of the corporation is promoted through actions that are responsible and accountable to these constituencies. Furthermore, they assert that, where human and social costs occur as a result of choices made in the interests of efficiency and profitability, corporations have an obligation to see that these costs are shared as fairly as possible.

Coleman arrives at much the same pluralistic notion of corporate responsibilities, but from a slightly different perspective. In his view, the flaw in conventional theories about corporate functioning (economic, legal, or sociological) is that they are much too aggregative; specifically, they fail to recognize that there are "interests and resources at each position in the corporation's structure." He then investigates how different allocations of rights and reciprocal obligations in a corporation will condition behavior, postulating that "in every organization, there exists such an allocation, which may be called the 'constitution' of the organization, whether explicitly stated or implicitly recognized as the legitimate order." This thesis evokes the explicit and implicit contracts between different parties involved in corporate activities on which economists and lawyers often comment, although Coleman's conceptualization runs very much against the principal-agent notions at the heart of most legal and economic theories of corporate behavior.

Some observers move well beyond the multilateral interdependence or pluralism of Brooks and Maccoby, Gustafson and Johnson, or Coleman to suggest that some constituent groups may, in fact, have a superior claim to that of stockholders. In Japan, in particular, the suggestion is often made that corporations represent a community of interests and that, if any one interest is dominant, it is that of employees. As Peter Drucker has put it:

> It expresses the most profound conviction of modern Japan, that the large enterprise is run primarily for its employees, at least as long as it does not get into serious financial trouble. The strength of post-World War II Japan—or at least its unique characteristic—is that it sees itself as a community, as a kazoku, or family. Japan itself is a kazoku. So is Kawasaki Steel and the Fuji Bank—and also the Ginza Branch of the bank or the toy section in . . . the big department store.[17]

Indeed, the clearest normative statement in this book is probably Peck's quotation from Nishiyama:

> [The large Japanese corporation] exists to supply workers with their means of daily living, to satisfy their common interest, and further to provide for their common destiny. The management workers, on the basis of their position and dominant control of the business, are obviously members of the community. Their management objective is the perpetuation of the firm as a communal body, and the pursuit of profits is merely the means for achieving this objective.

As Peck points out, critical features of the Japanese employment system (e.g., lifetime employment) and other aspects of corporate policy are guided by this communal vision of society. Put more abstractly, the well-being of wholes takes primacy over that of stockholders, with the interests of employees and their security apparently assuming the highest priority. More inclusive communitarian visions of society may expand the range of persons and entities whose well-being is taken into account in the determination of corporate activity. When trade-offs are necessary, different interests and values will be given preference, depending on who and what belong to the whole envisioned. The mechanism and criteria for deciding these trade-offs remain somewhat obscure but apparently emerge from Japan's oft-cited propensity for consensus building.

In general, several chapters in this volume use *network* and similar terms to describe the relations of corporations to the larger social systems of which they are a part. Implied, almost, in these terms is an assumption that the well-being of a corporation is so intertwined with that of other institutions that the corporation must take into account a wider context of considerations, a larger whole, if only for its own good.

Whether corporations are run for the benefit of stockholders or employees or others, the question of risk bearing is perhaps more complex than is normally stated in economics or legal textbooks. As noted by Brooks and Maccoby (and others before them), the labor force engaged in a given enterprise can acquire very specialized skills. The longer the employment in a particular activity, the more likely it is that an employee will have skills of special value to that enterprise but with limited applicability or marketability to other enterprises. In a parallel fashion, many suppliers to an enterprise are likely to acquire particular skills and abilities, which, again, may often have limited applicability or marketability elsewhere. Finally, most economic activities are specific to certain locations. If a location is isolated or dominated by a particular enterprise, the value of investments in housing or commercial real estate may depend crucially on the fortunes of that enterprise.

If a locally dominant enterprise fails, not only are stockholders wiped out (in terms of their investments in the enterprise), but almost as surely the stakeholdings of some employees, local businesspeople, and suppliers will diminish. In addition, the quality of local community services such as public education and of voluntary associations such as churches can be adversely affected. Indeed, if one accepts that it is more difficult to diversify risk attached to investments in human capital, housing, small businesses, and commercial real estate than in publicly marketed common stocks, these various other players may be at a higher risk. To some extent, of course, some of these risks can be attenuated or even eliminated (especially for suppliers and employees) by writing long-term contracts; in practice, however, writing contracts that encompass all contingencies may be so expensive that it is more efficient to proceed on an implicit contract: for example, an understanding that an employee who acquires employer-specific skills will have a job as long as the employer is solvent and will receive pay raises roughly consistent with productivity gains and general price inflation.[18]

An argument can be made, in fact, that much of the observed gain in share prices associated with takeovers is not really due to any efficiency gains but rather is attributable to transfers of wealth from suppliers and employees to stockholders.[19] Stockholder value enhancements from transfers created by mergers have long been recognized, of course, with tax benefits (transfers from the general taxpayer) and enhanced market power (permitting higher prices to extract transfers from consumers) most commonly mentioned. Even senior debt holders, who usually have relatively rigid contractual arrangements with the firm, may lose in takeovers, for example, when their debt is downgraded, and therefore loses value, as a consequence of the increased leverage commonly associated with takeovers.[20] In essence, the takeover can become a device for shareholders to appropriate wealth by reneging on prior contracts, both explicit and implicit, that for some reason are no longer advantageous to them, as well as by, possibly, extracting transfers from taxpayers and consumers.

To the extent, moreover, that any implicit contracts are based on the perceived trustworthiness of management, managements may understandably be opposed to their abrogation. If management grew up in an organization, suppliers and employees are likely to be friends, neighbors, and acquaintances—people to whom the managers feel some loyalty. Furthermore, management may believe that, without trust and the implicit contracts that go with it, they cannot manage efficiently. Certainly, in the long run, costs could be higher without implicit contracts, just as, in the long run, costs could rise if debt contracts became less flexible.[21]

Accordingly, much of the gain realized by stockholders in takeovers, especially those of a hostile character, may be mainly at the expense of others and, even worse, may eventually harm economic efficiency and performance by eliminating much of the trust on which day-to-day operations and implicit contracts are built. Under such circumstances, it is not difficult to see why democratically elected legislatures may become concerned when hostile takeovers occur. They may see no particular equity in the transfers created by takeovers or in the underlying precept of stockholder rights being dominant. To correct for the perceived unfairness in the common law and to limit downside outcomes for the communities they represent, legislatures may turn to various expedients to redress the balance. Plant closings must be announced in advance and discussed with the local employees and community before proceeding. Limitations may be proposed on the voting rights of certain stockholder groups—for instance, those of particularly recent vintage. More time may be introduced into the hostile takeover process so that nonstockholder groups and interests can better voice their concerns. Community impact statements could even be mandated. Special tax advantages might be created to permit greater employee participation as stockholders in order to align ownership interests in seemingly greater consonance with risk exposure. Finally, punitive taxes might be suggested on gains realized from takeovers.

The great disadvantage of these potential or actual dilutions of stockholder primacy, according to many economists and lawyers, and even many business-men, is that they may dissolve much of the basic discipline of a free-market economy. In this view, recognition of all of these other interests—of employees, suppliers, senior debt holders, local business people, and so forth—confuses the issue, which is obfuscated further by the resulting legislative modifications of corporate governance multiplying the number of corporate goals to be achieved. By attenuating market discipline, such changes may also permit inefficient or even incompetent management to persist when it should be replaced. This may have larger implications for the economy as a whole since, ultimately, the continuation of incompetent managements will result in a less efficient national economy less capable of competing in world markets. Indeed, the contrary argument that takeovers could result in less efficiency appears to these partisans to be obviously specious; otherwise, why would takeovers take place and why would stock values seem so undeniably enhanced by most takeovers?[22]

Weaver's critical examination of the doctrine of corporate social responsibility, "After Social Responsibility," provides a particularly strong statement of these concerns. His chapter is a complex historical and analytical argument from which one can infer the general moral point of view that influences both his analysis and prescriptions. His basic conclusion and general prescription is stated succinctly:

> Corporations must abandon an old self-legitimation that subordinated economics to politics . . . [and] embrace a new concept of the corporation based on the original liberal tradition of individual right, limited government, rule of law, free markets, and peaceful, nonimperial international relations.

"In today's competitive world," he concludes, "corporate welfare is a recipe, not for success, but for disaster."

While recognizing and responding to much the same competitive consider-ations as Weaver, Knowlton and Millstein (in their chapter provocatively entitled, "Can the Board of Directors Help the American Corporation Earn the Immortality It Holds So Dear?") advocate a rather moderate approach. Specifically, they feel that modification of existing corporate governance procedures could solve most recognized difficulties (e.g., balancing different social and employee responsi-bilities) without creating additional problems, such as eliminating market disciplines on inefficient managements. They approve of what they perceive to be the recent evolution of boards from being inside dominated to outside dominated, largely passive to more active, and less diligent to more diligent. However, the new context for corporate decisions is also more complex: more general social responsibilities but less detailed regulation and antitrust; rapidly changing technologies that quickly break down market barriers; ever-larger and more competitive global markets; and so on. All of these place greater responsibility on the governance of the corporation. Unfortunately, outside board members typically lack the time to understand the corporation's problems in depth and thus tend to base their analyses and decisions on information provided by management (even though they simultaneously may consume a lot of time going by the book when making routine decisions, in order to avoid future legal liability questions). To correct these deficiencies and imbalances, Knowlton and Millstein advocate that boards have control over their own agendas and be chaired by outside (nonmanagement) directors who have the resources to study and to hear alternative points of view. They also recommend restrictions on the number of boards on which directors may sit and exemptions from monetary liability for board members.

Knowlton and Millstein argue that these changes would improve corporate governance so that the need for destabilizing takeovers would be reduced substantially. However, their proposals do not question the basic primacy of stockholder interests. The corporation would continue, as an established and self-perpetuating economic and legal entity, to toil primarily for the stockholders, albeit, it is hoped, in a more responsible and competent fashion.

Whether or not the Knowlton-Millstein proposals would be enough to satisfy the critics and establish a new political consensus is an intriguing question. Ironically, Japanese corporations — which by all accounts are at least somewhat less stockholder and more employee oriented, if not employee dominated, than those of North America and Europe—have by most accounts also been at least as efficient and productive. There may be reasons for doubting how universal and relevant the productive superiority of the Japanese is and how far it will persist.[23] But the Japanese experience at least suggests strongly that orienting the business enterprise more to employee interests does not necessarily diminish efficiency; indeed, such an orientation is consistent with commonsense notions about improving incentives and motivation.

Suggestions, in fact, increasingly are made that employee compensation should be tied more closely to the general profit performance of firms, thus making employees not only implicit risk sharers but also explicit participants in the residuals resulting from corporate operations. As Coleman points out, and economists have long stressed, bonuses can be a means of bringing a particular worker's compensation into better alignment with his or her marginal product (or contribution); this can be in the firm's self-interest as well, because it reduces the odds of losing particularly productive employees to other firms where effective markets exist for their special skills. The ostensible benefits of such arrangements include not only potential improvements in worker efficiency but also a possible reduction in cyclical variations in unemployment.[24] To the extent that economic malaise might be attributable to a misdirection or misuse of corporations' free cash flow, as some critics and takeover advocates have asserted, it could at least be hypothesized that some diversion of such flows to employee benefits and incentives might be as beneficial economically as simply paying them out to stockholders. In short, the diagnosis that too much discretionary cash flow in the hands of management breeds trouble might be correct, while the prescribed solution, takeovers that place such funds in stockholders' hands, might not be. Needless to say, Wall Street and union halls might be expected to propose very different solutions, even if agreeing on the diagnosis.

In these matters of making workers' compensation more discretionary and incentive oriented, the Japanese have again been very much in the lead. As Peck points out, they pay a higher percentage of total annual employee compensation perceived to be profit-related (mostly as biannual bonuses) than elsewhere in the capitalist world. This practice may have arisen for reasons unrelated to employment stabilization or efficiency, but, nonetheless, the Japanese economy has experienced relatively stable and low levels of unemployment by Western standards, and the productivity and motivation of Japanese workers is reputedly very high.

American employers, while still lagging well behind the Japanese, greatly expanded the number of profit-sharing or discretionary portions of pay packages in the 1980s. Specifically, the U.S. Bureau of Labor Statistics reports that between 1983 and 1986 bonus provisions in major labor agreements in the United States rose from a negligible level to about 40 percent. The American Productivity Center, which regularly surveys the pay practices of 1,600 or so companies, reported in 1986 that about 75 percent of those surveyed used some form of nontraditional compensation.[25]

Obviously, it is not too great a step from changes in employee participation in residuals to changes in the legal or economic status of employees. This has been particularly true in the United States wherever the performance of a business enterprise has been unprofitable. In many failing businesses or activities (most prominently, in airlines, meat packing, and steel making), employees have proceeded from loss sharing (usually via wage reductions or postponements) to ownership sharing.[26] Various tax or other governmental incentives for creating greater employee stock ownership only heighten these tendencies, as in formal employee stock ownership plans (ESOPS) and tax-privileged stock options for management. Better funding of pension plans (often because of stricter government regulations) typically results in extensive institutional ownership of corporate stock and can provide still another route to greater employee ownership (especially if the pension fund is under trade-union control).

Such developments, if pursued far enough, could portend still another answer to the corporate governance issue, potentially quite dramatically different from current practice. The corporation would toil more for employee benefit than for outside stockholders, albeit with the distinction becoming increasingly blurred or nonexistent. A further question naturally arises as to whether similar ownership-participation solutions should be extended to suppliers and local communities. Are community ownership of the Green Bay Packers and local government ownership of several short-line railroads harbingers of the future?

These different approaches to corporate reform are not necessarily mutually exclusive. More responsible and responsive boards of directors obviously would be welcome regardless of who claimed the residuals on corporate performance. Boards could probably also enter into many different kinds of profit-sharing arrangements without incurring legal challenges. Similarly, creating incentives for employees to be more productive and efficient would be deemed desirable under most circumstances, again regardless of who benefits from corporate performance (and especially if the resulting economic gains were somehow shared among all the contributing parties). If suppliers and local communities assume a greater explicit ownership role, demands for legislative or political actions to reduce potential damages from takeovers might diminish.

Nevertheless, internal reform, if it improved the general performance of the corporation, should attenuate demands for realignment of ownership rights. Internal reform also has the apparent advantage of being less disruptive of existing arrangements, including the use of the takeover threat as a disciplinary device. Of course, even with a more attentive board, the temptations might still exist for stockholders to transfer wealth to themselves by abrogating implicit contracts.

In the end, however, the fate of any implicit contracts and any reform of internal corporate governance can be properly assessed only in the larger context of general public policy. The ultimate public policy question with regard to corporations is to define the role they should play in U.S. society, a role that involves social and political dimensions as well as economic. In essence, the question is where does the corporation fit into the broad fabric of the U.S. political system and economy?

Not surprisingly, this issue has received a good deal of attention, with the literature reflecting a broad range of views. On the one hand, Charles Lindblom, in the widely cited conclusion to his *Politics and Markets,* argues that the large private corporation does not fit with "democratic theory and vision."[27] To Lindblom, the modern business corporation is inconsistent with a pluralistic democratic society because corporations have so much more power than other interest groups that the checks, balances, or countervailing tendencies necessary for the proper implementation of democratic procedures are lacking.[28] At a minimum, Lindblom's observations have raised serious challenges to much conventional wisdom about the effectiveness of pluralistic processes in a democratic society.

While not necessarily rejecting Lindblom or even taking sides on the political concepts involved in his challenge, economists have usually adopted a more benign view of the corporation. Thus McCraw reports some particularly poignant endorsements of U.S. corporate behavior by economists. As might be expected, economists evaluate the corporation's performance mainly in terms of economic contribution, and few would deny that corporations have made important contributions to economic development and growth. Some, as already noted (e.g., Galbraith and Schumpeter), have gone even further, suggesting strongly that very large corporations are fundamental to a modern economy, specifically to develop complex modern technologies.[29] At an emotional or visceral political level, Schumpeter probably did not take pleasure in this finding; he reached what, for him, was the rather melancholy conclusion that the need for large organizations might well undermine much of the political support for capitalism. Galbraith, by contrast, found this possibility to be less inevitable and, in the event, less objectionable; certainly, if big corporations were necessary to develop economically, this was a fact that Galbraith could recognize, perhaps even welcome, and a reality to which public policy should adapt.

Nevertheless, many economists, even while acknowledging a corporate role in economic growth, would probably still be rather more suspicious of corporate bigness than Galbraith or Schumpeter. In the first place, like Coleman (a sociologist) in this volume, they might not be convinced that scale is necessary to promote research and development.[30] Secondly, they might retain a good deal of skepticism about how large corporations wield their power.[31]

The best litmus to separate those harboring continuing suspicions of corporate bigness from those holding more benign views probably is found in attitudes toward antitrust laws. Virtually all economists readily state that economic growth should be a major goal of public policy. Once that is accepted and the large corporation is deemed useful (perhaps indispensable) to its achievement, the large corporation is not likely to be viewed antagonistically, and antitrust laws become suspect. On the other hand, if the large corporation is viewed as less essential for growth and also capable of abusing its power, antitrust enforcement is viewed more favorably and government aids to business become less of a priority.

In this volume, at least three chapters—those of Gustafson and Johnson, Bower, and Weaver—deal explicitly with public policy recommendations on the future political role of the corporation, covering a very broad spectrum of policy possibilities.

Gustafson and Johnson are very much the centrists. They recommend an evolutionary adaptation of the corporate role in alignment with what they perceive to be a basic trend toward U.S. corporations inheriting larger and more explicit social and political responsibilities. Not only should corporations recognize the implications of these developments, they should develop institutional and managerial capabilities to cope with them. This would involve a continuing dialogue between business and government over laws and regulations defining which responsibilities are also not likely to serve their economic purposes and interests well.

Bower takes this argument a significant step further, portraying a need for corporations to become involved even more actively in external affairs, at a pace well beyond that of historic trends. He contends that contemporary corporations are part of a network of institutional arrangements by which public policy and business are conducted in modern industrialized societies, much after the pattern of Galbraith and Schumpeter before him and Reich contemporaneously.[32] Together with the other ''three estates''—politicians, government administrators, and scientists—corporate managers make and implement national policy. In Bower's view, neither political operatives nor corporate leaders have recognized fully that all corporations are inevitably caught up in a web of interdependencies with other companies and institutions and that many strategic decisions taken by company managements have considerable political content. This is perhaps most glaringly obvious in such areas as environmental legislation, nuclear power, tort law, or trade policy, but Bower argues that, to some degree, it permeates virtually all major business decisions. This leads him, in turn, to a belief that society should be much more aware of and ready to support the collaborative efforts of the various estates to shape policy more intelligently.[33]

Weaver's views are almost diametrically opposed to Bower's, and perhaps to Gustafson's and Johnson's as well. To Weaver, the economic well-being of the corporation is the single end that should govern its policies and relations with government and other institutions; he feels that the highly interdependent and interacting worlds described, for example, by Bower and Badaracco, are detrimental to this well-being. The whole whose interests are to be taken into account by managers should be restricted, defined by law, the marketplace, and a vision of society that looks more to the benefits of competition than to those of cooperation.

Weaver thus rejects explicitly and forthrightly *any* notion of corporate social responsibility; he sees it as being strictly propaganda, perhaps even a lie, used to manipulate the political system into giving business undue benefits or entitlements. Furthermore, he has very serious doubts, in striking contrast to Lindblom, about the ability of business to succeed in these manipulations.[34] Weaver also considers any extension of corporate social responsibility to be inconsistent with recent trends, a reversion to the old autocratic, conservative notion of the right to incorporation being limited to those pursuing or rendering some special public or royal purpose. In his view, corporations have done better historically, and will do better in the future, when they focus exclusively on their economic purposes and goals. By serving these economic goals better, and particularly the needs of their customers and stockholders, corporate managers will also be serving the general well-being of society better than if they were to divert some of their energies to obscure and ill-defined social responsibilities. As he eloquently concludes: "The new capitalist corporation's sharpened sense of self-interest will make it a better, more thoughtful producer, employer, neighbor, and citizen."

Weaver clearly believes that corporations, left alone and leaving government alone, would behave in a generally constructive manner; the market, defined by so-called natural economic forces of supply and demand, would be sufficient discipline to ensure that happy outcome. This contrasts with a long-standing American political tradition of skepticism concerning reliance on markets unaided by public policy.[35] While those espousing the American populist tradition might share Weaver's suspicion of forums bringing together labor, government, and businesses and might abhor the notion of industrial policies devised and administered by such collectives, they probably would not subscribe to Weaver's laissez-faire. In particular, they would probably judge antitrust laws to be a keystone of good procompetitive public policy, in need of strengthening rather than dilution.

Widely differing views about the social responsibilities and role of the corporation have very diverse implications for corporate governance and other related issues. Weaver's dismissal of any kind of corporate social responsibility might be construed as quite compatible with a reliance on financial markets to discipline managerial performance. As a corollary, he might be expected to resist public policies that would reduce takeovers or other externally generated corporate restructurings. Certainly, there is little room in Weaver's view for arguments about the political rights or needs of other groups involved in corporations.

Bower, on the other hand, has more in common with those who advocate a more activist or interventionist government role. In his view, a more explicit recognition of the interdependencies among the different functionary groups in society would be the best way to enhance values or improve economic performance. This vision does not totally discount the traditional role of the manager: "In the end, the strength of the economy depends on the strength of individual companies." However, "managers must be careful to recognize when they are functioning in their traditional roles and when they are functioning as representatives or stewards for a group of economic and human assets that are part of the nation's economic and social potential." In the second role, they must "develop a broad view of the national interest" in order to play their proper role in the public policy debate.

Even without formalization or institutionalization of Bower's suggestions, a development of his thoughts almost inevitably leads away from externally imposed financial restructurings as solutions to corporate problems. To the extent that American business leadership became ever more intertwined with the other estates, takeovers and other externally imposed restructurings would become more difficult; certainly, they would meet with even more substantial or entrenched opposition than is already the case. As empirical proof that this might not undermine economic efficiency unduly, Bower might point to Japan, where more cooperative mechanisms appear to make financial takeovers and externally generated restructurings less necessary. The evolution of entirely new forms of cooperative interaction between different corporations (through joint ventures, cooperatives, etc.), as described by Badaracco, could be cited as still another institutional mechanism for achieving these same goals, again with strong Japanese precedents in the keiretsu.

By contrast, the more centrist political role suggested for the corporation by Gustafson and Johnson would align better with the internal governance reforms advocated by Millstein and Knowlton. In both chapters, there are strong suggestions that the corporation is a useful economic institution that adapts reasonably well to changed circumstances, though perhaps not always with optimal promptness. Both imply that most of what is wrong with corporate behavior could be corrected with relatively modest evolutionary changes.

These diverse views pose the policy options starkly, with three major alternatives being identifiable. The first would embody an evolutionary adaptation or reform of corporate governance procedures (along the lines advocated by Millstein and Knowlton), while at the same time permitting a collective corporate sense of social and competitive responsibilities to develop (as advocated by Gustafson and Johnson). Under this "pluralist adaptive" approach, modest changes might be made in corporate laws, particularly as they apply to takeovers and related practices. The objective would be to limit the more pernicious aspects of these activities to make them more politically or socially acceptable while maintaining basic financial market disciplines. In essence, the law would be changed to make takeovers more orderly, perhaps more time-consuming, and certainly more cognizant of the multiplicity of interests involved. One might also expect some better effort to balance stockholder interests against those of other groups. Limitations might be placed on two-tier takeovers in exchange for the elimination of greenmail practices by management; or elimination of management devices for delaying or preventing takeovers (such as the "poison pill") might be traded for prompter revelation of takeover intentions followed by greater delays between such announcements and the actual expiration of takeover offers (to give boards of directors more time to ensure that stockholder and other interests were represented and protected properly). Finally, this evolutionary approach would be aided by and consistent with tax policies and other policy initiatives realigning ownership rights more closely with risk exposures and social costs.

A second distinct public policy response would involve far more substantial changes, specifically, a significant restructuring and redefinition of the corporate role in American political life. In this approach, corporations would be encouraged to consult more widely with one another and with other groups in society. At the extreme, this approach would pursue a vigorous industrial policy; implemented more modestly, it would permit, even encourage, the creation of broadly based policy forums wherein points of view would be exchanged among different participants (competitors, trade unions, government officials). Such a policy would thus establish greater consultation, and perhaps consensus, among all concerned before major policy changes were initiated or undertaken. Under this approach, there would almost certainly be some attenuation, perhaps even a virtual elimination, of conventional antitrust remedies in American law. Even if these were largely retained, explicit exemptions might be introduced to permit more experimentation with various cooperative or joint ventures among different corporate players, unions, and nonprofit research organizations. As noted by Badaracco, such arrangements are almost infinitely variable, so it is rather difficult to define precisely what form this approach might eventually take.

The third and final possibility would be a return to the economic fundamentals, with distinct focus on the economic role of the corporation, much in the fashion advocated by Weaver. In this approach, public policy would undertake few or no changes in corporate laws. In particular, nothing would be done to lessen the incentives for financial restructurings. The burden of proof for change would be very much upon its proponents, on the grounds that the present system was getting the job done—that job being to ensure that more competitive management is in charge of American corporations and that corporations redirect their investment policies to enhance efficiency and productivity. In this approach, there would also be little incentive to change greatly the antitrust laws, although some adherents of this particular approach might view them as being archaic or ill-intended. Underlying this approach is a clear reliance on competition as the major means to motivate economic actors and decisionmakers. Less emphasis would be placed on corporations achieving noneconomic goals, since such activities divert corporate energies from their highest and best use—producing goods and services efficiently. With this reduction in social and other noneconomic responsibilities, the corporation would also, according to Weaver, become less involved in governmental activities and undertakings; consultative forums, and even very weak forms of industrial policy, would be excluded.

What mix of these public policy options *might* prevail? Obviously, no one really knows. The American political system perhaps has a built-in bias in favor of centrist compromises, which seems best respected in the first, or centrist, alternative. On the other hand, democratic systems do tend to swing back and forth; to the extent that any such pendulum analogy holds, one or both of the two less centrist approaches might have at least a temporary ascendancy. In fact, some have argued that the United States in the early 1980s has seen the pendulum swing very strongly toward laissez-faire solutions and that public policy may now turn the other way in reaction.

What mix of public policy options *ought* to prevail? If the accent is on liberty, the individual range of private choice, and a sense that persons are heavily accountable for the outcomes of their activities, public policy will tend to minimize state intervention and other forms of collaborative corporate activities. If the accent is on compromise and cooperation between persons and interest groups, public policy will promote institutional arrangements that facilitate voluntary cooperative activities and favor only those regulations that exclude outcomes that are deleterious to society. If it is guided by a more corporatist view of the common good that mirrors the old view of estates, public policy will likely support more central planning. If it is based on a very egalitarian conception of distributive justice, public policy might assume at least some of the welfare norms known in Northern European countries.

Whatever value preferences are stated, at best they can only give direction to public policy, which necessarily takes place within the possibilities and limitations of political, economic, and social realities. However, the outcome, whatever it may be, almost surely will make a difference. Some very deep and abiding public policy issues are involved, which go to the very root of American constitutional and political experience and perceptions of the national interest. Indeed, the term *national interest* functions in contemporary discourse much as the term *common good* did in the oldest moral traditions of the West, which held that persons should pursue not only proper individual self-fulfillment but also the common good and that these two ends were mutually implicated. A generally organic metaphor was used in this tradition both to interpret society and to direct the moral conduct of persons. This vision of the common good lost much of its forcefulness during the Enlightenment, eroded by the emphasis on individual liberties, societies as contractual arrangements, and the potentially oppressive outcomes of giving the common good precedence over individuals. Bower, Gustafson and Johnson, and other authors in this volume seem to be proposing at least a qualified reintroduction of these older concerns.[36]

Also notable is the invocation by several contributors of certain ideals of democratic process. While these are justified by the authors in terms of their benefits to the corporation, one can reasonably infer that a respect for persons and for their cooperative participation in making decisions also provides a certain nonutilitarian moral backing. Signs of this can be found, for example, in the chapter by Brooks and Maccoby. Participation and cooperation ascend as values in their discussion of labor relations, as means to ends but perhaps not merely as that. Similarly, in the Gustafson and Johnson chapter, the values of democratic process for establishing participatory arrangements are invoked both for their utility and because they respect the dignity of the individual.

Many, if not most, of the contributors thus combine both implicit and explicit social visions with concerns about the performance (or efficiency or utility) of the U.S. economy. To varying degrees, they all see policy choices about corporate governance and law as having major implications for the efficiency of the American economy and, therefore, for the American standard of living as well. The efficiency with which U.S. society achieves other broader social goals, and even how we feel about one another as a society, may also be involved. Of course, it is perhaps not surprising that an institution that accounts for the vast majority of U.S. economic activity has acquired such importance. It would only be surprising if it had not!

NOTES

1. This point is perhaps most closely associated with John Kenneth Galbraith, *The New Industrial State* (Boston: Houghton Mifflin, 1967).

2. For an early statement of this point, see E. A. G. Robinson, *The Structure of Competitive Industry* (Chicago: University of Chicago Press, 1958). Subsequent elaborations can be found in several sources, particularly Oliver E. Williamson, "Hierarchical Control and Optimum Firm Size," *Journal of Political Economy* 75, no. 2 (April 1967):123–38; idem, *Corporate Control and Business Behavior* (Englewood Cliffs, N.J.: Prentice-Hall, 1970); and Robin Marris, "A Model of the Managerial Enterprise," *Quarterly Journal of Economics* 77, no. 2 (May 1963): 185–209.

3.   J.A. Schumpeter, *Theorie der wirtschaftlichen Entwicklung (Leipzig: Duncker and Humblot, 1911)*; idem, *The Theory of Economic Development* (Cambridge: Harvard University Press, 1934).

4.   Idem, *Capitalism, Socialism and Democracy* (New York and London: Harper and Brothers, 1942)

5.   For an interesting discussion of these points, see the commemorative volume honoring Schumpeter's one-hundredth birthday, Dieter Bos, Abram Bergson, and J. R. Meyer, eds., *Entrepreneurship: The Bonn-Harvard Schumpeter Centennial* (Vienna and New York: Springer-Verlag, 1984).

6.   For a good review of the extensive literature testing and evaluating the Schumpeter hypothesis, see William L. Baldwin and John T. Scott, *Market Structure and Technological Change* (Schur, Switzerland, and New York: Harwood Academic Publishers, 1987). For a sampling of some of the earlier literature on the subject, see F. M. Fisher and P. Temin, "Returns to Scale in Research and Development: What Does the Schumpeterian Hypothesis Imply?" *Journal of Political Economy* 87 (January/February 1973):56–70; Kenneth J. Arrow, "Economic Welfare and the Allocation of Resources for Invention," in National Bureau of Economic Research, ed., *The Rate and Direction of Inventive Activity* (Princeton, N.J.: Princeton University Press, 1962), pp. 609–25; Morton I. Kamien and Nancy L. Schwartz, "On the Degree of Rivalry for Maximum Innovation Activity," *The Quarterly Journal of Economics* 90 (May 1976):245–60; Almarin Phillips, "Concentration, Scale and Technological Change in Selected Manufacturing Industries 1899–1939," *Journal of Industrial Economics* 4 (June 1956):179–93; idem, "Patents, Potential Competition, and Technical Progress," *American Economic Review* 56 (May 1976): 301–10; F. M. Scherer, "Firm Size, Market Structure, Opportunity, and the Output of Patented Inventions," *American Economic Review* 55 (December 1965): 1097–1125; William Comanor, "Market Structure, Product Differentiation, and Industrial Research, *Quarterly Journal of Economics* 81 (November 1967):639–57; W. J. Adams, "Firm Size and Research Activity: France and the United States," *Quarterly Journal of Economics* 84 (August 1970):386–409; Steven Globerman, "Market Structure and R&D in Canadian Manufacturing Industries," *Quarterly Review of Economics and Business* 13, no. 2 (Summer 1973):59–67; and R. W. Wilson, "The Effect of Technological Environment and Product Rivalry on R&D Effort and Licensing of Inventions," *The Review of Economics and Statistics* 59, no. 2 (May 1977):171–78.

7.   See Zoltan J. Acs and David B. Audretsch, "Innovation, Market Structure, and Firm Size," *Review of Economics and Statistics* 49, no. 4 (November 1987):567–74.

8.   R. B. Reich, *Tales of a New America* (New York: Times Books, 1987).

9.   For a good summary and review of issues relating to environmental and fuel standards, see L. G. Kincaid, "General Motors and the Corporate Average Fuel Economy Standards," case C15–86–671.0 (Cambridge, Mass.: Kennedy School of Government, 1986). On the effects of shifts in the market, see R. W. Crandall, H. K. Gruenspacht, T. E. Keeler, and L. B. Lave, *Regulating the Automobile* (Washington, D.C.: The Brookings Institution, 1986); and Jose A. Gomez-Ibanez, Robert A. Leone, and Stephen A. O'Connell, "Restraining Auto Imports: Does Anyone Win?" *Journal of Policy Analysis and Management* 2, no. 2 (Winter 1983):196–219.

10.   For examples, see Robert Crandall, *The U.S. Steel Industry in Recurrent Crisis: Policy Options in a Competitive World* (Washington, D.C.: The Brookings Institution, 1981); Donald F. Barnett and Louis Schorsch, *Steel: Upheaval in a Basic*

Industry (Cambridge, Mass.: Ballinger Publishing, 1983); Walter Adams and James W. Brock, *The Bigness Complex: Industry, Labor, and Government in the American Economy* (New York: Pantheon Books, 1987); M. C. Jensen, "Takeovers: Folklore and Science," *Harvard Business Review*, November-December 1984, no. 6: 109–21; and Irwin M. Stelzer, "Fairy Tales about a 'New America,' " *The Public Interest* 88 (Summer 1987):118–24.

11.   The seminal statement on this hypothesis is, of course, that of Adolf A. Berle, Jr., and Gardiner C. Means, *The Modern Corporation and Private Property* (Chicago: Commerce Clearing House, 1932). For a critique, see George J. Stigler and Claire Friedland, "The Literature of Economics: The Case of Berle and Means," *Journal of Law and Economics* 26 (June 1983):248–54. For a more modern formulation as a principal-agent problem, see Michael Jensen and William Meckling, "Theory of the Firm: Managerial Behavior, Agency Costs, and Capital Structure," *Journal of Financial Economics* 3 (October 1976):305–60.

12.   The perpetuity characteristics of the corporation only intensify any tendencies toward conglomeration and separation of ownership and control. Obviously, with self-renewal or self-perpetuation of governance, it is easier for corporation managements to develop their own agendas.

13.   See W. F. Sharpe, "Capital Asset Prices: A Theory of Market Equilibrium under Conditions of Risk," *Journal of Finance* 19 (September 1964):425–42; and John Lintner, "The Valuation of Risk Assets and the Selection of Risk Investments in Stock Portfolios and Capital Budgets," *Review of Economics and Statistics* 47 (February 1965):13–37. A somewhat more positive case for conglomerates, resting mainly on managerial and innovative considerations, while minimizing transaction costs, can be found in Williamson, *Corporate Control and Business Behavior*. Excellent reviews of the arguments pro and con can be found in Dennis C. Mueller, "A Theory of Conglomerate Mergers," *Quarterly Journal of Economics* 84 (November 1969):643–59; idem, *The Modern Corporation* (Brighton, Sussex: Wheatsheaf Books, 1986), part 3, pp. 155–222; and John Lintner, "Optimum or Maximum Corporate Growth under Uncertainty," in R. Marris and A. Wood, eds., *The Corporate Economy* (Cambridge: Harvard University Press, 1971), pp. 172–241.

14.   David J. Ravenscraft and F. M. Scherer, *Mergers, Sell-Offs, and Economic Efficiency* (Washington, D.C.: The Brookings Institution, 1987), p. 44.

15.   For a good summary of these tax issues, see R. A. Musgrave and P. B. Musgrave, *Public Finance in Theory and Practice* (New York: McGraw-Hill, 1984), chs. 18 and 19, pp. 383–430.

16.   See W. J. Baumol, P. Heim, B. G. Malkiel, and R. E. Quandt, "Earnings Retention, New Capital and the Growth of the Firm," *Review of Economics and Statistics* 52, no. 4 (November 1970):345–55. Very suggestive evidence of such misinvestment occurs when the book value of a publicly traded corporation exceeds the market value of its equity, especially in inflationary periods. Some empirical evidence on the surprising extent of this phenomenon in the early 1980s in the United States can be found in John S. Strong, "Essays on Valuation" (Ph.D. diss., Harvard University, 1986).

17.   Peter F. Drucker, "Japan's Choices," *Foreign Affairs* 65, no. 5 (Summer 1987): 938.

18. Oliver E. Williamson, *The Economic Institutions of Capitalism: Firms, Markets, Relational Contracting* (New York: The Free Press, 1985).

19. A thorough development of this argument can be found in Andrei Shleifer and L. H. Summers, "Breach of Trust in Hostile Takeovers," in Alan J. Auerbach, ed., *Corporate Takeovers: Causes and Consequences* (Chicago: University of Chicago Press, published for National Bureau of Economic Research, 1988.) Among those reporting and documenting gains are M. C. Jensen, "Takeovers: Folklore and Science;" idem and R. S. Ruback, "The Market for Corporate Control: The Scientific Evidence," *Journal of Financial Economics* 11 (April 1983):5–50; and D. K. Dennis and J. J. McConnell, "Corporate Mergers and Security Returns," *Journal of Financial Economics* 16 (June 1986):143–87. For less sanguine views about the extent and, perhaps particularly, the permanence of these gains, see John L. Commons, *Tender Offer* (Berkeley: University of California Press, 1985): Peter F. Drucker, "Corporate Takeovers—What Is to Be Done?" *The Public Interest* 82 (Winter 1986):3–24; Moira Johnston, *Takeover* (New York: Arbor House, 1986); Warren A. Law, "A Corporation Is More than Its Stock," *Harvard Business Review* May-June 1986, no. 3:80–83; George Lodge and Richard Walton, "The American Corporation and Its New Relationships" (Harvard Business School, Boston, Mass., April 18, 1987, Mimeographed); Louis Lowenstein, "Pruning Deadwood in Hostile Takeovers: A Proposal for Legislation," *Columbia Law Review* 83 (March 1983):249–334; idem, "Management Buyouts," *Columbia Law Review* 85 (May 1985):730–84; Donald G. Margotta, "Finance Theory: Its Relevance in Corporate Control," working paper 85–14 (Boston: College of Business Administration, Northeastern University, March 1986); David J. Ravenscraft and F. M. Scherer, *Mergers, Sell-Offs, and Economic Efficiency*; and Andrei Shleifer and Robert W. Vishny, "Management Buyouts as a Response to Market Pressure," in Alan J. Auerbach, ed., *Corporate Takeovers: Causes and Consequences*. For an excellent summary of the empirical evidence and further citations, pro and con, see R. E. Caves, "Effects of Mergers and Acquisitions on the Economy: An Industrial Organization Perspective" (paper for "Conference on the Merger Boom," sponsored by the Federal Reserve Bank of Boston, October 12–14, 1987).

20. Solid statistical evidence on this point seems to be somewhat elusive. Using data mostly for the period prior to 1980, Dennis and McConnell, "Corporate Mergers and Security Returns," report neither gain nor loss for nonconvertible debt holders of both acquired and acquiring firms. Contemporary news reports on post-1980 experience, on the other hand, indicate substantial losses for debt holders in acquired and acquiring firms, because of ratings downgradings and the like. See S. W. Prokesch, "Merger Wave: How Stock and Bonds Fare," *New York Times*, January 7, 1986, p. A1. Similarly, Mueller and associates came to much more pessimistic views about the benefits of mergers, even prior to 1980. See Dennis C. Mueller, ed., *The Determinants and Effects of Mergers: An International Comparison* (Cambridge, Mass.: Oelgeschlager, Gunn and Hain, 1980).

21. As pointed out by Shleifer and Summers, "Breach of Trust in Hostile Takeovers," and to a considerable extent confirmed, at least indirectly, by the empirical evidence. See, for example, Caves, "Effects of Mergers and Acquisitions"; Ravenscraft and Scherer, *Mergers, Sell-offs, and Economic Efficiency*; and Mueller, *The Determinants and Effects of Mergers*.

22. For the seminal statement of this view, see Jensen, "Takeover: Folklore and Science;" and idem and Ruback, "The Market for Corporate Control."

23. Drucker, "Japan's Choices," provides some compelling reasons why there may be limits on Japanese industrial capabilities.

24. See Martin L. Weitzman, *The Share Economy* (Cambridge: Harvard University Press, 1984).

25. It should be noted that some of these categories of nontraditional compensation (profit sharing, lump-sum bonuses, earned time off, etc.) may be overlapping (i.e., nonexclusive). See Carla S. O'Dell and Jerry McAdams, *People, Performance and Pay: A Full Report on the American Productivity Center/American Compensation Association National Survey of Non-Traditional Reward and Human Resource Practices* (Houston: American Productivity Center, 1987).

26. For example, see John R. Meyer and Clinton V. Oster, Jr., "Productivity, Employment, and Labor Relations," chapter 6 in *Deregulation and the Future of Intercity Passenger Travel* (Cambridge: MIT Press, 1987); or Harvey Brooks and Michael Maccoby, "Corporations and the Work Force," in this volume.

27. Charles E. Lindblom, *Politics and Markets: The World's Political Economic Systems* (New York: Basic Books, 1977).

28. For a review of Lindblom's contributions and an assessment of their applicability to modern political circumstances, see David Vogel, "The New Political Science of Corporate Power," *The Public Interest* 87 (Spring 1987):63–79.

29. Galbraith, *The New Industrial State*; Schumpeter, *Capitalism, Socialism and Democracy*.

30. For a pungent and incisive statement of this case, see Stelzer's review of R. B. Reich's *Tales of a New America*, "Fairy Tales about a 'New America.' "

31. As in Adams and Brock, *The Bigness Complex*.

32. Galbraith, *The New Industrial State*; Schumpeter, *Capitalism, Socialism and Democracy*; and Reich, *Tales of a New America*.

33. This echoes, incidentally, a vision of human society from a distant past. How strongly Bower would use the historical analogy is not clear.

34. Lindblom, *Politics and Markets*.

35. As, say, expressed by Adams and Brock, *The Bigness Complex*.

36. A continuing bearer of the common good tradition has been the social thought of the Roman Catholic papacy, a literature largely ignored by most writers on economics and society. For two important documents see, Leo XIII, *Rerum Novarum* (1891); and Pius XI, *Quadragesimo Anno* (1931). For very recent discussions, see National Conference of Catholic Bishops, *Economic Justice for All: Pastoral Letter on Catholic Social Teaching and the U.S. Economy* (Washington, D.C.: United States Catholic Conference, 1986); and Oliver F. Williamson and John W. Houck, eds., *The Common Good and U.S. Capitalism* (Lanham, Md.: University Press of America, 1987).

INDEX

ABOUT THE EDITORS

John R. Meyer is James W. Harpel Professor of Capital Formation and Economic Growth at the John F. Kennedy School of Government, Harvard University. He has been vice chairman of the Union Pacific Corporation, president of the National Bureau of Economic Research, Inc., and a consultant on housing and transportation policy to U.S. government agencies, congressional committees, and foreign governments. His recent publications include *Deregulation and the Future of Intercity Passenger Travel* and *Deregulation and the New Airline Entrepreneurs* (with Clinton V. Oster, Jr.)

James Gustafson is Henry R. Luce University Professor of Humanities and Comparative Studies, Emory University. Previously he was university professor of theological ethics at the Divinity School and Committee on Social Thought, University of Chicago, and professor and chairman, Department of Religious Studies, Divinity School, Yale University. He is an ordained minister in the United Church of Christ. His publications include *Ethics from a Theocentric Perspective*: vol. 1, *Theology and Ethics* and vol. 2, *Ethics and Theology*; *Protestant and Roman Catholic Ethics: Prospects for Rapprochement*; and many scholarly articles.

ABOUT THE CONTRIBUTORS

Joseph L. Badaracco, Jr., is an associate professor of business administration at Harvard Business School and a member of the school's General Management Area. Professor Badaracco's first book, *Loading the Dice: A Five-Country Study of Vinyl Chloride Regulation*, compared business-government relations in five countries. His latest book on business leadership, with Richard Ellsworth, is entitled *Integrity and Leadership*. His current research focuses on cooperative relationships among businesses—joint ventures, consortia, and so forth—that lead to a blurring of firms' boundaries.

Joseph L. Bower is the senior associate dean for external relations and the Donald Kirk David Professor of Business Administration at the Harvard Business School, as well as a faculty member of the John F. Kennedy School of Government. Professor Bower has written several books, including *When Markets Quake, Business Policy: Text and Cases, Managing the Resource Allocation Process* (winner of the McKinsey Foundation book award in 1971), and *The Two Faces of Management: An American Approach to Leadership in Business and Government*, as well as many articles on corporate strategy and public policy. He has consulted widely on problems of strategy and organization with companies here and abroad, and with the U.S. government.

Harvey Brooks is Benjamin Peirce Professor of Technology and Public Policy, emeritus, John F. Kennedy School of Government, and former president of the American Academy of Arts and Sciences (1971–1976). He served as a member of the President's Science Advisory Committee from 1959 to 1964 and of the National Science Board from 1962 to 1974. From 1967 to 1972 he was chairman of the Committee on Science and Public Policy, National Academy of Sciences. He has also served on boards of various educational and scholarly organizations. In addition to numerous publications in nuclear engineering, physics of solids, underwater acoustics, and science and public policy, his writings include *The Government of Science*.

James S. Coleman is university professor, Department of Sociology, University of Chicago. He is a member of the National Academy of Sciences, the American Philosophical Society, the American Academy of Arts and Sciences, and the Royal Swedish Academy of Sciences. His publications include *The Asymmetric Society* and *Individual Interests and Collective Action*. He was principal author of *Equality of Educational Opportunity*.

Elmer W. Johnson practices law with Kirkland & Ellis, Chicago, of which he is managing partner. Until mid-1988 he was executive vice president of General Motors Corporation. He served as general counsel for International Harvester Company during its reorganization from 1981 to 1983, and as special counsel to the chairman of Ameritech Corporation in 1983. Mr. Johnson is a trustee of the University of Chicago, where he has been a visiting professor, and of the Aspen Institute. He is also a member of the Legal Advisory Committee to the New York Stock Exchange.

Winthrop Knowlton is research fellow, John F. Kennedy School of Government, Harvard University and president of Knowlton Associates, Inc. He was the Henry R. Luce Professor of Ethics, Business and Public Policy and director of the Center for Business and Government at the John F. Kennedy School of Government. He has been an investment banker and assistant secretary of the treasury for international affairs. From 1970 to 1981, he served as chief executive officer of Harper & Row Publishers, Inc., of which he is chairman of the board. Mr. Knowlton is the author of two nonfiction books, *Shaking the Money Tree* with John Furth and *Growth Opportunities in Common Stocks*, and two novels, *A Killing in the Market* with George Goodman (also known as Adam Smith) and *False Premises*.

Michael Maccoby directs the Project on Technology, Work and Character in Washington, D.C., and the Program on Technology, Public Policy and Human Development at the John F. Kennedy School of Government, Harvard University. He is a consultant to business, government, and unions. Dr. Maccoby has participated in several pioneering change programs, including the Bolivar Project for Harman Industries and the United Auto Workers, which was the first American joint labor-management effort to improve work, and became a model for the automobile industry. Dr. Maccoby holds a B.A. in social psychology and a Ph.D. in social relations from Harvard. He also studied philosophy at New College, Oxford, and psychoanalysis with Erich Fromm. Among his books on management are *The Gamesman, The Leader,* and *Why Work: Leading the New Generation*.

Thomas K. McCraw is professor of business administration at the Harvard Business School where he also serves as a director of research and chairs the Business, Government, and Competition Area. He is author of *Morgan Versus Lilienthal* (William P. Lyons Award, 1970) and *TVA and the Power Fight* (1971) and editor of *Regulation in Perspective* (1981) and *America Versus Japan* (1986). His most recent book, *The Prophets of Regulation*, won both the 1985 Pulitzer Prize in History and the 1986 Thomas Newcomen Award, which is given for the best book on the history of business published during the preceding three years.

Ira M. Millstein is a senior partner with Weil, Gotshal & Manges, New York City. In addition to practicing law, he writes and lectures on antitrust, government regulation, and corporate governance. He has been associated with New York University Law School, Yale University School of Organization and Management, and the John F. Kennedy School of Government, Harvard University, and is now director of the Henley Program of Business and Law at the Columbia University Graduate School of Business. A member of the American Law Institute, Mr. Millstein is co-author of *The Limits of Corporate Power* and co-editor of *The Impact of the Modern Corporation.*

Merton J. Peck is Thomas DeWitt Cuyler Professor of Economics at Yale University. He has served as a member of the President's Council of Economic Advisers and as deputy assistant comptroller and director of systems analysis in the Office of the Secretary of Defense. He has also been a fellow at Kobe University, a visiting scholar at the Economic Planning Agency in Japan, and a consultant to the US-Japan Economic Relations Group. His publications include *The World Aluminum Industry in an Era of Changing Energy Prices* (editor and contributor) and *Economic Aspects of Television Regulation* (with Roger Noll and John McGowan), as well as articles on deregulation, technology, and economic growth, often with special reference to Japan.

F. M. Scherer is the Joseph Wharton Professor of Political Economy at Swarthmore College. From 1972 to 1974 he was senior research fellow at the International Institute of Management, Berlin, Germany, and from 1974 to 1976 he was chief economist at the Federal Trade Commission. Dr. Scherer is vice president of the American Economic Association and president-elect of the International J. A. Schumpeter Association. He has written numerous articles and books, including *Industrial Market Structure and Economic Performance, The Economics of Multi-Plant Operation: An International Comparisons Study, Innovation and Growth: Schumpeterian Perspectives,* and *Mergers, Sell-offs, and Economic Efficiency* (with David J. Ravenscraft).

Paul H. Weaver served for two years as public-affairs executive at the Ford Motor Company. A former writer and editor at *Fortune* magazine, he is now at the Hoover Institution at Stanford University. His most recent publication is *The Suicidal Corporation.*